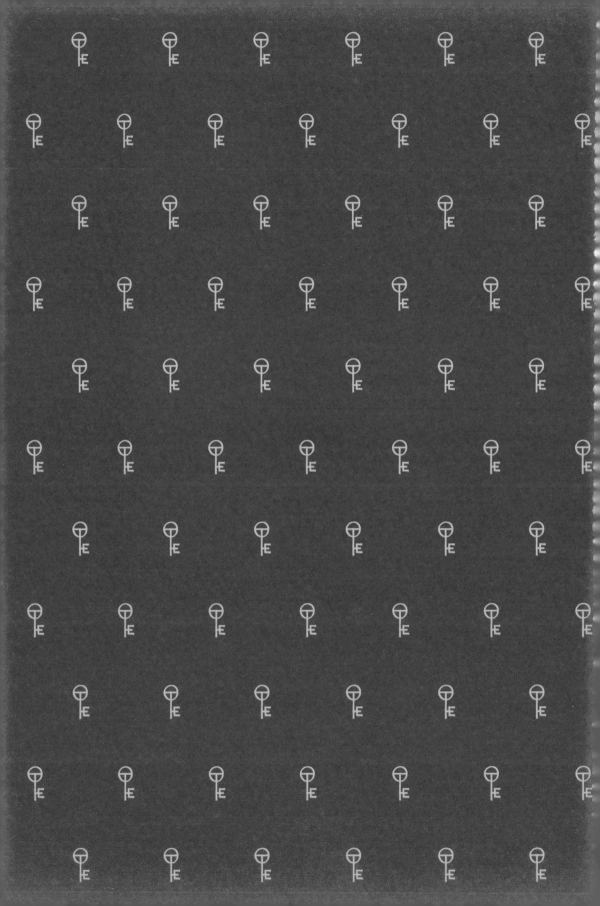

THROUGHOUT THE AGES, METAPHYSICAL
TRADITIONS HAVE BEEN TRANSLATED
INTO SACRED AND VISIONARY ART.
THE LIBRARY OF ESOTERICA
EXPLORES THE SYMBOLIC LANGUAGE
OF OUR MOST POTENT UNIVERSAL
STORIES, THE TALES WE TELL THROUGH
PAINT AND INK, COSTUME AND CLAY.

THE LIBRARY
OF
ESOTERICA

WITCHCRAFT

FOREWORD BY
Pam Grossman

DESIGN BY
Thunderwing

EDITED BY
Jessica Hundley
Pam Grossman

TASCHEN

WITCHCRAFT

SPELLBOUND

*The witch cooks
love down in a pot.
She feeds herself to herself;
she grows stronger.*

— SONYA VATOMSKY,
excerpt from the poem "Groundmeat" from her book *Salt Is for Curing*, 2015

I've been under the witch's spell for most of my life — first falling in love with her stories as a child through fairy tales and fiction, and then taking on her mantle in a more personal manner as a pagan-curious teen. She'd fix her gaze on me from the frames of alluring old paintings and sing me irresistible incantations through the throats of alt-rock queens. Whenever she was close by, I felt electrified and expanded. And then one day she slipped her cloak around me and claimed me as her own.

When I call myself "witch," I do so mindful of the dark charge of persecution that has haunted anyone who has been deemed a threatening outsider. But it is also an archetypal energy of enchantment, mystery, and divine femininity that I am consciously connecting to. Ray Bradbury wrote, "A Witch is born out of the true hungers of her time." Like so many, I am now ravenous for alternative models of beauty and power that upend the status quo.

And so when the wondrous Jessica Hundley invited me to collaborate with her on this bewitching visual banquet, I was ecstatic.

What follows is a kaleidoscopic, wide-lensed look at depictions of witches throughout history — both as we've imagined them and as they self-identify. This tome spans time and space, gender, and geography. You'll find real rites and contemporary rituals in its pages alongside wild, unbridled visions by artists through the ages.

Witchcraft. A doubly potent word, for it is brewed from two intoxicating ingredients: the ever-entrancing *witch*, and the *craft* that creates her anew.

So come feast upon the witch's image magick. Get nourished and full as the moon.

— Pam Grossman
Brooklyn, New York, 2021

(frontispiece) **Laura Tempest Zakroff** · *Starbody Sigil* · **United States** · **2021** Air, fire, water, earth, and spirit, our bodies mirror the elements. Born of stardust, we align with the shape of the pentagram — each of us the embodiment of magick.

John William Waterhouse · *The Magic Circle* **England** · **1886** Brimming with magick symbolism, the famed Waterhouse painting shows a witch drawing a flaming circle with one hand, while clutching an athame in the other. The ghostly cauldron steam consumes her gaze.

Preface by
JESSICA HUNDLEY
Series Editor

WE ARE ALL WITCHES

Yes, I'm a witch
I'm a bitch
I don't care what you say
My voice is real
My voice speaks truth
I don't fit in your ways

— YOKO ONO, "Yes, I'm a Witch" from the album *A Story*, 1974

Yoko Ono wrote these words in 1974, bristling at media backlash over her relationship with John Lennon, targeting her righteous indignation at the press, at the patriarchy, at the brittle unyielding edifice of the cultural establishment. Ono was and remains a witch – defiant, powerful, a magickal being, manifesting the spell of creative action. By her very existence, she defies stereotype. By proclaiming herself a witch, she transforms a legacy of persecution into an expression of empowerment.

The archetype of the witch is in a state of constant evolution. The foundations of witchcraft are murky, its history hidden and suppressed. The archaic brutality of the witch hunts remains resonant even now – fear manifested as judgment, ignorance exhibited through violence. And yet, the witch not only endures, but thrives, a symbolic embodiment of victory, of the triumph of magick over the tyranny of oppression. With this book, we attempt

to unveil the origins of an ancient narrative, an expansive, enchanted practice that encompasses a myriad of traditions. Although we focus predominately on the history of Western witchcraft, we are honored to include conversations with a diverse range of self-identifying witches, each embracing their own uniquely individual practices.

Witchcraft is culled from countless cultural and ancestral influences. Rituals can be passed down or self-created, solitary or communal. We hope to showcase and celebrate witches in all their multiple manifestations. The witch, after all, is a shape-shifter, continually transforming and evolving. And in this way, YES, we are *all* witches, seeking self-realization through experience and connection through the coven of community.

We cast the circle and step inside.

– Jessica Hundley
Los Angeles, California, 2021

Bev Grant · *W.I.T.C.H. Hex on Wall Street* · United States · 1968 The Women's International Terrorist Conspiracy from Hell marched down Wall Street on Halloween to curse the capitalist patriarchy within the lair of New York's Financial District. The Dow Jones average had a steep decline the following day.

PART I

—

The

Initiation

CONJURING
THE CRAFT

THE KEY OF HEKATE

A Brief History of Witchcraft in the Western World

We gaze up at the same stars, the sky covers us all, the same universe encompasses us. What does it matter what practical system we adopt in our search for the truth? Not by one avenue only can we arrive at so tremendous a secret.

— SYMMACHUS, 384 CE

To trace the origins of witchcraft in the Western world is to explore a narrative birthed in ancient mythology and folklore and subsequently expressed through a long and brutal legacy of persecution. That the witch has emerged in modern times as a symbolic emblem of empowerment has been a development of the late 19th century, the result of a seemingly endless battle between ignorance and enlightenment, oppression and catharsis.

Like so many other human histories, the story of the witch has been formed through fear — fear of the other, to be exact, be it the radical fringe, the creative thinkers, the defiant outsiders, the nonconformers. The shift from polytheistic culture to strident monotheism and the ongoing desire of many in power to crush individuality in favor of a more subservient collective are also key

factors in witchcraft's blood-soaked evolution. For far too long, religious tyranny, violent misogyny (as well as passive misanthropy), and repressive patriarchal power have subjugated our innate curiosity for the magickal.

What exactly is a witch? The definitions are fluid and never final. References to witchcraft or magick in some form find their place in the histories of nearly every culture around the globe. And although the focus of this book is predominantly to survey the visual representations of Western traditions, even within these confines the characterizations are vast, varied, and continually evolving. The witch transforms according to the era and environment — shape-shifting through the ages, but a muse, always — the subject of creative idolatry, showcased in countless paintings, sculptures, books, and plays. As an enduring archetype, the witch most likely first evolved from

(previous) Oli Scarff · Imbolc Fire Festival England · 2016 One of eight annual pagan celebrations, the ancient Celtic Imbolc celebrates the sun's return, the reawakening of the natural world each spring, and the fire goddess Brigid.

Hans Baldung Grien · *The Witches* · Germany 1510 A powerful chiaroscuro woodcut depicts a sabbath-preparation scene of witches gathered around the ointment urn. The salve contained within, when rubbed over their bare skin, was said to enable flight.

potions in her mortar and pestle that transform men into swine and back again. There is Hekate, the triple-figure goddess associated with the darkened night, the crossroads between death and life, the underworld, plant magick, and sorcery. Euripides's great tragedy, *Medea*, embodies the vengeful power of a woman scorned. After she is rejected by her husband, Medea's fury becomes murderous and potent. In the polytheistic worship of the Egyptians, Isis is perhaps the most obvious embodiment of the witch archetype. Representing rebirth and magick, she is the mother goddess, capable of resurrecting the dead and granting new life. In Norse mythology, Freya holds the powers of fertility and divination as well as love, beauty, and war; her magickal chariot is pulled by twin cats, and around her shoulders, a cloak of falcon feathers gives her the gift of flight. In Celtic traditions, Brigid is the goddess of hearth and home, a guide to healers and to all those who experiment in the magickal arts.

matriarchal worship, the rituals of ancient goddess cultures and the mythic legacies of early civilizations. Again, these spiritual traditions of course exist throughout the world, but the lineage of the Western witch can be traced back to Mount Olympus, to the myths of the Greeks and Romans and to the earliest folk traditions and sacred rites of Egyptian, Germanic, Norse, and Celtic cultures.

The Greek bards were particularly enamored of the witch. In Homer's epic *The Odyssey*, the hero, Odysseus, encounters Circe, a witch and goddess with powers inextricably linked to the plant and animal worlds. At her home on the enchanted island of Aeaea, she lives among tamed lions and docile wolves, mixing

In Christian mythologies, one of the first-known recorded appearances of the word *witch* occurs in the Old Testament, in the books of Exodus 22:17 and Leviticus 20:27. Most likely written around 560 BCE, the passage in Exodus commands brutally, "Thou shalt not suffer a witch to live." Leviticus expands on this with another demand, that "A man also or woman that hath a familiar spirit, or that is a wizard, shall surely be put to death: they shall stone them with stones: their blood shall be upon them." In the Book of Deuteronomy, practices associated with many polytheistic religions, such as soothsaying or conjuring and spellwork, were also condemned. In the

Ulrich Molitor · *Women Drawn as Witches* · Germany 1508 Though considered an apologist for witchcraft, Molitor supported the eradication of witches. An early woodcut demonstrates his contradictory beliefs, as women brew a cauldron of live snakes and chicken parts.

Books of Samuel, the Bible's most infamous sorceress, the Witch of Endor, practices necromancy at the bidding of King Saul, communicating with the dead to predict the king's fate in battle. The 1597 treatise on witchcraft by King James VI of Scotland (later to become James I of England), *Daemonologie*, refers to the biblical Witch of Endor as "Saul's Pythonese," referencing the mythologies around the Pythia, priestesses who could fore-see the future. The publication of the book came just a few years after King James had overseen the first witchcraft trial in Scotland, and he penned *Daemonologie* in part to rational-ize the viability of magick and the existence of witchcraft. Sadly, the king was not the first

nor, at all, the last to ignite violent retribution against those accused of sorcery. And, like so many others, he would reference key biblical passages to support his cause.

Since its inception, the concept of mono-theism has fueled adversity for those who might be seen to be empowered by spirit or self – any forces beyond those of one Almighty God. In the early manifestations of Christianity, witchcraft – or rather, paganistic worship and ritual – would present a particu-lar obstacle. Beginning in the seventh century, as Christian missionaries began to arrive in Northern Europe, they sought to dismantle deep-seated indigenous belief systems. By this

Unknown · *Riding Witch* · Russia · 18th Century
A wood engraving depicts the forest witch Baba Yaga, a Slavic folkloric sorceress who rides into bat-tle on her wild boar, often called Hildisvíni ("battle swine"). She is both feared for her wicked wrath, and sought for help and healing in times of distress.

time, the Anglo-Saxons had already begun to Christianize Ireland and the British Isles, in part by adaptation and transformation — elements of pagan rites and symbols were mutated and morphed, and then integrated in various ways into Christian myth. The goddess Brigid became Saint Brigid. Christianity spread in part through symbiosis.

In this way, the Western world was essentially disenchanted, the magickal act an impossibility — the capability for the miraculous possessed by God and God alone. The Church was not yet intimidated or threatened by the witch, in part because of the resolution that the witch's powers did not, in fact, exist. This conviction was due in many ways to the fact that the influence exerted over the Church by theologian Augustine of Hippo was still powerfully resonant. In the early 400s CE, Augustine had argued that sorcery, witchcraft, and the like should not be feared, because they were simply not threats, their presence merely an "error of the pagans" to believe in "some other divine power than the one God."

For a moment, a kind of "live and let live" policy reigned regarding paganism, with Christian leaders busy with other battles. But ultimately, this attitude began to change, not surprisingly in parallel with shifts of power and challenges to the Church's imminent domination. As always, the uncontrollable must be reined, the dissidents placed into submission by any means necessary.

The act that may have first ignited the most murderous era of witch hunts can be traced to a proclamation made by Pope Innocent VIII in 1484. At the request of Heinrich Kramer, an inquisitor charged by the Church to root out heretical uprising, Innocent VIII issued a declaration supporting Kramer's allegations of witchcraft being practiced in Northern Germany. The Pope's statement read, "It has recently come to our ears, not without great pain to us, that in some parts of upper Germany, many persons of both sexes, heedless of their own salvation and forsaking the Catholic faith, give themselves over to devils male and female, and by their incantations, charms, and conjurings, and by

Daniel Hopfer · *Gib Frid (Let Me Go)* · Germany ca. 1515 Three witches hold down and threaten the Devil as he fights against the birth of a wild boar. Boars personify the Great Goddess with their crescent-shaped tusks, symbols of fertility and strength.

Mahiet and the Master of the Cambrai Missal Artwork from *Grandes Chroniques de France* · France ca. 1340 From the fifth through the eighth century CE, the Merovingian dynasty allegedly tortured and burned witches, marking the earliest period of known witchcraft annihilation.

other abominable superstitions and sortileges, offenses, crimes, and misdeeds, ruin and cause to perish the offspring of women, the foal of animals, the products of the earth, the grapes of vines, and the fruits of trees, as well as men and women, cattle and flocks and herds and animals of every kind, vineyards also and orchards, meadows, pastures, harvests, grains and other fruits of the earth."

Paranoia and hysteria ensued. Kramer, spurred on by rumors and hearsay, would go on to document his investigations into witchcraft, compiling his "research" into the book *Malleus Maleficarum* (*The Hammer of Witches*), first published in 1487. Reprinted 13 times over the next 40 years, the book, a detailed manual for hunting down and identifying

witches, would cause a conflagration of accusation and torture, a funeral pyre of persecutions upon which countless souls would burn. Through the early 1500s and onward, the Reformation era would see innumerable witchcraft trials throughout Europe and the British Isles. Mass executions, many by burning at the stake, were conducted across the continent. In 1515, courts in Geneva, Switzerland, are thought to have tried and killed hundreds of people for practicing witchcraft. In Italy, a decade later, the number surged into the thousands.

Both the Catholic and the Protestant churches were leaders of the charge, the sectarian battles between the two faiths resulting in turmoil and strife, a fury taken out on

Charles Stanley Reinhart · *The Ducking Stool*
United States · 1885 A rendering of a witch dunking, an early form of waterboarding, captures the atrocious behavior of the accusers. Supposed witches were dunked in and out of freezing water to torture them into admitting to witchcraft.

the easily targeted – predominantly women. Blame was laid heavily across the shoulders of innocents, for everything from thunderstorms to shipwrecks, diseased crops to stillborn babies. In the late 1500s, the madness had swept into France. Fueled in part by the publication, in 1580, of French lawyer Jean Bodin's treatise on witchcraft trial methodologies, *On the Demon-Mania of Sorcerers*, it seemed that witches were everywhere – their malevolence hidden among midwives and weavers, brewers and potters, young maidens and crones alike.

Bodin's book encouraged torture, entrapment, and the testimonies of children against their parents. From 1500 to 1660, it is believed that 50,000 to upwards of 80,000 suspected witches were executed in Europe, a large percentage of them women. In 1973's *Witches, Midwives, and Nurses*, historians Barbara Ehrenreich and Deirdre English make the claim that women schooled in midwifery and other healing practices represented a particular threat to the patriarchy. The persecution of the witches, "was born in feudalism and lasted – gaining virulence – well into the 'age of reason.' The witch craze took different forms at different times and places, but never lost its essential character: that of a ruling class campaign of terror directed against the female peasant population. Witches represented a political, religious, and sexual threat to Protestant and Catholic churches alike, as well as to the State."

Many men were also certainly accused of witchcraft and executed. But despite the fact there were numerous occultists and astrologers in high positions within the royal courts, witchcraft and the study of magick were, for the most part, considered entirely separate. John Dee, the favorite astrologer of Elizabeth I and renowned for his ability to speak with angels and foresee the future in his crystal ball, was never accused of witchcraft. As the scholar Ronald Hutton explains in his 2017 book, *The Witch: A History of Fear*, "magic had nothing to do with witchcraft because the former was mostly the preserve of men, who sought to control demons, while the latter was mostly that of women, who were servants and allies to them. The self-image of such magicians, in the medieval and early modern periods, drew on the established ideals of the clerical, monastic and scholarly professions, representing themselves as part of the elite of pious and learned men."

In 1590, the aforementioned King James, along with his betrothed, Princess Anne of Denmark, would play key roles in instigating some of the most notorious witchcraft hunts, a series of trials that took place nearly simultaneously in both Denmark and Scotland. When the princess's ship was hit by storms while she was en route to marry King James, the boat's captain conveniently blamed the mishap on witches, a group of Danish men and women who subsequently confessed under torture. Soon after, King James, seized with paranoia, decided to hold investigations of his own, resulting in the condemnation of a dozen supposed witches in Scotland in what became known as the North Berwick trials. After prolonged questioning and horrific torture (in some instances overseen by the king himself), the victims confessed and were burned at the stake in what would be the largest witch hunt in British history.

The trials became sordid tabloid fodder of the times, with the pamphlet *Newes from Scotland* documenting the confessions of a young woman named Geillis Duncan who, under torture, named numerous individuals as fellow witches: "Agnes Sampson the eldest witch of them all, dwelling in Haddington; Agnes Tompson of Edenbrough; Doctor Fian alias John Cuningham, master of the school at Saltpans in Lowthian, of whose life and strange acts you shall hear more largely in the end of this discourse. These were by the said Geillis Duncan accused, as also George Motts's wife, dwelling in Lowthian; Robert Grierson, skipper; and Jannet Blandilands;

Gustav Klimt · *Die Hexe* · Austria · 1898 The lithograph *The Witch* was among many vibrant original works published in the Vienna Secession art movement's radical magazine, *Ver Sacrum*. Klimt and other Austrian artists created the publication to protest normative art styles.

with the potter's wife of Seaton; the smith at the Brigge Hallis, with innumerable others in those parts, and dwelling in those bounds aforesaid, of whom some are already executed, the rest remained in prison to receive the doome of judgment at the Kinges Majesties will and pleasure."

In scholar Silvia Federici's *Caliban and the Witch*, published in 2004, the trials were "the first persecution in Europe that made use of multi-media propaganda to generate a mass psychosis among the population. Alerting the public to the dangers posed by witches, through pamphlets publicizing the most famous trials and the details of their atrocious deeds, was one of the first tasks of the printing press." News pamphlets and detailed books on witch hunting helped to push forward the propaganda. In 1647,

the self-proclaimed "Witchfinder General" Matthew Hopkins published his infamous tome, *The Discovery of Witches*, in which he intricately outlined his witch hunting methods. As word spread, the hysteria and horror would continue, and trials were held throughout most of Europe. In France, in a span of two years, 1643 to 1645, more than 600 people were arrested for witchcraft in the Languedoc area alone. Throughout the battles of the Thirty Years' War, a series of conflicts that flared in Europe between 1618 and 1648, witch hunts continued relentlessly, with countless put to death under false allegations; they were tortured until they confessed, and subsequently executed. Political unrest and economic instability became harbingers for persecution to come – those in power placed blame on the poor, the weak, and the vulnerable.

Claude Gillot · *Errant pendant la nuit…* · France ca. 1700 Known for his detailed mythological landscapes, Gillot depicts an imagined scene at a witches' sabbath.

The genocide of witches would continue unabated for generations, until the Age of Enlightenment in the late 1680s would begin to shift perspectives and philosophies. In 1682, an elderly woman named Temperance Lloyd became the last person executed for witchcraft in England. The trial was highly criticized, particularly by Lord Chief Justice Sir Francis North, an outspoken advocate against witchcraft persecution. In his investigation of the case, he wrote, "The evidence against them was very full and fanciful." Eventually, North's beliefs became widespread throughout the British Isles and Europe, and the horror, at long last, seemed to be over. Until a decade later, that is, when witch hunt hysteria finally hit the shores of the New World.

There had been scattered trials and executions throughout New England since the late 1640s, but the frenzy of persecutions that took place in Salem, Massachusetts, in 1692 were some of the most horrifying of all. Ignited in part by the writings of local theologian Cotton Mather, Salem became a hotbed of witchcraft activity after several young girls claimed that three women – colonists Sarah Good and Sarah Osborne and an enslaved woman named Tituba – had bewitched them. More "witches" were eventually accused and tortured for confessions. The first hanging would take place on June 10, 1692, and the last on September 22 of that same year. Nineteen people were ultimately killed over three months of horrifying trials in that infamous summer full of paranoia, accusation, and death.

Over the course of the next two centuries, witchcraft myth would merge in part with the study of occult arts, while the witch archetype endured throughout the art and literature of each era. Forgoing the exploitative spectacle of depictions created in the 1500s and 1600s, the witch was instead romanticized, both in artwork and in written works such as Jules Michelet's *La Sorcière*. Published in 1862, the book would rewrite the archetype of the witch, arguing that witchcraft was the last surviving vestige of pagan worship, celebrating rites of fertility and nature. Although full of misrepresentations and historical errors, *La Sorcière* became an immediate best seller, sparking in many ways the modern witchcraft movement to come – with its concept of the witch as the last of the pagan freedom fighters, relentlessly persecuted by the tyranny of the Church. The idea spread and was embraced by others in the Romantic movement.

The archetype of the witch as the persecuted "other" was also used by early suffragettes as the bleakest example of patriarchal tyranny. In a powerful speech at the 1852 Woman's Rights Convention, scholar and suffragette Matilda Joslyn Gage made this claim: "Witches too often were educated women who challenged existing power structures… The witch was in reality the profoundest thinker, the most advanced scientist of those ages.…No less today than during the darkest period of its history, is the church the great opponent of woman's education, every advance step for her having found the church antagonistic." Gage, an author and scholar, was also an ardent abolitionist and defender of Native American rights. Her son-in-law also happened to be L. Frank Baum, who would go on to create perhaps the most powerful fictional witches in Western culture in his multivolume children's book series, which included *The Wonderful Wizard of Oz*.

By the late 1800s, the witch had become both an emblem of injustice and a subject of romantic speculation. In America, the writer Charles Godfrey Leland would explore the origins of the archetype in *Aradia: Gospel of the Witches*. Published in 1899, his book helped introduce the concept of witchcraft as descended from the rites of ancient goddess worship and influenced several key figures in the development of modern witchcraft. The Theosophists and Transcendentalists, meanwhile, were exploring themes of nature and the supernatural throughout their vast output of literature and art of the late 19th century. Magick and the study of the occult were embraced by such organizations as the Hermetic Order of the Golden Dawn, whose members boasted the poet W. B. Yeats and the artist Pamela Colman Smith, who would go on to illustrate the iconic *Rider Waite Smith* Tarot deck. The infamous occultist Aleister Crowley was also a member and author of several books on ceremonial magick as well as his own Tarot deck, *The Thoth*, illustrated by British artist Lady Frieda Harris.

Another member of the Golden Dawn who would influence the ongoing evolution of witchcraft was writer, scholar, and ceremonial magician Dion Fortune. Her novels and nonfiction work, particularly her book *The Cosmic Doctrine*, were purported to have been penned through channeling from 1923 to

1925 and would have a profound effect on 20th-century witchcraft. A few years prior, in 1921, the anthropologist Margaret Murray had published her now rather infamous study, *The Witch-Cult in Western Europe*, in which she claimed that witchcraft was indeed pagan in origin. Murray introduced the terms *olde religion* and *sabbat*, claiming that medieval witch cults gathered in groups of 13 for nature and fertility rites. There is little to back up the historical veracity of actual witch cults in Europe, and many of Murray's theories have since been debunked by scholars. Murray herself based much of her book on themes she found in the 1890 discourse *The Golden Bough*. Written by scholar Sir James George Frazer and published in two volumes, it was a

Stewart Farrar · Janet Farrar in Osiris Position **England · 1971** Wiccan high priestess Janet Farrar, a prolific author on modern witchcraft, poses in the crossed-wrist Egyptian god posture in a drawing-down-the-moon ritual. Performed in sacred circles, covens practice the ceremony to invoke the energies of gods and goddesses.

comparative study of mythology, religion, and magick. *The Golden Bough* incited controversy concerning Frazer's theory that religion and myth were primitive ways to explain the mysteries of the natural world.

Although the historical legitimacy of both Murray's and Frazer's publications have since been questioned, the books played key roles in the foundation of modern witchcraft, particularly in the beliefs expounded by British occultist Gerald Gardner. Considered the founder of 20th-century witchcraft, Gardner spent much of his life living in India, Malaysia, and Sri Lanka. He had purportedly studied the practices of Hindu Sufis and Freemasons, studied with Theosophist Annie

Besant, as well as with the occult organization Fellowship of Crotona, and been a member of Aleister Crowley's Ordo Templi Orientis — all before forming his own unique tradition, now known as Wicca. Claiming he had first been taught what he termed "the craft" in 1939 by a woman he referred to as "Old Dorothy," Gardner would write fictional work on the topic under a nom de plume, in part because witchcraft laws were still in place in Britain. When these laws were finally repealed in 1951, Gardner published two books using his own name: *Witchcraft Today* in 1954 and, five years later, *The Meaning of Witchcraft*, which essentially outlined the tenets of what would become the predominant modern tradition of the practice.

David Teniers the Younger · *Witches' Initiation*
Flanders · ca. 1648 A mentor and neophyte are shown among a multitude of demonic beings and a possible devil character in an imagined initiation requiring sworn allegiance to darkness.

Francisco de Goya · A Scene from *El Hechizado por Fuerza* · Spain · 1798 A demon holds the lamp that Don Claudio, the protagonist of Antonio de Zamora's play, must always keep lit and full of oil because his life depends on it.

Gardnerian Wicca spread rapidly, in large part due to the efforts of British poet and author Doreen Valiente, who remains one of the most influential women in modern witchcraft. Through her engaging writing and interviews, Valiente helped to introduce Gardner's concepts of Wicca to a global audience. Her books and lectures detailed a magickal practice centered on nature, inclusion, and self-discovery. She quoted Dion Fortune in 1978's *Witchcraft for Tomorrow*: "'All the gods are one god, and all the goddesses are one goddess, and there is one initiator,'" adding that the "one initiator is one's own high self, with which the personality becomes more and more integrated as the path of spiritual evolution is followed."

Gardnerian Wicca would eventually be joined by several other witchcraft practices,

among them the Dianic, goddess-centered Neopaganism, influenced in part by Murray's writings as well as Leland's *Aradia*. Founded in the 1970s by Zsuzsanna Budapest, Dianic practices worship only the Goddess, primarily in the form of the Roman goddess Diana. There were also the Neoclassical and Alexandrian sects, the latter made famous by Alex and Maxine Sanders, whose theatrical, erotic rituals made headlines around the world.

The Sanderses would appear in a number of films and documentaries throughout the late 1960s and early 1970s, openly showcasing and sharing their coven's secrets, rites, and beliefs. After the couple separated in 1972, Maxine continued to run her Temple of the Mother coven in London, and it is still renowned and respected for its charitable work within the local community.

Throughout the 20th century, the embrace of occult practice would also serve as creative inspiration for a generation of rebellious, inventive female artists who would transform the witch archetype into a reflection of their own complex identities. A circle of Surrealists that included Leonora Carrington, Remedios Varo, and Leonor Fini would form a kind of coven of their own, translating the concept of witchcraft into a representation of imaginative individuality and fertile, fecund, distinctly female power. During the same era, writers like Anaïs Nin and filmmaker Maya Deren would also explore a future feminine through their sensual, revelatory works.

Unknown · Portrait of Gerald Gardner · England ca. 1960 Considered the founder of modern Wicca, Gardner's writings had a massive influence on the evolution of the practice in the late 20th and 21st centuries.

Later, the occultist, poet, and artist Marjorie Cameron would bring her esoteric aesthetic to Hollywood's cult underground, appearing in films by experimental filmmakers Kenneth Anger and Curtis Harrington, as well as producing her own prolific output of paintings and writings. The red-haired, wild-eyed dancer, artist, and unapologetic bohemian Vali Myers established a studio and wildlife sanctuary on the Italian coast in the mid-1960s, becoming known as a countercultural icon, the beautiful and mysterious "Witch of Positano." In 1968, the popular astrologer and occult author Louise Huebner was proclaimed, "Official Witch of Los Angeles County" at a ceremony at the Hollywood Bowl. A year later, Huebner released an album of spells and incantations entitled, "Seduction Through Witchcraft". New Zealander Rosaleen Norton, who went by the name Thorn, was another painter, occultist, and freethinker; she was known through the 1960s and 1970s as the "Witch of Kings Cross."

During this period, the burgeoning women's rights movement ushered in a new era of the witch as activist, the archetype emerging as a signifier of a feminine revolution. One of the most explicit examples of this can be found in the work of 1960s radical feminist activist group W.I.T.C.H. (Women's International Terrorist Conspiracy from Hell). The organization fought for women's and civil rights and equality, participated in the antiwar movement, and, among other acts of theatrical rebellion, put a hex on Wall Street. Their manifesto read, "W.I.T.C.H. is…theater, revolution, magic, terror, joy,

garlic flowers, spells….the living remnants of the oldest culture of all – one in which men and women were equal sharers in a truly cooperative society, before the death-dealing sexual, economic, and spiritual repression of the Imperialist Phallic Society took over and began to destroy nature and human society."

The women's rights movement would essentially reinterpret aspects of Gardnerian Wicca and Neopaganism into various facets of new-era witchcraft, the archetype remaining fluid and adaptable. Gardner himself had famously stated, "The witches do not know the origin of their cult." Many felt this meant that the craft itself, without origin, subsequently could be reinterpreted according to the individual, forgoing the rigidity of organized religion to allow for future evolution.

In an attempt to define the tenets of modern witchcraft, a group known as the American

Unknown · Doreen Valiente with Ceremonial Sword · England · ca. 1970 Considered the high priestess of modern witchcraft, Valiente is photographed with a ritual implement. As a co-conspirator of Wicca founder Gerald Gardner, she revived witchcraft as a legitimate religion and helped lift a ban that forbade practice. Her pioneering feminist efforts transformed the future of the craft.

Council of Witches reported in 1974, after much outreach, that the craft was varied and inclusive. Each coven was considered autonomous; each explored various symbologies and rituals. In her seminal 1979 tome, *Drawing Down the Moon*, journalist and witchcraft practitioner Margot Adler wrote, "That's why Wicca is flexible, it's religion without the middleman." She added, "It doesn't matter whether your tradition is forty thousand years old or whether it was created last week...dogma is the worst thing you can have in the Craft."

The same year that Adler's densely researched book drew back the veil on witchcraft in the modern world, the California-based practitioner Starhawk pioneered a new, empowered, goddess- and nature-centric approach with her groundbreaking book *Dreaming the Dark: Magic, Sex and Politics*.

In it, Starhawk made the claim that "a society that could heal the dismembered world would recognize the inherent value of each person and of the plant, animal, and elemental life that makes up the earth's living body; it would offer real protection, encourage free expression, and reestablish an ecological balance to be biologically and economically sustainable. Its underlying metaphor would be mystery, the sense of wonder at all that is beyond us and around us, at the forces that sustain our lives and the intricate complexity and beauty of their dance."

With books like *Dreaming the Dark* and Luisah Teish's *Jambalaya*, an exploration of African American spiritual traditions, and later academic works such as Silvia Federici's *Caliban and the Witch*, a wave of authors and artists helped to push forward the concept of witchcraft as empowering spiritual practice. Today, the craft is considered nothing less than a visionary venture. It rejects dogma in favor of creativity, and celebrates diversity and inclusion over exclusion and division. The modern witch encompasses a vast range of identities and expressions. Practitioners of the contemporary craft are most likely to defy definition and to honor the full spectrum of identifiers like gender or race. Ritual is considered a method of connection to the cosmos and the natural world, to our bodies and to each other. Rites are flexible and varied.

The practice can be explored in a myriad of manners, through activism and rebellion, meditation and movement, or cathartic works of art. As Starhawk states in *The Spiral Dance*, "There are two kinds of power. One is power over, which is always destructive, and the other is power from within, which is a transcendent and creative power." With that in mind, perhaps the most magickal act of all is the ongoing discovery of ourselves.

Hans Baldung Grien · *The Three Ages of Man and Death* · Germany · 1541–44 The early metaphorical work starkly presents the transient nature of youth, and how it is intrinsically linked to death.

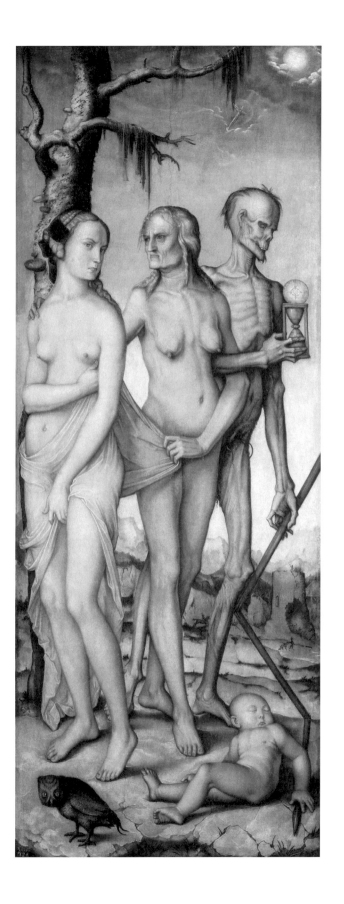

TRANSMUTATION
OF THE WITCH

Persecution into Empowerment

Like the word wild, *the word* witch *has come to be understood as a pejorative, but long ago it was an appellation given to both old and young women healers, the word* witch *deriving from the word* wit, *meaning wise. This was before cultures carrying the one-God-only religious image began to overwhelm the older pantheistic cultures which understood the Deity through multiple religious images of the universe and all its phenomena.*

— CLARISSA PINKOLA ESTÉS, PH.D.,
Women Who Run with the Wolves: Myths and Stories of the Wild Woman Archetype, 1992

The witch is both an archetype with ancient roots and an identity with modern origins. Forged in a syncretic cauldron of Christianity and paganism, fact and fiction, myth and history, witches defy simple definitions. They appear in disparate cultures and costumes. They run the gamut from good to evil to the liminal in between. Beyond their mercurial allure, witches have arguably endured as cultural icons because of their persecution. "The witch hunts of history have had the most drastic social consequences of all kinds of witch beliefs," Johannes Dillinger explains in *The Routledge History of Witchcraft*, published in 2020. The witch hunts and their legacy of brutality dictate how we understand the witch today.

Witches first emerge in ancient Greek, Hebrew, and Roman texts. These predominantly female figures used their magick to commune with the dead, poison their enemies with herbal remedies, and divine the future. They inspired awe and fear and were often outliers within their communities – but not quite the targeted outcasts they would later become. As Ronald Hutton clarifies in his 2017 book, *The Witch: A History of Fear, from Ancient Times to the Present,* "ancient traditions played an important role in the formation of European witchcraft beliefs in more complicated and subtle ways, and over a long period of time." But it wasn't until Christianity took root in Europe during the first millennium that the wicked witch of the Western world began to materialize.

Kiki Smith · *Pyre Woman Kneeling* · **United States**
2002 A bronze female figure tops a pyre. In Smith's narrative style, the statue commemorates women who were burned for witchcraft.

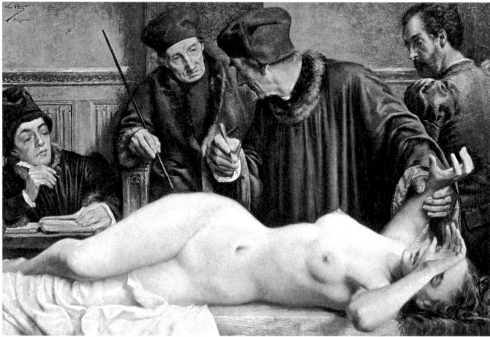

Amid plague, famine, war, and the religious conflict of the Middle Ages, Christian theologians began to explore the nature of evil. Drawing on Church doctrine and popular folk beliefs alike, scholars from Saint Augustine to Thomas Aquinas proposed various theories about harmful magick, *maleficium*, and the servants of Satan who practiced it. As the Church set its sights on differentiating Christian from pagan and the holy from the heretic, these demonological writings became indispensable to fleshing out the diabolical witch. Though there were no large-scale witch hunts during the medieval period, it was during that time when "concerns about harmful magic coalesced with those about demonic presence and power in the world," the historian Michael D. Bailey avers in his essay, "Witchcraft and Demonology in the Middle Ages," in *The Routledge History of Witchcraft*. This culminated, he continues, "in the ready acceptance, at least by many authorities, of an automatic and inevitable relationship between the practitioner of *maleficium* – the witch – and the devil."

By the 15th century, the satanic witch had crystallized into an agent of disaster and disorder. The invention of the printing press allowed witch hunting tracts to be disseminated far and wide, and publications like Heinrich Kramer's *Malleus Maleficarum* (*The Hammer of Witches*), first published in 1487, set an early standard for witch persecution and prosecution. Building on centuries of Christian sexism that trace back to Eve harkening the downfall of mankind, Kramer asserted that "all witchcraft comes from carnal lust, which is in women insatiable."

Although this passage has at times been employed to oversimplify the complex motivating factors behind the witch hunts, gender undoubtedly played a pivotal role.

According to contemporary estimates, 70 to 80 percent of those tried for witchcraft between the 15th and 17th centuries were women. In some regions, men were predominantly accused, but older, poor women made up the overwhelming majority. "The themes of the witch trials recur with monotonous regularity across Western Europe," Lyndal Roper emphasizes in his 2014 tome, *Witch Craze: Terror and Fantasy in Baroque Germany*, "featuring sex with the Devil, harm to women in childbed, and threats to fertility, all issues which touch centrally on women's experience."

Demonologies published after the *Malleus Maleficarum* would continue to shape and refine beliefs about witches and witch hunting. However, it was Kramer's book that served as a prime source for the witch imagery that still captivates us today. Spurred in part by that work, Ulrich Molitor's witchcraft treatise, *On Female Witches and Seers*, published in 1489, finally put a face to the satanic sorceress with accompanying woodcut prints of witches kissing demons, casting spells to change the weather, and flying on pitchforks disguised as animals. These images were far more accessible to the general populace than demonological texts in Latin, allowing early modern people to get a glimpse of the witch. Molitor and the *Malleus Maleficarum* also emboldened artists like Albrecht Dürer, Hans Baldung Grien, and countless others to engage with witches, transforming them into wildly popular subjects of fine art.

Tompkins Harrison Matteson · *The Trial of George Jacobs, 5th August 1692* · **United States** · **1855** Accused of witchcraft by his family, Jacobs was convicted and hanged during the Salem witch trials.

Edmond Van Hove · **Scientists Look for a Mole on a Woman's Body** · **Belgium** · **1888** Believed to be a branding by the Devil, a "witch's mark" was used as evidence in convicting witches.

Witch hysteria continued to spread across Western Europe and, eventually, North America, serving as a catchall supernatural explanation for illness, infertility, blights, pestilence, death, and intercommunity conflict. At times, some of the accused did engage in folk magick or practices that were contrary to dominant Christian traditions,

Unknown · Matthew Hopkins, Witchfinder General · England · 1647 The frontispiece of the book *The Discovery of Witches* portrays the infamous man responsible for hundreds of witch executions.

Albert von Keller · *Witches' Sleep* · Germany · 1900 Known for his occult art, Keller was also a practitioner of mysticism. The calm demeanor of the victim alludes to her ability to use magick – leaving behind her body and the suffering as other women agonize over her departure.

but most witchcraft accusations were pure fabrications. Laws and lore varied from region to region, but cruelty and corruption were endemic to most witch trials and the "confessions" of the accused were often elicited through horrific methods of torture. Throughout the early modern era, at least 50,000 people were executed for the crime of witchcraft.

By the early 18th century, however, witch hunts began to wane as religious and secular authorities questioned the efficacy and ethics of witch persecution. But witches didn't fade into the background; they merely grew in popularity as fantastical subjects to be mined by creative minds.

A new fate awaited the witch in the 19th century, when writers began to look to witches and witch hunts with a sympathetic eye. Inspired by ancient mythology, Romantic occultists, and freethinkers of

his time, French historian Jules Michelet penned *La Sorcière* in 1862, a vivid account of the witch hunts with a protofeminist twist. According to Marion Gibson in her 2018 book, *Witchcraft: The Basics*, Michelet "saw witchcraft prosecution as a general means of oppression, especially of women." His explicit prose captured the attention (and ire) of many, but also took significant liberties with historical fact by incorrectly suggesting accused witches were all "skilled herbalists and psychics, valued by the poor and anti-feudal activists."

A few decades after *La Sorcière* made waves, American suffragist Matilda Joslyn Gage published her 1893 manuscript, *Woman, Church and State*. Moved by Michelet, Gage took similar liberties with history, positioning the formerly persecuted witch as "a woman of superior knowledge" to galvanize readers in the fight against patriarchy and misogyny of her time. Gage's

Jörg Merckel · *The Derenburg Witch Trial* · Germany 1555 Claiming partnership with Satan, a woman named Gröbischen was burned with another condemned witch during the five-year-long Derenburg

trials. The popular print reads that she was saved from the flames by the Devil himself. Her husband also depicted, was burned for fornicating with her sister, thereby bedeviled by association.

work resonated with other fin de siècle suffragists and sparked her son-in-law L. Frank Baum to include a good witch character in his book *The Wonderful Wizard of Oz*, first published in 1900. No longer just an evil, child-murdering hag or a devilish seductress, the witch began to shape-shift in the decades that followed. Drawing from a heady brew of fact and fiction, the witch eventually blossomed into a martyr mascot for feminist activists in the 1960s and '70s as well as a figurehead for Wiccan and other neo-pagan groups looking to reclaim the divine feminine in their religious and spiritual practices.

This lightning-fast trip through the annals of "witchtory" leads us back into the 21st century, where witches are indeed everywhere: in art, fashion, literature, film, and television. The witch is now a spiritual identity, a political identity, and an evergreen archetype of

female power and persecution. You'll find the witch on protest signs at rallies in support of gender justice and in millions of Instagram posts tagged #witchesofinstagram. Witches make the news every time a politician cries "witch hunt" or a group of witchcraft practitioners leads a public hex against oppression or inequity.

Make no mistake, however, real witch hunts still rage in certain parts of the world, and there are few countries today where women aren't scapegoated in some way for society's ills. But though witch hunts won't likely ever go away, neither will the witch. For when the witch appears — regardless of culture or costume or gender — it is usually as a beacon or a bellwether. Reviled or revered, witches always echo our deepest, darkest desires and fears.

Lee Balterman · Yippie Protesters Dressed Like Witches · United States · 1969 Women don classic witch costumes to object to the infamous Chicago Eight trial of anti–Vietnam War protesters, which they deemed a witch hunt. The accused were convicted of conspiracy to riot, but the ruling was overturned.

My initial contact with witchcraft probably began before I was even born. My parents named me Lilith, that's my given name. And they always had a connection to that particular goddess, even though they weren't in a formalized practice. They got married in the late 1960s and were one of the first interracial couples to be legally married in New York state. For me, there was already an element of magick and witchcraft in my life. I knew I had a different relationship to the universe around me. My Scottish grandmother had a lot of Celtic witchcraft practices. And as I got older and more in touch with my Native American and Black family, I began to shape my own practices from all these influences. A lot of my writing and magick recently has been surrounding protest magick and trying to change things that maybe we've put up with for way too long. Now we know that we have these tools. Witchcraft and magick for the first time is not subject to the negative oppression that it was subject to for hundreds if not thousands of years. So this allows us to take back our power in a very real and practical and effective way. I'm really proud that I live in a time when this is possible.

— LILITH DORSEY, Filmmaker, Dancer, Scholar,
& Author of *Orishas, Goddesses, and Voodoo Queens*, 2020

Vali Myers · *Blue Fox* · Australia · 1972–74
A free-spirited visionary connection to nature and
specifically to animals was intrinsic to Myers's being.
Her art often portrayed her with her pets in scenes
of wildness.

MAGICKAL CULTURES

Reconciling Witchcraft & Global Folk Traditions

I come from a Chicana background and was raised observing Dia de Los Muertos and keeping altars in the home. In my family and culture, keeping an altar is a typical part of your everyday home and life. Observing my people's traditions in these contexts taught me to think about and search for spiritual insights outside of any organized or colonial religion. It suggested to me that there are many ways to talk to the divine and to connect with what we want and what we love.

— REBECCA ARTEMISA, Artist & Witch, 2020

The allure of modern witchcraft lies in the promise that anyone can reclaim their power through a hodgepodge of spiritual mysticism. In contrast to religion, witchcraft purposely avoids strict rules, with no definitive "right" or "wrong" ways to practice. But there are ways to practice magick without perpetuating damage. Whether it's educating oneself about witchcraft's colonialist history, avoiding practices not meant for you, or creating your own rituals, many Asian, Latinx, Indigenous, and Black witches who practice their craft offer guidance on how to respectfully incorporate other cultures' practices into your own. Of course, no one group is a monolith, and individuals from disenfranchised communities have vastly different opinions on these issues.

Brought over to North and South America by European colonizers, the word *witch* was used to demonize the spiritual practices of Indigenous peoples and survivors of the transatlantic slave trade. Not everyone who practices spiritualities commonly associated with the witch aesthetic identifies with the word, and labeling their sacred rituals or medicinal practices "magick" is considered offensive; it was also a tactic used by colonizers to justify violence against Black and Indigenous people — and continues to be used by those in power today.

People around the world are still being persecuted and killed over accusations of witchcraft. In Nigeria, for example, children deemed "witches" are abandoned and ostracized by society. While the Afro-Brazilian religion Candomblé, which has historically been practiced in secret, is no longer banned in Brazil, its followers are being victimized by an evangelical Christian movement that denounces their worship as demonic, calling it witchcraft as a reason to condemn it.

Tsukioka Yoshitoshi · *The old devil woman retrieving her arm* · Japan · 1889 A woodcut from a series of illustrations created for a 19th-century Japanese collection of ghost stories and folktales.

Identifying as a witch should be an *intentional* self-declarative act. Formal power structures that gatekeep communication with the divine are antithetical to modern witchcraft (a fact that sets it apart from many other religions). Magick, in many ways, is everywhere and for everyone. Some practitioners may be more experienced and knowledgeable, but no witch can rightfully claim a monopoly on spiritual access.

On the other hand, certain terms, rituals, and herbs that are often commodified and marketed today are appropriated from marginalized spiritualities that would not consider them magickal at all. The widely used term *chakra* is specific to the South Asian religion of Hinduism. Another example is the term *gypsy*, which has been used for centuries as

a racial slur to persecute Romani people, but is now used by countless brands to market a bohemian look associated with fortune-telling and crystals. Smudging with palo santo and white sage is considered a sacred practice for many native North American tribes, one that was only passed down to members of their community and previously was done in secret. Until the American Indian Religious Freedom Act was passed in 1978, it was illegal for Native North and South American tribes to practice many of their ceremonies, including burning white sage, yet now one can find sage bundles offered at retailers across the globe.

Aspiring witches must respect the boundaries of closed practices that explicitly state they can *only* be practiced by people who are descendants of a cultural heritage. Hoodoo, for example, originates from slavery and was created specifically for Black people.

And while a modern reclaiming of witchcraft is about women taking back neo-pagan religions like Wicca from the men who made them, these late-20th-century feminist reclaimings often still grounded witchcraft in cisheteronormative gender binaries. While the "lady witch" archetype is empowering to some, it erases the queerness in many of the disenfranchised practices New Age witchcraft grounds itself in. Two Spirit, for example, is a pan-Indian term coined in 1990 to describe the social title given to members in the community who fulfill a traditional "third gender" role.

In Yoruban-based spiritualities across the transatlantic slave trade diaspora, from Candomblé in Brazil to voodoo in New

Wiele & Klein · **Two Malayan exorcists dressed in elaborate ritual costume** · **Malaysia** · **Early 20th Century** These embellished sorcerers were able to invoke real states of frenetic trance that were said to liberate cursed victims from evil possession.

Gromyko Semper · *Alchemy of a Babaylan* · **Philippines 2013** As the artist explains, "The Babaylans were the spiritual leaders of the tribe in pre-colonial Philippines. A warrior-priest/priestess of ancient Filipinos, they presided over the religious rites and were thought to serve as mediators between gods and humans."

Orleans, guardian spirits (or Iwa and Orishas like Eshu-Elegbara, Olokun, Abata, and Inle) are often depicted as gender-fluid, intersex, homosexual, or androgynous. Forced assimilation to Christianity then transformed them into more binary, heteronormative, cis deities. None of the aforementioned is synonymous with witchcraft, to be clear. But for those who do identify with the term, it's powerful to learn of the rich queer history in spiritualities from around the world.

The multiplicity of traditions offers seekers inclusivity and fluidity and spirit-centered and magick-based rituals that can be adapted to the needs of each practitioner,

while bringing together both ancient and future-forward spiritualities, accepting of all, without judgment or limitation. The folks turning to modern witchcraft were often made to feel othered, ostracized, or excluded from more mainstream faiths. Ultimately in witchcraft they find a more accepting, diverse, empowering collective — to call their own.

Myrlande Constant · *Haitians, Lend a Hand to Mother* · Haiti · 2008–17 Constant's Haitian ceremonial vodou flags, or drapo vodou, intentionally sparkle to engage the attention of Iwa spirits. Every color in the flag is highly symbolic and codified based on the different attributes of the Iwa.

André Hora · *Obaluaiye* · Brazil/England · 2010 Called Orisha and considered deities in the Yoruba tradition, the Obaluaiye are spirits who incarnate as humans to relieve suffering in the Earth realm.

I've always been drawn to the magickal and mysterious. I am multiracial, so that in itself is reflected in my magick, the rituals, and the spellwork that I practice and share. I infuse elements of my cultures, utilizing aspects of traditional folk healing from my Indigenous Mexican and African American ancestors. I've learned and implemented many useful rituals from witches and healers from my own family, and from those that I've met along my journey. I trust my intuition, and let it guide me. I study plants and minerals for their healing properties. I implement color, astrology, candles, oils, and natural resins. If my magick had a name, it could be defined as natural magick. Creating magick IS my life. There is no differentiation in my world between the mundane and the mystical — both coexist together. My intention is powerful and in my creative rituals I am often going between worlds and dedicating myself completely to my desired outcome. At this time, there is a very powerful, yet subtle, shift taking place on our planet, the awakening of the divine feminine energy. Witches, especially witches of color, are reclaiming their personal power and that scares people. This power or energy has been inside of us for many years. It is an ancient wisdom that has been suppressed due to societal conditioning, pressures to conform into what is deemed "acceptable" behavior. Many young women have been taught to ignore or discredit things like their intuition, or "psychic senses," for fear of being ridiculed or called "crazy". Eventually we are taught to forget about our natural gifts. We lose the connection to living with the cycles of nature and, sadly, to ourselves. Magick is our birthright. The witch is like no other archetype, because the witch embodies autonomy over one's self, but most importantly over one's soul. To me, it means freedom, the power to boldly and unapologetically embrace nature, heal yourself, heal your community, respect the seen and unseen realms. The freedom to be your most authentic self. To embrace ALL aspects of whoever you may be — fiercely. The witch prevails from now until eternity because the witch knows how to survive and shape-shifts with cycle and season. The witch transcends all time and space, and will prevail in the hearts and minds of anyone who wishes to shed their soul like a serpent. The witch lives because the witch has never died.

— BRI LUNA, Founder of The Hoodwitch, Visual Storyteller, & Bruja, 2020

Katelan V. Foisy · *Queen of Sticks* from *The Hoodoo Tarot* · **United States** · **2020** A collaboration between artist Foisy and writer Tayannah Lee McQuillar, the *Hoodoo Tarot* deck explores arcana archetypes through the lens of American rootwork traditions and hoodoo symbolism.

Essay by
DR. KATE TOMAS

BEYOND OPPRESSION

The Power of the Witch

A history of women...must begin with struggles [of] the medieval proletariat...Only if we evoke these struggles...can we understand the role that women had and why their power had to be destroyed for capitalism to develop, as it was by the three-century-long persecution of the witches.

— SILVIA FEDERICI, *Caliban and the Witch*, 2004

Perhaps the thing that connects all people who self-identify as witches and who would be described as such by others is a particular type of access to hidden knowledge and power. The witch is someone who — rather than follow the traditional and culturally endorsed pathways to power, either via necessity or choice — pursues wisdom, knowing, and the ability to impact their own life and the lives of others through alternate means that are not culturally endorsed or seen as valid.

The witch is part of a wider culture, and at the same time exists on the fringes of this culture. The witch represents hidden knowing because they have access to information and knowledge that they *should not* have access to. If you want money and power, capitalist culture says you must get an education, get a "good job," work hard. The witch refuses such dictates and asks, "Is there another way?" There is always another way.

The sort of knowledge and power that the witch has access to is ancient and infinite; at the heart of all forms of witchcraft is an understanding that there is more to the world than meets the eye, and that if one establishes relationships (with herbs, animals, plants, elements, any others), one can count on their help and power to bolster one's own. The witch is always open to expansion, to learning, to growth. This makes them a dangerous threat to any human-imposed structure of power (and oppression).

But it is not just this access to unauthorized ways of knowing that has associated the witch with danger. Witchcraft is ultimately concerned with access to power, and with changing the material reality of the life of the witch and those who need their help. The wise woman who acts as midwife and gynecologist to women who would otherwise have no choice around planning their families is not just helping women in need. She is actively subverting the very structure of society as it is set up under patriarchy. The witch who shares knowledge of parsley tea with a person who does not want to be pregnant is not just sharing information — they are redistributing power.

Frances F. Denny · "Shine" from *Major Arcana: Portraits of Witches in America* · United States · 2017
Modern witch Shine Blackhawk is a channeler of animal spirits and ancestors. Blackhawk practices her own synthesis of hoodoo (Black Native American spirituality) and shamanism.

This is the power that the witch holds, a power that comes from a way of engaging with the universe that is open to its infinite nature. This ability to redistribute power that cannot be controlled provoked the frenzied witch hunts in Europe and America, and it is the fear of this ability that sustains the animus against witchcraft still very present today. The witch cannot be controlled; their access to power cannot be taken away. For this reason they are a threat to those whose power is reliant on maintaining structures of oppression.

Many cultures need the figure of the witch in order to define what is and is not "ordinary" or "mundane." Many people turn to witchcraft when they feel all else has failed them. Witchcraft and the witch act, therefore, as a sort of constantly evolving metric for what society considers acceptable, and for who has power and access to it.

Who, then, is a witch? They are anyone with the ability to see beyond — beyond structures of power and oppression, beyond the idea that there are only certain "valid" ways to know and only certain things to know. They are anyone who uses this ability to see beyond, to redistribute power, and to combat oppression. They are me. They are you. They will always be.

Kay Turner and Rosina Lardieri · *The Turning* United States · 2017 From "What a Witch, Part 6: Before and After: What the Witch's Nose Knows That Andy Warhol's Nose Doesn't Know." Document of a performance by Kay Turner with photographer Rosina Lardieri, A.I.R. Gallery, Brooklyn, NY, 2017.

Lauren Lancaster · W.I.T.C.H. (detail) · United States · 2017 The Women's International Terrorist Conspiracy from Hell was founded in 1968 by feminist antiwar protesters. The black-dressed, pointy-hatted, faceless witches were an undeniable vision and significant force during a time of political urgency.

A WORLD
BEWITCHED

A Timeline of Witchcraft

1200 and 165 BCE · The word *witch* is first mentioned in the Old Testament in verses from the Books of Exodus, Deuteronomy, and Leviticus.

1230s CE · The Catholic Church institutes its policy of Inquisition in an effort to root out heretics.

1258 · The Church makes demon worship and sorcery punishable acts of heresy.

1316–34 · Pope John XXII issues several papal bulls connecting heresy with witchcraft, thereby inciting a growing paranoia and persecutions against those accused of practicing "sorcery."

1484 · At the request of the monk Heinrich Kramer, an inquisitor charged by the Church to root out heretical uprisings, the *Summis desiderantes affectibus* is issued by Pope Innocent VIII. This papal bull gives monks permission to investigate crimes of witchcraft and heresy.

1486–87 · The *Malleus Maleficarum* is published. Penned by Heinrich Kramer and Jacob Sprenger, the book is a detailed

manual for hunting down and identifying witches.

1536 · Anne Boleyn is executed. Although accused of witchcraft by her husband, King Henry VIII, she was ultimately found guilty of treason in conspiracy with her alleged lovers, not of witchcraft.

1542 · As fear of witches continues in England, the country passes its first Witchcraft Act, making witchcraft a secular crime.

1580 · French lawyer Jean Bodin publishes his treatise on witchcraft trial methodologies, *On the Demon-Mania of Sorcerers.*

1580–1650 · Witch hunt hysteria sweeps through Europe. Thousands of people are accused of witchcraft, tried, and executed.

1584 · Reginald Scot of Kent publishes *Discoverie of Witchcraft*, which expresses doubts as to the veracity of witchcraft.

1590–92 · King James VI of Scotland (later to become James I of England) personally oversees the condemnation of a dozen supposed witches in Scotland in

what will become known as the North Berwick trials.

1597 · King James VI of Scotland (later James I of England) publishes his study of magick and witchcraft, *Daemonologie.*

1604 · The Witchcraft Act of King James I of England expands the list of punishable offenses related to witchcraft.

1610–30 · Throughout Europe and England, an immense wave of witchcraft persecutions kill countless innocent people.

1612 · Twelve people are accused of witchcraft in the Pendle trials in Lancashire, England. Of the accused, one is found not guilty, one dies in prison, and 10 are put to death.

1634 · In Loudun, France, a group of nuns claims to be possessed and blames Father Urbain Grandier for practicing sorcery. Even after Father Grandier is executed, the "possessions" continue to occur for the next three years.

1647 · The self-proclaimed "Witchfinder General" Matthew

1200 ———— 1500 ———— 1600

Hopkins publishes his infamous tome, *The Discovery of Witches*, in which he intricately outlines his witch hunting methods.

1662 · Isobel Gowdie is executed after confessing to witchcraft without being tortured. She claimed to have led a coven for many years and to have been in direct league with the Devil.

1682 · King Louis XIV of France outlaws witchcraft trials.

1692 · Salem, Massachusetts, is swept up in terrifying witch hunt fervor. Nineteen people are killed over the course of three months of horrifying trials in the New England village.

1862 · Jules Michelet publishes *La Sorcière*, which argues that witchcraft is the last surviving vestige of pagan worship, celebrating rites of fertility and nature.

1887 · The Hermetic Order of the Golden Dawn is founded.

1890 · *The Golden Bough* is published. Written by scholar Sir James George Frazer and published in two volumes, it is a comparative study of mythology, religion, and magick.

1890 · Scholar and ceremonial magician Dion Fortune is born. Her writings, particularly *The Cosmic Doctrine*, penned through channeling from 1923 to 1925, will have a profound effect on 20th-century witchcraft.

1893 · American suffragist and human-rights activist Matilda Joslyn Gage publishes *Woman, Church and State*, claiming the number of women executed in the witch hunts was in the millions.

1899 · Charles Godfrey Leland explores the origins of the witch archetype in *Aradia: Gospel of the Witches*.

1900 · L. Frank Baum publishes *The Wonderful Wizard of Oz*.

1921 · The author Margaret Alice Murray publishes her book on the witch trials, *The Witch-Cult in Western Europe*.

1948 · American artist and scholar Kurt Seligmann publishes his now classic overview of the occult practice over the ages, *The Mirror of Magic: A History of Magic in the Western World*.

1951 · The Fraudulent Mediums Act is passed in England, making witchcraft essentially legal and helping to spur the Wiccan Movement as witches could now go public.

1954 · Gerald Gardner publishes the books *Witchcraft Today* and, five years later, *The Meaning of Witchcraft*, outlining the tenets of modern Wicca.

1950s–70s · Occultist, poet, and artist Marjorie Cameron brings her esoteric aesthetic to Hollywood's cult underground, appearing in films by

experimental filmmakers Kenneth Anger and Curtis Harrington, as well as producing her own prolific output of paintings and writings.

1960s–70s · The artist and dancer Vali Myers establishes a studio and wildlife sanctuary on the Italian coast in the mid-1960s and becomes a counter-cultural icon, the beautiful and mysterious "Witch of Positano."

1960s–70s · New Zealander Rosaleen Norton, known as the "Witch of Kings Cross," influences many as a painter, occultist, and freethinker.

1950s–90s · Doreen Valiente, initiated by Gerald Gardner into his Wiccan coven, helps adapt many important Wiccan texts. Valiente introduces Gardner's concepts of Wicca to a global audience and remains one of the most influential women in modern witchcraft.

1968 · The Church of All Worlds begins publishing their influential Neopagan magazine, *Green Egg Magazine*.

1968 · Sybil Leek publishes her book *Diary of a Witch*.

1968 · W.I.T.C.H. (Women's International Terrorist Conspiracy from Hell), a collective of feminist activists, is founded. The organization fights for women's and civil rights and participates in the antiwar movement.

1970s · The women's rights movement ushers in a new phase of witchcraft as translated through a feminist lens.

1970s · Dianic, goddess-centered Neopaganism is founded by Zsuzsanna Budapest.

1970s · The Alexandrian sect of witchcraft is made famous by Alex and Maxine Sanders.

1970 · Scholar and Wiccan priest Raymond Buckland releases *Witchcraft: Ancient and Modern*.

1973 · *Witches, Midwives, and Nurses* is published by historians Barbara Ehrenreich and Deirdre English. The book makes the claim that women schooled in healing practices represented a particular threat to the patriarchy.

1974 · In an attempt to define the tenets of modern witchcraft, the American Council of Witches reports that the craft is varied and inclusive. Each coven is considered autonomous, exploring various symbologies and rituals.

1977 · Author, scholar, and practicing witch Laurie Cabot is proclaimed the official witch of Salem by Massachusetts governor Michael Dukakis.

1979 · With her seminal tome *Drawing Down the Moon*, journalist and witchcraft practitioner Margot Adler draws back the veil on modern witchcraft.

Jo Freeman · *W.I.T.C.H. '69* · United States 1969 According to scholar, activist, and author Freeman, "W.I.T.C.H. was more of an idea-in-action than an organization. Founded in 1968 by a group of radical women in New York City who wanted to do guerrilla theater, covens rose and fell around the country as opportunities to do zap actions presented themselves."

1979 · The California-based witchcraft practitioner Starhawk pioneers a new goddess- and nature-centric approach to the tradition with her groundbreaking book *The Spiral Dance*.

1980s · The New Age movement popularizes esoteric practices, including a revival of pagan and goddess-worship traditions.

1983 · Italian scholar Carlo Ginzburg's historical study *The Night Battles: Witchcraft and Agrarian Cults in the Sixteenth and Seventeenth Centuries* is published in English.

1983 · Marion Zimmer Bradley releases her feminist reinterpretation of the Arthurian legend, *The Mists of Avalon*.

1985 · Luisah Teish publishes *Jambalaya*, exploring African American spiritual traditions.

1986 · Janet and Stewart Farrar publish their influential book, *The Witches' Way: Principles, Rituals and Beliefs of Modern Witchcraft*.

1988 · Influential Wiccan, scholar, and author Scott Cunningham debuts his now-classic book *Wicca: A Guide for the Solitary Practitioner*. More than a million copies will sell.

1990s · Information on witchcraft becomes accessible through the self-publishing zine boom and witchcraft websites formed in the nascent days of the internet.

1992 · Raymond Buckland publishes *Buckland's Complete Book of Witchcraft*.

1994 · Silver RavenWolfe releases *To Ride a Silver Broomstick: New Generation Witchcraft*, influencing countless young witches.

1996 · The hugely popular Hollywood witchcraft movie *The Craft* is released.

1997 · The J. K. Rowling book *Harry Potter and the Philosopher's Stone*, the first book of the Harry Potter series, is published in the United Kingdom.

1999 · Renowned author and scholar Ronald Hutton releases his seminal tome, *The Triumph of the Moon: A History of Modern Pagan Witchcraft*.

2001 · *Harry Potter and the Sorcerer's Stone* debuts in U.S. theaters — marking the first in a series of global blockbuster films based on J. K. Rowling's books.

2004 · Silvia Federici publishes her book *Caliban and the Witch*.

2000s to present · Witchcraft is embraced by a new generation exploring individual expression, inclusivity, and community. Seeking to find connection outside the limitations of organized religions, they redefine and reinterpret the practice in a multitude of ways.

1970 ——— 1980 ——— 2000

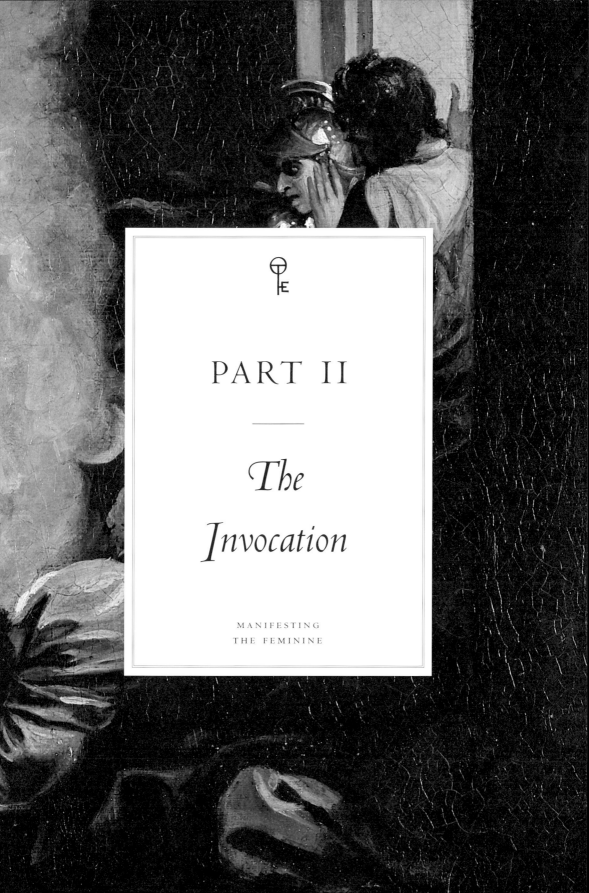

PART II

—

The

Invocation

MANIFESTING
THE FEMININE

FROM THE
ISLAND OF AEAEA
The Witch in Myth & Religion

O night, faithful friend of mysteries; and you, golden stars and moon, who follow the fiery star of day; and you, Hecate, goddess with threefold head, you know my designs and come to strengthen my spells and magic arts; and you, earth, who offer your potent herbs to magi; and airs, winds, mountains, streams, and lakes, and all you woodland gods, and all you gods of the night: Be present now.

— Prayer of Medea to Hecate from Ovid, *The Metamorphoses*, 8 CE

Mythological witches travel between worlds. In high culture they might appear as goddesses. In patriarchal religions, witches often appear as monsters. The witch embodies what writer Clarissa Pinkola Estés calls "the Old Wild Powers." And though the witches of myth are not easy to pin down, we know where to find them. Search the remote, wild places, places of isolation and enchantment. The witch loves to go where even the most valiant hero finds himself unnerved. She rides the wolves and calls the storms, she calms seas, stirs the whirlwinds, and summons forests back to life. Subduing the natural world is often the work of heroes, but the howling wilderness finds its guardian in the witch.

Medea prowled the cypress and olive groves of Corinth by light of a waxing moon, slicing herbs from their stalks with a bronze boline. Women in classical antiquity were barely allowed out of the house, but Medea was a witch, a woman alone, black hair loose and long, silk cloak open and ungodly. At midnight she spun three times then knelt, knees to dirt, charging Hekate to aid her work. She called upon the powers of the earth and the dark waters, she called upon the wild demons of nature and of night. "I calm rough seas and stir the calm by my magic spells," she sang, "bring clouds, disperse the clouds, raise storms and storms dispel; and, with my incantations, I grind the

(previous) Benjamin West · *Saul and the Witch of Endor* · England · 1777 In the Bible, Israel's King Saul consults a witch, who then summons the ghost of Samuel. The ghost appears and scolds them both before he predicts Saul's demise in a fated battle.

John William Waterhouse · *Circe Offering the Cup to Ulysses* · England · 1891 Waterhouse's painting imparts Circe's mesmerizing powers of seduction. In Homer's *Odyssey*, she changes Ulysses's crew into pigs, offering him the same poison.

serpent's teeth…" Here was a woman confident in her powers, commanding herbs to "return the flower of youth," not for herself, but as a favor to her husband. Later, when the ingrate betrayed her, she extracted her toll in the blood of his children.

In Ovid's *Metamorphoses*, written more than two millennia ago, we see one of the most famous witches of the classical world acting in ways common to witches throughout time. Witch time is not ordinary time; for her it's circular, cyclical, weird. It skips beats. Spend a day in her world, and you may return home to find your toddler now has a long gray beard. Witches don't heed the time clock, they writhe to the rhythms of the moon, the

seasons, the cosmos, and the mysteries of nature. A witch does not hustle. She will not be compelled. Witch time recalls a pre-Christian, pre-capitalist era, when humans and nature were one.

Consider Grendel's Mother, the old-world ogress defending her fanged, furry child. She lured Beowulf leagues beneath a savage sea to a cave as dark as the womb. In the Babylonian Talmud, the witch Lilith evaded the wrath of God by commanding a legion of demons from her desert refuge. Hekate, the three-headed patron deity of witches, performs her liminal rites at the crossroads, while Frau Hilda, the Teutonic nature goddess, can only be reached by descending into the cold, shining waters of a well. The Russian crone Baba Yaga haunts the deep dark woods, just like the contemporary witches in the *Blair Witch Project* or the recent film *The Witch*, where she plagues the heretic family in the form of a hare.

Witches are shape-shifters. They can transform into animals, sometimes into mist. A witch recognizes the numinous spirits in nature. She knows their names; they come when she calls. Her familiars are her friends: sleek black hellhounds, snakes, crows, horses, hawks, owls, goats, spiders, cats big and small. All with personality. In the Tarot – a compendium of myths and symbols from the Western mystery traditions – the witch rides the lion in the Strength card and is known as the Lady of the Beasts. As the High Priestess she slips into trances; as the Empress she enchants with love spells. When the witch appears as the Queen of Wands, she wields the occult powers of plants.

Unknown · *Diana the Huntress* · Italy · ca. 55–79 CE This fresco of Diana, Goddess of the hunt, is from an ancient villa in Stabiae.

Erté · *Medusa* · France · 1956 A classic Erté drawing depicts the mythological witch Medusa in fashionable attire.

The witch of myth is both poisoner and healer. She knows the secrets of the poppy, brewing henbane, monkshood, and mandrake root into venoms, entheogens, and intoxicants. The Celtic goddess Ceridwen stirs her cauldron and brings forth Awen, the name for both the underworld and the mystical elixir of divine inspiration. Hygeia, the daughter of Asclepius, the god of medicine, is really an older goddess. Can anyone doubt she is a witch when her symbols are the snake and the pentagram? She is also a medicine woman, a doctor, and a scientist, refining her materials. From bubbling substances, witches prepare ointments with menstrual blood, wax, mercury, and salt. The witch goddess Diana, a midwife, uses her powers to call forth life. But witches are also necromancers. They summon the spirits of the dead as the Witch of Endor did for the king of the Hebrews.

In the German myth of Tannhäuser, Queen Sibyl lived in a magic mountain where vapors hissed from the center of the Earth. To get there, the hero descended past dripping cairns, and dragons guarding heavy wooden doors. Long after the Christian conversion of the Germanic tribes, pagans still insisted on making offerings to this witch at the foot of her mountain. Similar myths are found across Europe, ranging from the highlands of Scotland to the smoldering ashes of Mount Etna. Queen Sibyl was witch as priestess, or perhaps the Goddess herself, leading us into the underworld, a shamanic journey into the interiors of the Earth, and our own unconscious minds. Like Isis, she can glide through the upper worlds and the lower, gathering information to use here in the middle world, to achieve her will and make her medicines. In the legend of Tannhäuser, the witch gives the hero a green wand, symbol of the

Peter Paul Rubens · *Medusa* · Flanders · 1618
A painter of many mythological subjects, Rubens depicted an iconic beheaded hag who lives beyond death. The severed serpents birth smaller ones by way of Medusa's toxic and enchanted blood, as her decapitated head maintains its cursed wrath.

regenerative powers of nature. When the wand sprouts flowers, defying the will of the Pope, it wins Sibyl the hero's soul.

Often antagonists, witches are not afraid of the hero, his men, or their weapons. Consider the Greek witch Circe. While Odysseus's wife, Penelope, sulks around the family home – accosted by suitors, silenced by her son, praying for her husband to return from his adventures – Circe waits for no one. From her garden island of Aeaea she exults and enjoys; if Odysseus's men try to harm her, she turns them into swine. Witches live outside civilization and its rules. In fact, it's the witch's disinterest

in the hero and his adventures that the patriarchal authorities despise. They want her toiling in the nursery waving hankies at the hero while he expands his empire. But witches in a nursery just turn the children to changelings, and witches only care about empire when they want to burn it down.

Frank Dicksee · *La belle dame sans merci* · England 1901 John Keats's poem of the same name tells of a powerfully magickal woman who enchants a knight with her seductive yet destructive beauty. Their romantic romp through winter's landscape ends in death, creating the mythology of the femme fatale.

John Collier · *Circe*
England · 1885
The daughter of a god
and goddess, Circe was
adept in witchcraft.
Collier elegantly
painted her living
in nature among
animals, as she had a
propensity for turning
humans into beasts.

(top) Emil Johann Lauffer · *Merlin Presenting the Future King Arthur* · Bohemia · 1873 Donning stag horns, Merlin is depicted as the master of animals while caring for the infant Arthur. In Arthurian myths, the future king was said to have been placed in Merlin's care to be raised to adulthood in secrecy.

Eugène Delacroix · *Furious Medea* · France · 1838 Medea holds the blade against her children, whom she intends to kill in vengeance after her husband, Jason, has abandoned her to marry Creusa. As a sorceress linked to Hekate, she had used her magick to help Jason in his search for the Golden Fleece.

Witch *comes from* wicce, *a 5,500-year-old word that meant a wise woman, a shaman, a seer of the sacred. Discovering the indigenous wisdom of my ancestors, I came out of the broom closet 40 years ago, which made me one of America's first public witches. I became a priestess and created my own tradition, the Temple of Ara, the first to fuse core shamanism with Wicca. Of course, there've been many challenges, especially being public long before it was acceptable, but when I found my purpose, I found my strength. I've very joyfully spent my life making the impossible possible — helping witchcraft become the fastest-growing spirituality in America. There are countless ways of practicing witchcraft now. My own tradition is deeply rooted in reverence for Mother Earth, with practices that reconnect us to her and to the lost and sacred parts of ourselves. The results are magickal. The most important is the truth of who the witch is — the wise one who knows spirit and world are one. Witchcraft awakened my magic; it awakened me to the magic of Creation. It's been a path home to a re-enchanted world, a path to my place and purpose in that world. Witchcraft is a deeply personal spiritual practice and if you work it, it will work. It heightens and expands all of my senses, especially my sense of the sacred. And that connection to the sacred — in realms of spirit and embodied by nature — is the source of all real magick.*

— PHYLLIS CUROTT, Author, Attorney, & Wiccan Priestess, 2020

(previous) William Blake · *The Night of Enitharmon's Joy* (formerly *Hecate*) · England · 1795 The triple goddess and patroness of witchcraft is depicted with a book of spells, a donkey, an owl, and a toad. In Blake's mythology, her magick is expressed through her feminine power and liberated sexuality.

Evelyn de Morgan · *The Love Potion* · England · 1903 Rich in symbolism, the lush painting transcends the idea of the witch as diabolical, and portrays her as a philosophical alchemist, using potion to invoke the divine for spiritual pursuits.

John Collier · *Lilith*
England · 1887 Lilith,
the first woman, is
often thought of as Eve.
She radiates beauty,
grace, and connection
to the natural world
in Collier's portrayal,
as opposed to the
male-centric narrative
of the demon woman
who refused subser-
vience to her male
counterpart.

Martina Hoffmann
Isis · United States
2018 The Egyptian
goddess of magick and
healing is the ruler of
destiny and protector
of women. Isis's
nature is loving and
compassionate in
the realistic painting
style of Hoffmann,
who fuses archetypal
symbology with sacred
feminine grace.

Michelangelo Merisi da Caravaggio · *Head of the Medusa* · Italy · ca. 1597–98 The famed portrait of Medusa was painted on a jousting shield. Once a beautiful priestess, Medusa was cursed and disfigured, attaining the power to turn men to stone.

Unknown · Balinese Actor in Fanged Mask for
Play · Indonesia · Date Unknown In Bali the spirit
of the mask is said to incarnate the living flesh of
the dancer. Performers trance-channel the wisdom
of their culture through this art form, sometimes
used to drive out evil spirits from a village.

(following) Jacob Cornelisz van Oostsanen · *Saul
and the Witch of Endor* · Netherlands · 1526 Depicting a scene in the Old Testament, when King Saul
and his companions arrive to seek the council of
the Witch of Endor.

Sepultru Samuelis

I grew up with the classic "wicked witch" fairy tales, but they never caught my interest. It wasn't until I encountered Medea in Greek myth that I began to be intrigued. Medea led me to Circe, whose power of transformation I found deeply compelling. I was also drawn to the idea that witchcraft functions outside of normal societal rules for women — that it isn't something you are born with, or something that others confer on you. Magick is something you create for yourself, and women were often punished for their attempts to use it. Once I understood the strong ties between feminism and the study of witchcraft, I was fascinated. I consider myself an admirer, more than a practitioner. I see witchcraft as an art, like theater, writing, painting, or dance — it offers insight, creates beauty, interrogates and reshapes the world. So for me, witchcraft and the creative process feel like one and the same. A key tenet is the crucial understanding that we cannot wait to be given our strength, we must find it ourselves, and when we do, we must use it to uplift others. I think we need that more than ever in our world today. For me, a witch is a person (often but not only a woman) who works outside of traditional structures to transform the world. Fears of women wielding power and independence are old, and very much still with us. A witch is a woman with more power than can be controlled by the society around her. They represent figures of justice, equality, complexity, and mental discipline. I hope that we can use the history of witches as a way to remember that the fear of women is one we are taught early and often, and to continue to question our biases about those whom society says we should disenfranchise and condemn.

— MADELINE MILLER,
Scholar & Author of *Circe* & *The Song of Achilles*, 2020

(following) Unknown · *Women on the Island of Aeaea* Unknown · 1890 Circe and her nymphs lure Odysseus and his men to the banks of the hidden island of Aeaea.

Anthony Frederick Augustus Sandys · *Morgan-le-Fay* England · 1864 The witch of Avalon is painted in stunning detail with occult symbols adorning her clothing. Once King Arthur's protector and healer, she weaves an enchanted robe that will consume him – an example of religious revision of witch as monster.

Karina Kulyk (Fosco Culto) · *Hecate Crowned*
Italy/Ukraine · 2016 A contemporary work
depicts the bejeweled queen of the underworld,
deity of the night, and three-faced ruler of witchcraft, magick, and the moon.

Chris Ramirez · *Hecate* · United States · 2020
An ink rendering of the great triple goddess features her three faces, symbolizing the phases of
the moon and the cycles of womanhood.

THE POISONED APPLE

The Witch in Literature, Fairy Tales, & Folktales

O well done! I commend your pains;
And every one shall share i' the gains;
And now about the cauldron sing,
Live elves and fairies in a ring,
Enchanting all that you put in.

— Hecate in William Shakespeare's *Macbeth*

She awaits lost children in the dark wood, her gnarled hand outstretched, tempting with a crimson fruit. She calls out to her coven, her path lit by a pale moon as she rides her broomstick through the midnight sky. She shifts her shape to suit the one to which she casts the spell – crone, nymph, or beguiler.

For most of us, the archetype of the witch first appears within a book's pages, fairy tales read aloud – the wicked queen setting Snow White to sleep, the crouched hag hidden in the hut as Gretel and Hansel leave their trail of breadcrumbs. Literature has been enamored of the witch since the mythic tale of the sorceress Hekate, first thought to have been put to page in *The Theogony*, a Greek epic from the 8th century BCE. In Homer's great *Odyssey*, the witch Circe is all-powerful. In the Welsh *Mabinogion*, a compilation of oral folktales first published sometime in the 12th century, the sorceress Ceridwen oversees her Awen, a magick cauldron representing inspiration and knowledge.

Across the centuries, Celtic literature has been rife with powerful women practicing potent magick, most notably in the tales of Taliesin, a 6th-century bard and poet who was said to serve in the court of King Arthur. In Arthurian legend, magick and witchcraft feature prominently – from the wizard Merlin to the enchantress Morgan le Fay. The latter shape-shifts through varied retellings – from a sheerly malevolent incarnation in T. H. White's *The Sword in the Stone*, to the empowered and misunderstood feminist of Marion Zimmer Bradley's *The Mists of Avalon*.

(previous) **John Boydell · *Macbeth, the Three Witches and Hecate* · England · 1805** Hekate, goddess of witchcraft, scolds the three witches for offering Macbeth assistance. The toads, sacrificial infants, ouroboros, and other supernatural figures foreshadow impending doom.

Jos. A. Smith · Illustration from Erica Jong's *Witches* · United States · 1981 The drawing is based on the classic fairy-tale offering of a poisoned apple.

In the canon of great writers, Shakespeare was in particular thrall of the witch, offering up some of the most enduring fictional depictions of all time. He would feature a magician witch in *The Tempest* with the legend of Sycorax, a character that appears only as a memory in the play, a dark shadow cast from the past. Perhaps most memorable are his Weird Sisters in the first folio of *Macbeth*, three witches who in many ways mirror the ancient Fates, but who guide Macbeth's destiny into darkness rather than into light. In part inspired by mentions of witchcraft in *Holinshed's Chronicles of England, Scotland, and Ireland*, first published in 1577, *Macbeth's* witches are culled from traditional stories rife in British folklore, tales of faeries and magick, intertwined with a wry nod to Greek and Roman mythology.

Later incarnations of Shakespeare's Weird Sisters would borrow heavily from fellow Jacobean playwright Thomas Middleton, whose play *The Witch* is thought to have been written around 1613 and who himself took inspiration from Reginald Scot's treatise disparaging the verity of witches, 1584's *Discoverie of Witchcraft*. Each writer seems to have influenced the next, drawing prolifically from existing literature, historical tomes, and most likely from *Daemonologie*, a study of demonology written and published by King James VI of Scotland himself, in 1599.

Later, with each new interpretation and incarnation, *Macbeth's* witches would evolve and transform, taking on various forms, depending on era and execution of the play itself. The witch as writer's muse would

continue to transmute as well, an iconic subject appearing in stories from around the globe. In Japan, the witch is the central protagonist in countless ghost and fairy tales, her appearance in literature dating back to early medieval Edo-period manuscripts. A type of female demon called a yamauba is often shown white-haired and wild-eyed, destroying all who have the misfortune to cross her path.

In Eastern European folklore she appears as Baba Yaga, a decrepit child-eating sorceress, sometimes also depicted as one of three sisters and often shown peering wickedly from the door of her home, a ragged hut set upon a foundation of enormous chicken legs. Baba Yaga, like Hekate, is seen as all-powerful and transmutable, showcasing a variety of magickal abilities — most of them malefic. The Brothers Grimm began collecting and transcribing folk stories told over centuries, many with the witch as the central villain, resulting in generation upon generation of childhood nightmares. The Grimms's stories are now woven deeply into the fabric of our shared subconscious, our intimacy with the witch born through bedtime stories and the darker side of Disney fantasies.

The witch also rides across the pages of the elevated literary canon. She is the faerie enchanter, the "belle dame" of the ballad "La Belle Dame sans Merci," and she cavorts with her coven on the stormy Brocken peak of the Harz Mountains in Johann Wolfgang von Goethe's *Faust*. In early-20th-century fantasy literature she takes precedence. The malevolent sorceress Queen Jadis in C. S. Lewis's *The Chronicles of Narnia* is the cruelest of witches,

Henry Fuseli · *Macbeth, Banquo and the Witches* **England · ca. 1793** Depicting Act I of Shakespeare's tragedy, Fuseli portrays the moment the witches offer three prophecies to Macbeth and Banquo. One of the revelations, which comes to be, is that Macbeth will become king of Scotland.

freezing the once fecund lands in a Hundred Year Winter and serving as a formidable foe to the great Lion and his followers. And then of course there are the witches etched perhaps most indelibly on the global imagination through the Oz books of L. Frank Baum. The Wicked Witch of the West and Glinda the Good Witch are the finely sketched archetypes that have found their way onto the yellow brick road of our dreams.

In 1953, Arthur Miller revisited the court-room terrors of the Salem witch trials with his harrowing play *The Crucible*. Meanwhile, amid the brew and bubble of modern feminism, the witch would be represented by a slew of writers, themselves confrontational and fearless. In the pages of Virginia Woolf, Sylvia Plath, Audre Lorde, Anne Waldman, and Lucille Clifton, we find her fury and her wrath. The feminist spirituality movement of the 1970s further evolved this renewed fascination with the witch as feminist, the dormant goddess rising up once again to take back her power.

In 1983's *The Mists of Avalon*, Marion Zimmer Bradley subverted the stories of King Arthur, retelling the legend once again, this time from the point of view of the Druid priestesses of Avalon facing the impending encroachment of Christianity. In Clarissa Pinkola Estés's seminal *Women Who Run with the Wolves*, first published in 1992, fairy-tale tropes are inverted and retold. Here the witch archetype has evolved into the "Wild Woman" fearlessly blazing a trail for self-realization, translating instinct into visionary energy, feminine strength into a form of ancient magick.

And then finally, of course, we come to the young Hermione Jean Granger, the witch that reignited the sabbath bonfires, heating the cauldron over which an entirely new generation of young sorceresses would cast their spells. J. K. Rowling's character from the *Harry Potter* series and the series itself have influenced countless readers to delve deep into the old world of words and magick, and to reinvent in their own ways the ancient concept of the witch. And so on and on, the magick circle spins, the cycles moving ever forward, the wheel of the year marking the season, as the witch is born and reborn again upon the page.

William Henry Margetson · *She Was Known to Have Studied Magic While She Was Being Brought Up in the Nunnery* England · 1914 A captivating illustration from *The Legends of King Arthur and His Knights* depicts the young sorceress Morgan le Fay, who was raised in a convent where she became adept in the magickal arts.

Leo and Diane Dillon · *Jadis, the White Witch* **United States** · 1994 This contemporary illustration takes a mythical approach to the depiction of the enigmatic White Witch of C. S. Lewis's popular young adult series, *The Chronicles of Narnia*.

Unknown · *Le laboureur
alla trouver l'enchanteur*
France · ca. 1910
An illustration after a
painting by Hermann
Vogel about the Brothers
Grimm fairytale,
Daumesdick, this French
adaptation tells of a
peasant who seeks
magickal assistance in
his quest to have a son.

(opposite)
Eugène Grasset · *Three
Women and Three Wolves*
Switzerland/France
ca. 1900 Based on the
Russian folktale of Baba
Yaga, this Art Nouveau
watercolor shows
enchanted women and
wolves appearing feral
and wayward to sym-
bolize feminine intuition,
growth, and wildness.

(following, left) Kremena Chipilova · *The Three
Golden Hairs* · Finland · 2020 In Slavic fairy-tale,
three hairs from the sun are said to guarantee
marriage to a king's daughter. The godmother of
the sun agrees to pluck the hairs of the all-knowing
and get answers to three questions.

(following, right) Ivan Yakovlevich Bilibin · *The
Witch Baba Yaga* · Russia · 1900 The Russian folktale
"Vasilissa the Beautiful" is about a girl who visits Baba
Yaga, the forest witch, for help. In Art Nouveau style,
Bilibin portrays the traditionally disheveled crone of
lore, who lives in a hut supported by chicken legs.

J. Martin

(previous) John Martin *Manfred and the Alpine Witch* · England · 1837 A watercolor interpreting Lord Byron's poem of a man condemned to eternal sleeplessness. He summons a witch, imagined in a rare, glowing, Virgin Mary-esque style, who demands his soul in return.

Tsuruya Kōkei · Ichikawa Ennosuke III as the Witch of Adachigahara in *Kurozuka* · Japan · 1987 The legendary witch of the black mounds in Japanese folklore, a version of Baba Yaga, is often depicted as maniacal, with wild hair and a wretched mouth, and living in the forest.

W. W. Denslow · *The Wonderful Wizard of Oz* United States · 1900 Dorothy and Toto meet Glinda the Good Witch and a few of the friendly munchkins in L. Frank Baum's classic tale, which whimsically acknowledged magick as both good and evil.

My first introduction to witchcraft was through literature and fairy tales as a child. And as a woman growing into adulthood, I felt I had so much to learn from all those aspects of femininity that are portrayed in myth and fairy tales. And I found that was much richer than the images of women in pop culture around me. I also think that what drew me to the concept of witchcraft was that I'm quite interested in women. I'm interested in difficult women and bad women and strange women. And I think reclaiming those facets of yourself through witchcraft — I'm very fascinated by that conceptually. I started Sabat as a very visual project because I was doing visual journalism. We wanted to showcase artists who were utilizing elements of witchcraft or the occult within their creative process. What I personally love about witchcraft and about the witch as an archetype is this idea of standing strong as an individual and of daring to be "at the edge of the village"— whether that be a political village or a village of thought or whatever. To me, the witch is the alternative one, to be the one who questions the status quo. I love that about the witch as a figure. Someone who dares to be a bit difficult. I think that's what I need from the witch in my life, I need her willingness to be a bit contrary.

— ELISABETH KROHN,
Writer, Scholar, Founder, & Editor of *Sabat* Magazine, 2020

Rogelio de Egusquiza · *Kundry* · Spain · 1906
The mythology of the mysterious character of Kundry
is explored in a portrait depicting the classic witch
archetype in Wagner's musical drama *Parsifal*.

Viktor Britvin · *Vasilisa*
the Beautiful · Russia
Date Unknown On her
journey through dark-
ened woods, Vasilisa
clutches her magickal
doll on her way to witch
Baba Yaga's hut. The
modern illustration
from the Russian
folktale exemplifies the
wild-woman archetype.

(opposite, top) Walt Kelly · *Hansel and Gretel*
United States · 1935 Created the year Kelly joined
Walt Disney Studios, the previously lost illustration
was found in 1995 by a family member.

Arthur Rackham · Hansel and Gretel and the
Witch · England · 1909 The artist created a series
of colorful illustrations for the publication of the
classic Brothers Grimm fairy tale.

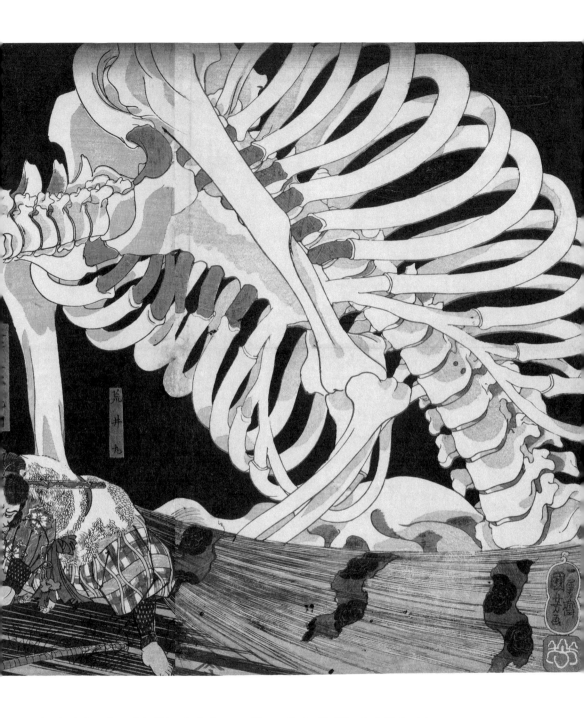

(previous) Pieter Bruegel the Elder · *Dulle Griet* (*Mad Meg*) · Belgium · 1563 The painting mocks the fury of the heretic in a scene from a famous Flemish folktale.

Utagawa Kuniyoshi · *Takiyasha the Witch and the Skeleton Spectre* · Japan · 1844 A colorful woodblock triptych captures the historical figure Princess Takiyasha using witchcraft to summon a giant skeleton from a spell scroll. She avoids the emperor's capture by setting the specter on Mitsukuni.

Kay Nielsen · Illustration from *East of the Sun and West of the Moon* · Denmark · 1914 Illustrated by Nielsen, this collection of Norwegian fairy tales includes a story of a girl who is able to communicate with animals, the wind, the moon, and the stars, and uses magick to free the prince from trolls.

William Rimmer · *Scene from Macbeth* · United States · 1850 The three witches from *Macbeth* conjure their "masters" for direct consultation, with the usual foreboding storm and wind. Rimmer's interpretation reveals the first of three apparitions, while the second lingers near the moon above.

SHAPE-SHIFTER

The Many Faces of the Witch

I've come to realize that the Witch is arguably the only female archetype that has power on its own terms. She is not defined by anyone else. Wife, sister, mother, virgin, whore — these archetypes draw meaning based on relationships with others. The Witch, however, is a woman who stands entirely on her own. She is more often than not an outsider, and her gift is transformation.

— PAM GROSSMAN, foreword to *Literary Witches: A Celebration of Magical Women Writers*, 2017

In perhaps the most famous witch film of all time, Dorothy is asked by Oz's effervescent enchantress, Glinda, "Are you a good witch or a bad witch?" Though MGM's 1939 release *The Wizard of Oz* popularized the idea that witches could indeed be kind and beautiful, it also solidified a bewitching binary: These magickal beings were either benevolent or wicked, and nothing in between. "Depictions of the witch seem to have swung with amazing regularity between these two mental and physical poles: hideous frenzy and beguiling grace," writes Lorenzo Lorenzi in his 2005 book, *Witches: Exploring the Iconography of the Sorceress and Enchantress.*

Upon closer inspection, however, the figure of the witch has gone through many iterations and mutations over time. Though there are now people who identify as witches — and there have always been people who have labeled others as witches — the witch is best

understood as an imaginal being. "Witch" refers to a protean canvas onto which humanity projects its fears and fantasies about feminine power. And it's an archetype that not only reflects these concerns, but also refracts them prismatically. Rather than putting a given witch into one of two boxes, there is a whole spectrum of ensorcellment to consider.

As Linda C. Hults writes in her 2005 seminal book, *The Witch as Muse: Art, Gender, and Power in Early Modern Europe*, "We know now that witchcraft beliefs were not a monolith of concretized superstitions inherited from the Middle Ages but an evolving bundle of ideas, often with unresolved internal contradictions, that varied from context to context…" The same can be said about witches themselves.

Despite this variety, we tend to know a witch when we see one. Witches wield otherworldly power, but they are, by and large, human.

(previous) **Henry Fuseli and John Raphael Smith** *The Weird Sisters* · England · 1783 Also known as the three witches from Shakespeare's *Macbeth*, they were thought to bear a parallel to the mythological three Fates who prophesied one's destiny.

Luis Ricardo Falero · *Faust's Dream* · Spain/England 1878 Mephistopheles takes Goethe's Faust to witness a witches' sabbath, complete with demons, humans for satanic offering, and invocation of pestilence. Nudity was typical of occult art from this period.

1878

And while there have been — and continue to be — male and non-binary witches, the visual iconography more often than not skews female. A witch may be attractive or repulsive, generative or destructive, divine or diabolical, and so on, in any number of combinations. Each witch occupies her own unique spot on a sort of hexen-matrix upon which we can map our endlessly complicated feelings about women's attractiveness, age, and agency. She transforms in response to the anxieties and desires of her time and place.

It's only fitting, then, that one of the most common tropes of the witch is her ability to

shape-shift. Witches are derived from much older tales about nocturnal creatures who could change form and wreak havoc. Ancient Romans believed in the *strix*, a woman who could turn herself into an owl or a bat at night. It had a bloodcurdling screech and sharp talons, and was said to murder children in their sleep. Most likely, *strigae* were a later incarnation of Mesopotamian demonesses called *lilitu*, who later morphed into Lilith, the defiant, potentially demonic quasi-goddess of Jewish mythology (and a character beloved by feminist witches today). The witch Pamphile in Apuleius's 2nd-century novel *The Golden Ass* could transform herself into an owl, and she is a clear successor of the *strix*. And of course witches and owls are still associated with each other to this day.

"Confessions" of alleged witches during the early modern European witch hunts often spoke of strange shape-shifting abilities, with some confessors telling of their tendencies to turn into everything from cats to hounds to toads. Most famously, accused Scotswoman Isobel Gowdie recounted her experience of transforming into a rabbit using the following chant: "I shall go into a hare,/With sorrow and sych and meickle care;/And I shall go in the Devil's name,/Ay while I come home again."

The idea that witches could turn into other creatures is both fanciful and threatening. These metamorphic women breach norms and traverse boundaries, and therefore cannot be trusted. As Serinity Young writes in her 2018 book *Women Who Fly: Goddesses, Witches, Mystics, and Other Airborne Females*,

Unknown · *Witch with Her Cat Familiar* · England 17th Century A hairy-faced, wart-nosed crone in profile grasps her wooden crutch instead of a broom. The black cat on her back seems to be mesmerized in the woodcut portrayal.

"Shape-shifters are unnerving because they cannot be contained within the primary categories of species, suggesting other, uncanny possibilities that subvert fundamental beliefs about what it is to be human. They are indifferent to differentiation, violating the established order, including the order of gender." In changing themselves, these witches become bestial, with sharpened senses and predatory urges. They turn into creatures of instinct – civility and morality be damned.

Whether or not a female witch can literally change shape, her looks are still a key element in how the archetype of the witch is signified. Perhaps the most common form the witch takes is that of the crone, with her bent back, hooked nose, and silver hair. She cackles and creaks, and is often shown hunched over a cauldron brimming with repugnant ingredients such as eyeballs and rotting bones. Everything about her reminds us of death – or, more accurately, decay. After all, the word *crone* roots back to the Old North French *charogne* or *caroigne*, meaning "carrion." That these witches are usually shown surrounded by skulls and carcasses underscores their own decomposition.

Depictions of witches – from Albrecht Dürer's engraving *Witch Riding Backward on a Goat* (ca. 1500) to the bony hags of Francisco de Goya's 18th-century series of etchings *Los Caprichos* – reinforce this further by showing horrid hags in the nude, with sagging breasts and wrinkled flesh exposed for all the world to see. Even more, we can glean from their poses that these old witches are shameless in their nakedness. Their heads are lifted and their arms are spread open

like leathery wings. There is an implied eroticism to these images, made all the more taboo due to their geriatric subjects. As Hults writes, "The aged female form, presented as an inappropriate, indecorous, and disconcerting spectacle, embodied social and moral disruption." As such, these are not images created to arouse, but rather to be mocked or rejected – and ultimately to be feared.

Prejudices against older women, especially those with sexual appetites, still exist today. Most often, December-May relationships are the subject of dismissal and ridicule, as evidenced by the usage of terms like *cougar* and the relative dearth of stories that laud these partnerships rather than satirizing them. A postmenopausal woman is still

Samuel Luke Fildes · *The Witch* · **England** · **19th Century** Fildes captures a witch in a tender manner. He would often paint for the purpose of changing public opinion.

Francisco de Goya · *Pretty Teacher!* · Spain · 1797–1799 In Goya's stunning etching, a maiden flies with her instructing crone. The act of flying on brooms was suggestive of sexual lust and liberation.

Adam Alessi · *MAGIC!* · United States · 2020 Masks often appear in Alessi's work, yet this classic portrayal of a witch needs no facial covering. Green-skinned with a gnarly nose, her four fingers motion the magick that extends from her being.

largely considered to be sexually invisible or outright abominable. The naked old witch is doubly disgusting, then, for she acts upon her own grotesque desires and does so without obfuscation. Even worse, particularly by early modern Christian standards, she is an erotic being who is unable to create life.

This leads us to a related aspect of the witch archetype: that of the antimother or monstrous mother. In Euripides's telling, the scorned witch Medea murders her own children in an act of retaliation against their father, Jason, her ex. Fairy tales from "Hansel and Gretel" to "Rapunzel" feature child-snatching witches, and in the 16th and 17th centuries, witches were said to abduct children (an extension of the Lilith/ *strix* legends, no doubt) and make "a flying ointment," an unguent that helped them fly, from the children's dead flesh. Presumably it was easier for early modern people to believe that the high infant mortality rate was due to malefic magick than that babies were dying because of illness. Tragically, this often led to witchcraft accusations and torturous, often terminal convictions for women over 40. For who better to accuse of infanticide than those who could no longer make babies themselves?

Still, the crone witch is not always depicted as malevolent. She is sometimes a healer or a helpful guide. In her guise as wise woman, her knowledge of plant properties and secret spells can certainly improve one's circumstances. This weird wisdom-keeper often lives alone and in liminal spaces: on the outskirts of town, in the heart of a forest, at the edge of the sea. Her intimacy with nature reveals her own wildness, and here we get a sense of so many witches' foremothers: the pagan goddesses and faerie beings of myriad flavors. These old witches are connected to ancient information, and will share it with the lucky and the lost — but often for a price. Because of this exchange, they can be ambiguous in their morality. One of the most iconic witches is the Slavic crone Baba Yaga, who was said to live in the woods inside a chicken-legged hut. In some stories, Baba Yaga is fearsome, but she also may assist in a maiden's initiation or quest, as she does with the light-seeking girl Vasilissa. "Old women do more complicated symbolic work in literature and myth than males in their third age," writes Marina Warner in her piece "Witchiness," published in the August 2009 issue of *London Review of Books*. And with that complexity comes intrigue, and power. This aspect of the witch archetype celebrates the accumulation of blessings and boons that can only come with time and experience — and the guts to live on one's own terms.

William Mortensen · *Isis* · United States · 1926
Goddess of the moon and magick, Isis is an archetype of fertility and the power of creation. She is always pictured with a horned cow, and the fire at her navel symbolizes the energy that gives life, more often pictured as a sun disk in Egyptian art.

Albrecht Dürer · *Four Witches* · Germany · 1497
Four witches convene in secrecy, as a demon lurks in the doorway. One of the earliest, pre-Renaissance examples of witches appearing nude in art, the engraving alludes to Hekate, patron of witchcraft.

The hag is the most recognizable version of the witch, thanks to centuries of fine-art renderings and the yearly reinforcement of Halloween iconography: "Witch" has consistently been one of the most popular costume choices for adults in the United States for the better part of the last two decades, according to the National Retail Federation. While witches can be any age, and have been depicted as such throughout history, in their younger forms, they are usually shown as supernatural seductresses, nubile and magnetic and dripping with charm.

Early modern European witch hunting pamphlets show images of witches with uncovered heads and long, flowing hair: a signifier of wanton, untamable energy. And in the artworks of the era, these sexy hexers were often depicted in the nude, implying sin and salacious behavior. The foursome of Dürer's *Four Witches* (1497) are youthful and voluptuous, and at first glimpse one might regard them as an innocent group of maidens in their prime. Until, that is, the skull on the floor and the demon in the doorway come into focus. "Beware of women who gather unsupervised," Dürer seems to imply.

Likewise, *The Weather Witches* (1523) by Dürer's protégé, Hans Baldung Grien, is an erotically charged image of two tempting nymphs au naturel, all swirling hair and swerving curves. They can not only change the climate, they can also derail one's life entirely. A lifted sheet between them

Unknown · Witch · England · 15th Century · Two sergeants at arms are cursed and chased off by a witch, a beggar, and a court fool in an image thought to be from from the illustrated 1376 poem by Jean le Fèvre *Le respit de la mort.*

Frans Francken the Younger · *The Witches' Kitchen* Flanders · ca. 1604 A witch prepares for her ascension up the chimney, surrounded by occult ingredients. Francken produced many paintings detailing witches' preparation for the sabbath.

reveals the presence of a goat – a sign of the Devil – and the promise that to give in to their temptation is to walk the path of eternal damnation. The bodies of the lusty witches are not only sites of sin, then, but are the progenitors of all that is harmful in the world. As Charles Zika writes, in the 2007 book *The Appearance of Witchcraft*, "[These witches] are identified as the source of disorder in nature by Baldung's depiction of the hair that flies out in all directions, fanned by the sulphurous clouds that presumably result from the women's evil." Beautiful, brazen witches like these are allegorical stand-ins for loose women – or any woman who stirred unholy feelings in the hearts and loins of good Christian men. Indulging in the

company of libidinous ladies was a sure way to tarnish one's soul.

This spellbinding seducer is a version of the witch that has long outlasted the European witch hunts, as evidenced in all manner of art and entertainment, from the soft-core witch photographs of William Mortensen in the 1920s and '30s to Frank Sinatra's crooning about "That sly come-hither stare/ That strips my conscience bare" in his 1957 hit "Witchcraft." But whether she's framed as a love-potion pusher, a vixen on a phallic broomstick, or a mistress of the night (wink wink), the implication is usually that she is not to be trusted. Her beauty may be genuine or an illusion (also known as a glamour), but

Manuel Orazi · *Witch within Magic Circle* · Italy 1895 Orazi's haunting and beautiful illustration depicting magick and alchemy was created for a calendar published in France in 1886.

Erik Theodor Werenskiold · *Troll Witch and Three Princesses* · Norway · 1900 In Norwegian folklore, witches are referred to as troll hags. Many stories abound with princesses being captured by these witches before being saved by a hero.

in either case it is to be understood as a trick, not a treat. She uses her dark allure to get what she wants — and she's a remnant of the centuries-old belief that a woman's desire is always dangerous.

Burgeoning female sexuality — and growing power in general — is a key aspect of the "magical girl" or "teen witch" trope. These characters are featured in countless young readers' books, from the Harry Potter series to *Akata Witch*, in films ranging from *The Craft* to *Kiki's Delivery Service*, and in TV series like *Chilling Adventures of Sabrina*. No matter the tale, the storylines follow a similar pattern: A young witch has to negotiate her newfound abilities, and makes many mistakes while doing so. It's a clear metaphor for the very real transformations that adolescents go through, with their suddenly unreliable, changing bodies, as well as the tension they feel between the pressure to meet familial and social expectations, and their longing for autonomy. The young witch may master her mystical skills or give them up entirely, but either way, she is able to exert control over her gifts and her destiny.

These stories also reflect a surprising development that started in the 19th century: The witch has shape-shifted yet again from a diabolical villain to a beloved protagonist. This is thanks in part to starry-eyed (if outrageously fanciful) reimaginings of witch "history" by thinkers such as *La Sorcière* author Jules Michelet and suffragist Matilda Joslyn Gage, who was L. Frank Baum's mother-in-law and an inspiration for the character Glinda and Oz's other good witches.

20th-century occult-oriented writers such as Charles Godfrey Leland, Margaret Murray, and Gerald Gardner each in their way promoted the notion that witches were in fact real but terribly misunderstood, mistreated, and maligned. Though many of their theories have been called into question, if not disproven outright, it's thanks to them and many others that we now have so many positive witch depictions. Today a witch is as likely to be shown as brilliant, beautiful, and brave as she is devilish, disgusting, or outright deadly.

It's certainly not a development that earlier generations would have predicted. As John Callow writes in 2018's *Embracing the Darkness: A Cultural History of Witchcraft*, "The transformation of the witch from a figure who had occasioned fear and loathing for the best part of 2,000 years into one perceived as sympathetic — even aspirational — is one of the most radical and unexpected developments of modern Western culture." The creepy crones and nocturnal nymphs are still with us, but now we have added inspirational, appealing change agents to the brew. From heroines in on-screen tales like *Bewitched* and *Siempre Bruja*; to the activist feminist witches and W.I.T.C.H.; to the intersectionally and ecologically minded members of the contemporary pagan movement, a witch is now something that many not only want to see, but want to be. This marks an archetypal evolution, to be sure.

More than that, it reflects a wider acceptance of complex feminine power in the cauldron of our shared consciousness.

Albrecht Dürer · *Witch Riding Backward on a Goat* **Germany · ca. 1500** An engraving incorporates the idea of reversal, that sorcery reverses the natural order of things. The witch rides reversed, but her hair blows the opposite direction. An initial of the artist's signature is also backward.

Frances F. Denny
Luna (Oakland, CA)
United States · 2017
Denny's series of pho-
tographs of present-day
witches, featured in her
book *Major Arcana:*
Witches in America,
was inspired by
the artist's family history,
when she discovered her
ancestors involvment
in the Salem witch trials.

(following, left)
French School
A Horned Witch · 18th
Century The portrait
is said to be of the
reputed witch Katharina
Kepler, mother to
the famous scientist
Johannes Kepler. She
made healing herbal
potions for neighbors;
one, with whom she
argued, would accuse
her of witchcraft.

(opposite, top) Asli Baykal & Princess Nokia
Still from the Music Video "Brujas" · United
States · 2017 The Baykal–directed music video for
"Brujas," a song by rapper Princess Nokia, explores
Taíno and Yoruban witchcraft rituals.

Leonard Baskin · *Wicked Witch of the West* · United
States · 1984 The crone in the fantasy children's
book *Imps, Demons, Hobgoblins, Witches, Fairies
& Elves* is characteristic of Baskin's work.

Jean-Baptiste Monge.

(previous, right)
Jean-Baptiste Monge
Annaick the Witch
Canada · 1997
Influenced by the
animated styles of
Norman Rockwell and
Arthur Rackham,
Monge brings a fairy-
tale witch to life as a
crone with a knack for
cauldron escapades.

Lumb Stocks · *The Witch of the Alps* · England · 19th
Century An illuminated engraving depicts a scene
from Lord Byron's poem *Manfred*. Manfred seeks to
quell his guilt over the death of his beloved Astarte
by summoning spirits who will create a spell to help
him forget her.

William Mortensen · *Preparation for the Sabbot*
United States · ca. 1930 In one of a series of photos of witches and their practices by the controversial
Mortensen, a young witch is rubbed with magickal
ointment to enable her flight to the unholy gathering.

There are four equally valid definitions of a witch circulating in the modern world. Two are as old as the English language, though they collide with each other: that a witch is somebody who uses magick for evil purposes, to harm others; or that a witch is somebody who uses magick for any purpose, good or bad, although those who employ it to help others are often distinguished by being called "good" or "white" witches. Two are distinctively modern, though now well over 100 years old: that a witch is a feisty and independent woman, often persecuted by those who wish to repress women, and that a witch is a practitioner of a pagan religion based on a veneration of the forces of nature. I do not identify publicly as a witch, as I have never had much personal use for magick in the traditional sense, and because of the serious stigma attached to the word. Even to be known to be studying the subject historically has done me real harm in the past. Each of the four different definitions retains considerable emotional traction. The concept of the witch as evil magician creates a formidable adversary, invested with millennia of fear, for fictions depending on a struggle between good and evil (and a believed reality for those modern people who still see the world in those terms). The concept of the witch as good magician taps into our growing awareness of the power of mind over matter and the efficacy of magickal acts as therapies. The feminist concept rests on the fact that the witch figure is one of the very few symbols of independent female power that traditional Western culture has recognized. The witch as pagan has given us a complex of viable and benevolent modern religions, embodying feminism, environmentalism, and personal growth.

— RONALD HUTTON, Author & Scholar, 2020

Hans Baldung Grien · *Two Witches* · Germany
1523 A common theme in depiction of witches in
art of the Middle Ages was of women as seducers
and sinners. To succumb to their lustful behavior
could result in contraction of syphilis, symbolized
by the vial of quicksilver one of them holds.

Edd Cartier · *Confronting the Witch* · United States Mid-20th Century An illustration of a witch was featured in a pulp magazine. Cartier worked predominantly in the science-fiction and fantasy realm.

Eduard Fuchs after Luis Ricardo Falero · *The Belated Witch* (detail) · Spain/England · 19th Century A sky-clad young witch ascends from a chimney on sabbath night. Her expression is one of uncertainty, being a neophyte.

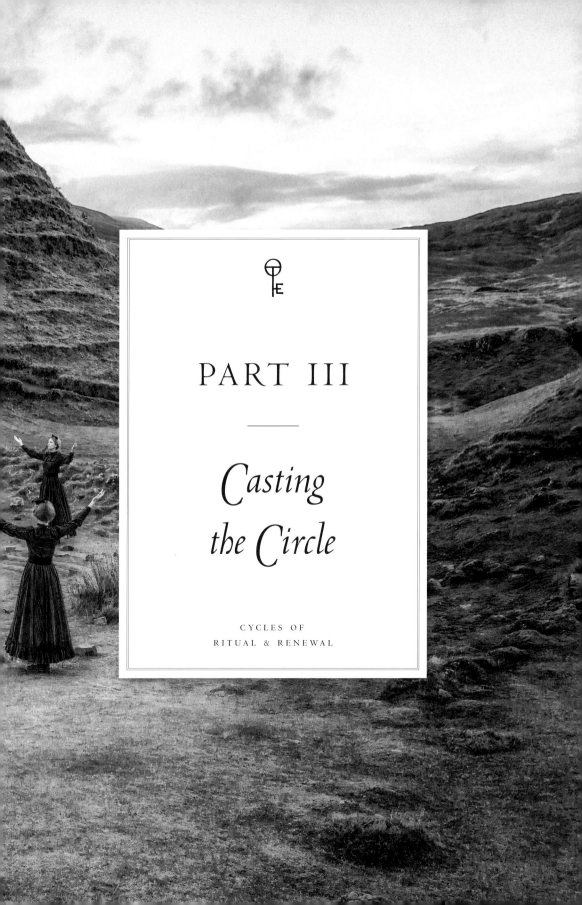

PART III

—

*Casting
the Circle*

CYCLES OF
RITUAL & RENEWAL

PART III

Essay by
PAM GROSSMAN

RING OF POWER

The Magick Circle in Witchcraft

The circle ranks among one of the most frequently used symbols in the western esoteric tradition. Geometry, astrology and other arts employ the circle as a map, guide or tool for the various ways in which the tradition manifests itself. It is a symbol of the totality of existence, of the divine, of the infinite, the ouroboros-like cycles of the seasons, the wandering stars, and the divine order of the celestial realm.

— WILLIAM KIESEL, *Magic Circles in the Grimoire Tradition*, 2012

Of all the symbols of witchcraft, perhaps the most universal is the magick circle. Whether outlined on the ground in salt, chalk, dirt, or stones, or simply visualized in one's imagination, it designates a sacred space that connects the terrestrial and celestial spheres. Magick circles exist in virtually every culture, and they are used by witches in many ceremonial contexts. They allow the caster to collect and focus energy, protect themselves from unwanted entities, and enter a portal that is "between worlds," as is often said.

A witch may cast a circle in solitude or in collaboration with their coven. After self-purification, it is a crucial step done at the beginning of a ritual or spell to signify

that the actions that follow therein will be consecrated and guarded. In Wiccan tradition, the circle is usually nine feet in diameter, but in truth it may be any size, so long as it can comfortably accommodate those within. In some instances, no circle is physically marked other than by the bodies of those gathered, or by a solitary witch's words and gestures.

Sometimes a coven can cast another sort of circle from within their circle, pooling their energies to form a "cone of power," which can be directed for a shared magickal outcome. But even when one is working alone, the magick circle can be thought of as a perimeter or boundary line: a container for the liminal.

(previous) **Psyché Ophiuchus** · *Ritual* · France 2019 A ceremonial circle takes place in Fairy Glen on the Isle of Skye at dusk, forming a protective barrier within which rites of sacred incantation summon particular energies.

Giuseppe Pietro Bagetti · *The Walnut Tree in Benevento* (*the Witches' Sabbath*) (detail) · Italy · 1820s Benevento saw large gatherings held around this iconic tree, which was said to be the meeting place for pagan ceremonies in honor of Isis.

Though there are many styles of circle casting, it generally entails calling in the directions, or "quarters," as well as any protective guides that may aid in one's magickal work. Some witches welcome the five elements of air, fire, water, earth, and spirit, or the seven directions, including east, south, west, north, below, above, and the center. In doing so, the caster becomes a fully oriented and integrated being: a microcosmic reflection of the magnificent macrocosm.

The magick circle also signifies the eternal pattern of life, for a circle has no beginning and no end. It symbolizes the holy loop of birth, death, and renewal, including the solar turn of the seasonal wheel and the lunar phases that repeat resplendently each month. The circle is forever; making use of it in ceremonies allows the caster to transcend space and time.

Though the circle may appear stationary to the human eye, its energy is anything but stagnant. In the enchanted realm, it may swirl, spin, crackle, or vibrate. It may expand outwards and extend upwards, forming a multidimensional forcefield or barrier. It simultaneously attracts and repels, encompassing the witch safely within.

A magick circle may also be inscribed on paper, worn as a talisman, or hung in the home. It may be used as a seal to conjure a spirit or invoke a deity; sometimes the names or glyphs of angels, demons, gods, or goddesses are incorporated, as well as potent words of summoning. In ceremonial magick, the circles may be intricate diagrams that blend multiple languages and sacred shapes. But even a simple round line when cast with intention can be a source of immense magickal potential.

Jesse Bransford · *Hills Become the Sun (Three into Four)* United States · 2015 The occult art of Bransford becomes magick itself. Serving as a spell, the large floor stave is based on old Norse mythology and thought to contain supernatural power.

Jesse Bransford · *Circle to the Four Corners (Kali, Hecate, Ishtar, Lilith)* · United States · 2016 The floor talisman invokes the directions and the dark goddesses from different traditions, with their respective symbols, languages, and elemental markers.

DRAWING DOWN
THE MOON

Covens in Witchcraft

The coven is a Witch's support group, consciousness-raising group, psychic study center, clergy-training program, College of Mysteries, surrogate clan, and religious congregation all rolled into one. . . . The structure of Witchcraft is cellular, based on small circles whose members share deep commitment to each other and the Craft.

— STARHAWK, *The Spiral Dance: A Rebirth of the Ancient Religion of the Great Goddess*, 1979

The word *coven* refers to a group of affiliated witches. It shares its root with the words *convene* and *covenant*, which indicate aptly both the word's meaning and the institution's function – the coven embodies both the gathering of witches and the action of binding them together in spiritual agreement. A coven may consist of two or more witches who come together regularly to observe ritual or to practice together, much like any other sort of religious congregation, meditation sangha, or therapeutic group. However, the intention of combining forces to achieve a spiritual end is what defines a coven more than its number of members, how often they meet, and who leads it.

The most widely embraced model of what a coven is and how it functions may be found in *A Witches' Bible* by Janet and Stewart Farrar. First published in 1996, the book provides a basic guide and liturgy to the Gardnerian tradition of witchcraft, based on the teachings of British scholar Gerald Gardner, who is credited with popularizing a form of neo-paganism during the mid-20th century. In *A Witches' Bible*, the Farrars outline Gardner's specific system, a practice of Wicca in which a high priest and a high priestess act as facilitators for rituals, offer guidance to the other members of the coven, and generally administrate the coven's business, as it were, defining the nature of the community's agreement, what the ritual is, and how and when to conduct it. Hierarchical structures like this, while often a facet of traditions of witchcraft and mysticism, are not as revered today as they were in the past.

Julia Soboleva · *The Healing Can Begin* · England 2020 Bird-headed women gather under beneficent skylights. A few of the women's heels are lifted, as if they are ready to take flight, invoking an eerie yet mystical hope as they commune with the cosmos.

There are covens today that are consensus-based groups that don't adhere strictly to assigned roles and power dynamics, while others have strict rules and guidelines of ascension into one's own power. A Gardnerian-style coven, for example, has initiatory rites and rituals of procession from one rank to another on a path toward high priest or high priestess. In her (widely debunked) book *The Witch-Cult of Western Europe*, Margaret Murray popularized the idea of covens and posited that they traditionally had 13 witches, based upon just one confession from a Scottish witch trial.

However, in Gardnerian tradition, covens do tend to contain no more than 13 people, so when a coven exceeds that number, a process called "hiving off" can take place. A higher-ranking coven member leaves the coven to start their own, taking with them some members of the previous coven. This mimicks the natural swarming process of honeybees, when some members of a hive that has become too crowded will establish a new bee colony.

It is not uncommon within covens for people to work in pairs in which the opposite charges of each partner's energy (in one form or another) can create a dynamic circuit that lends power to the pair's workings, the way the opposite poles of a battery create a charge between them. This is the essential function of a coven, regardless of its particular order or makeup: creating a network of different energies and channeling them toward a collective goal.

Boëtius Adamsz Bolswert · *Heks tovert demonen voor Willemynken* · Flanders · ca. 1600s A witch conjures demons over a village in an engraving from the renowned Bolswert. She stands outside of the elaborate magick circle as a villager stands within, startled by her summoning skill.

Meagan Boyd · *The Coven* · United States · 2021 Inspired by Matisse and made as a protection spell, the dance of witches under the moon explores the magick of sisterhood, and is infused with blessings that come from goddess celebration.

Kurt Seligmann
*Sabbath Phantoms
(Mythomania)*
Switzerland/United
States · 1945 With a
deep interest in alchemy,
Seligmann imbued his
Surrealist work with
occult symbolism. Once
a member of André
Breton's Surrealist
group, he was ejected
over an argument about
Tarot, yet continued his
alchemical interest and
creations.

Alison Blickle · *Courage* · United States · 2014
From part three of Blickle's "History of Magic"
series, *Uncrossing* presents patterned bodies in
ritual. Altars accompany the installations, often
bearing receptacles symbolizing the cosmic egg.
Uncrossing describes spellwork that reverses a hex.

(top) Nils Blommér · *Fairies of the Meadow*
Sweden/Italy · 1850 Swedish elves dance at twilight in the meadow of Gripsholm Castle, home to
the royal family. The soft, pink strip of sky hints at
the positive magick being stirred up by the nature
spirits and their playful tumbling.

Witchcraft is about empowerment above all else. One of the witchiest things you can do is unlearn all of the limiting beliefs we've been taught about who we are, what is possible, and how to act in alignment with your true needs and desires. Capitalism has shaped our lives in so many ways that make it hard to have faith in ourselves, trust our intuition, and create supportive communities. Witchcraft pushes back against all of that. It helps you imagine new realities and ways of knowing, outside of the ones handed down to us from oppressive structures meant to keep people struggling and suffering. A witch is anyone who believes they have the power to shape their own reality and acts on it. I am honored to identify as a witch, and I also think it's a huge responsibility to take on that identity when so many throughout history have been victimized by it. I strongly believe that reclaiming the word witch, *once such a powerful tool of oppression, will lead to some kind of collective liberation, but it is imperative that we make that connection. The archetype of the witch has endured because the kind of unruliness and power that it represents is an incredibly powerful force in the collective unconscious, especially as it relates to women and other marginalized folx. The witch contains multitudes — there are so many ways to extract meaning from that term. It can reference folk healers at the same time it can reference innocent victims. It can reference a rejection of societal norms, as well as someone who moves with uncanny ease through the world around them. From fairy tales to healers and midwives to radical feminists, the archetype endures because, like it or not, there is a little witch in all of us.*

— ERICA FELDMANN, Founder of HausWitch, Author, & Witch, 2020

Rik Garrett · *Untitled (from Earth Magic)* · United States · 2012 Garrett explored historical, fictional, and personal relationships between witchcraft, concepts of femininity, and nature in this series of photographs created between 2010 and 2013.

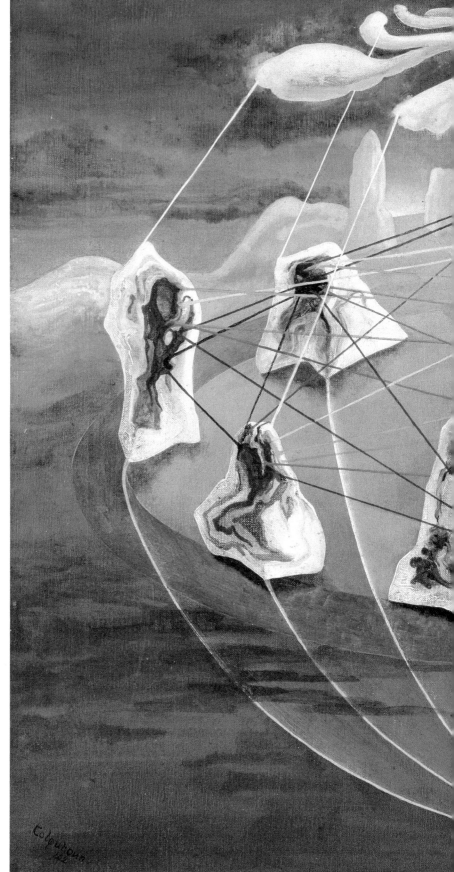

Ithell Colquhoun
The Dance of the Nine Opals · England · 1942
Nineteen maidens danced and performed ceremony on the Sabbath (Sunday), therefore being turned to stone for their heresy. Colquhoun draws the Merry Maidens as connected to ley lines in the earth, forming sacred geometric patterns.

DAUGHTERS OF THE NIGHT

The Witches' Sabbath

Witches bound for the Brocken are we,
the stubble is yellow, the new grain is green.
All our number will gather there,
and You-Know-Who will take the chair.

—JOHANN WOLFGANG VON GOETHE, *Faust*, 1808

The notorious ceremonial gathering of witches, warlocks, demons, and the Devil has perpetuated the most damning of witchcraft lore. The myth is responsible for vast paranoia, and became a method of rationalizing relentless prejudice and persecution. Yet modern research indicates that no such nefarious meetings actually occurred. In fact, the phrase "witches' sabbath" (or "sabbat") was rarely used prior to the 20th century. In his 2011 paper "The Pursuit of Witches and the Sexual Discourse of the Sabbat," the historian Scott E. Hendrix explains that accusations of witches gathering for orgiastic celebrations were simply paranoia, false conspiracies first fueled by the Christian Church. These misrepresentations were spread by those seeking to persecute "witches," mostly women who were past childbearing age.

These falsifications and distortions began with the dawning of Christianity, as the witch hunts began, rumors purported details on what occurred during these supposed witches' sabbaths became amplified and massively perverted. According to widespread misinformation, meant to encourage suspicion and distrust, these gatherings of witches were said to have occurred on those sacred nights each year, when the subtle veil between the living and the dead is most vulnerable. Supposed deplorable rites and rituals occurred in these gatherings, inciting frenetic activity and obscene manifestations. With Lucifer himself presiding over the festivities, witches were said to conjure spirits, curse the living, and incite pestilence. Demons and witches were thought to join together in orgiastic pleasure, fornicating indiscriminately.

Francisco de Goya · *Witches' Sabbath* · Spain · ca. 1797 The macabre abounds in a painting that symbolizes the mystic union between the divine and animal nature. The Devil appears as a Hathor-horned goat that is being offered sacrificial babies by witch maidens and crones, while the desolate landscape spotlights the ominous waning moon.

Necromancers were said to revive the dead, all among a plethora of grisly apparatus, fire, and unhallowed invocations.

Far from prying eyes, upon secluded European mountaintops, amid woodland groves, or in subterranean cellars, covens of witches would supposedly prepare for their legendary night flight to this macabre mass, concocting "flying ointment" out of entheogenic plants. They would smear it on their bodies and fly up chimneys via broom, or ride bareback on goats or other beastly creatures. Horrific tales of these alleged gatherings served to ignite fear and ensure punishment and persecution of those falsely accused of practicing witchcraft. Subsequently, the heinous killing of accused witches became far more atrocious than the imagined sabbaths themselves.

Yet, centuries later, the archetype of the witch remains and the concept of the sabbath has been reinterpreted and reclaimed. The practice of witchcraft persists and in covens around the globe, like-minded adepts now convening in order amplify, support and educate. Witchcraft itself now encompasses a rich and diverse array of cultures and practices. The myth of the sabbath has been completely redefined by a new generation to signify an inspired moment of coming together, a celebration of community, an empowering act of communal revelry. The contemporary sabbath gives present-day witches the freedom to unite and reclaim their own magickal traditions.

(page 156–57)
William Holbrook
Beard · *Lightning Struck
a Flock of Witches*
United States · Date
Unknown A kinetic
scene of turmoil and
drama, Beard captures
a fantastical view of
stormbound witches
in flight – the coven
sent reeling from a
slash of close lightning.

Salvator Rosa · *The Witches' Sabbath* · Italy · ca. 1650
A Baroque-period sabbath scene demonstrates
how Rosa often represented the myths of witchcraft
rituals and gatherings.

José Benlliure y Gil · *A Witches' Sabbath* · Spain
1890 A warlock conjures spirits from a small
cauldron for a more somber audience of witches
in Gil's fantastical lithograph.

Austin Osman Spare
Once Again to Earth
England · ca. 1920
From the artist's book
The Focus of Life,
the fine pencil drawing
is a portrait rumored to
be of his "witch-mother,"
Mrs. Patterson,
who lived for more
than a century.

(opposite, top) Jan van de Velde II · *The Sorceress* Netherlands · 1626 The Dutch printmaker created a series of engravings depicting a sorceress presiding over her cauldron.

(opposite, bottom) Salvator Rosa · *Witches at their Incantations* · Spain · ca. 1646 In this Baroque-period painting, the artist explores archetypal imagery associated with the fictional witches' sabbaths.

Matthäus Merian I
Zauberey · Switzerland/
Germany · 1626 A
helter-skelter sabbath of
witches, shape-shifters,
dead babies, necroman-
cers, beastly fornication,
and a merry line of
demon dancers descend
from Brocken peak.

Francisco de Goya · *Witches' Sabbath, Las Brujas*
Spain · 1798 Goya's usual sinister vision of witches
has them using ritual tools such as a voodoo doll,
infant body parts, and a spell book.

Jan or Frans Verbeeck · *The Witches' Sabbath* · Flanders
16th Century In a vivid and dramatic scene of
spellcasting, a swarm of witches awaken the dark
side while inspecting grimoires, possibly causing
the chapel fire in the background.

*In my exploration of women's lives, in both fiction and cultural history,
I have long been fascinated by the complexity of the figure of the witch
and her multilayered powers to enchant, to heal, and to do harm. From
childhood, I was enthralled by Circe and Medea, and have retained
my pleasure in magic, metamorphosis, and fantasy, especially in stories.
As I grew older, the horrors of witch hunts in Europe called out for
attention, so I began reading the historical material. These terrible,
unjust persecutions, in Europe and in many other parts of the world,
need to be understood and analyzed, as they have so many parallels
with other forms of scapegoating. The chief victims of the religious
trials were indigent old women, the least powerful members of society.
Accusations of witchcraft justified attacking the defenseless, while at
times accepting the blame was a way of claiming magical powers to
retaliate. I continue to be fascinated by what the human mind is capable
of conceiving. The tensions between the seduction of such dreams and
the beliefs they can instill, often with appalling consequences, continue
to baffle and torment me.*

— MARINA WARNER, Author & Scholar, 2020

(following) Frans Francken the Younger · *The Witches' Sabbath* · Belgium · 1607 Grisly images abound in this vivid sabbath scene featuring a fearsome, shape-shifting witch. Many magickal symbols line the floor, leaving one to ponder the imagination of the artist.

Rosaleen Norton · *Bacchanal* · Australia · Date Unknown A 20th-century rebel, Norton was a bisexual witch who rose above criticism, bans, and court cases aimed at censoring her art, beliefs, and open practice of sex magick.

THE TURNING
OF THE SPOKES

The Sacred Days of the Wicca

Although spellcasters often coordinate their activities with moon phases, witches' sabbats (or festivals) have historically been synchronized with the solar calendar. Lunar months are brief, roughly 28 days, and easily calculated just by gazing at the night sky. The solar calendar, however, is complex and requires expert astronomical and mathematical calculations.

The importance of these calculations to our earliest ancestors is documented by the proliferation of prehistoric archaeoastronomical sites scattered around the globe — architectural structures that were designed to align with specific celestial phenomena and that served as megalithic calendars. These structures occur in Africa, Asia, and the Americas, as well as in Europe. The oldest is currently believed to be the calendar circle at Nabta Playa, south of Egypt, which is estimated to have been erected in the fifth millennium BCE. Other sites include Stonehenge, Newgrange, Machu Picchu, and Angkor Wat.

Like the moon, the solar year also waxes and wanes: The sun increases in strength following the winter solstice, reaches its peak at the summer solstice, and then begins to decrease in power immediately afterward. These solar phases are reversed in the Southern Hemisphere. In response, Wiccans and pagans dwelling below the equator may also reverse sabbats to better reflect their reality, celebrating Beltane, for example, while their counterparts in the north are honoring Samhain, and vice versa.

Unlike a lunar cycle, a solar year lacks a distinct beginning or end; it has long been perceived as resembling a continually turning wheel, with the equinoxes and solstices serving as spokes. This reflects Earth's rotation around the sun, but also serves as the basis for the Wiccan sacred calendar.

Vivienne Shanley · *Wheel of the Year* · England 1999–2000 Painted in intricate detail, the wooden wheel is archived in the Museum of Witchcraft and Magic in Cornwall, England. The artwork symbolizes the eight sabbats, or festivals, of the Wiccan tradition. The concept of life and time and the repeating, cyclical nature of everything are celebrated to remain connected to the earth and the cosmos.

YULE

Light in the Darkness

In the Northern Hemisphere, Yule coincides with the winter solstice, the longest night of the year, signaling the gradual rebirth and strengthening of the sun. The date varies annually, but is on or near December 21. Its name may indicate Odin, the Norse deity and master magician who bears many names. Alternatively, it may reference the raucous, jolly mood characteristic of the season (the word *jolly* is thought to derive from *jól*, the Old Norse word for a midwinter celebration). Elements of modern Yule also derive from the Saturnalia, the Roman festival that corresponds with the winter solstice.

The name Yule is sometimes considered a synonym for Christmas. Pagan traditions that have crept into Christmas celebrations are incorporated into the Wiccan sabbat, such as burning the Yule log or gift giving, a vestige of the Saturnalia. In addition to Odin, a trio of Germanic witch goddesses are celebrated:

Berchta, Herta, and Hulda, also known as Holle, namesake of the Brothers Grimm fairy tale "Mother Holle." Any or all of these deities may lead the Wild Hunt, an anarchic procession of ghosts and spirits believed to fly overhead during Yule. Their passage is heralded by the cacophony of geese, owls, or crows cawing at night. Christians were taught to fear the Wild Hunt, but witches may venture outside to greet these night riders, seek their blessings, and dance with them.

Weather at this time of year, at least in northern climes, is likely to be inclement, so Yule is often celebrated indoors or at least close to home, rather than with the outdoor festivities so closely associated with other sabbats. Houses are decked with greenery and candles are lit, heralding the rebirth of the sun. It is the season for ghost stories and an opportunity to welcome visiting souls of ancestors and the mighty dead.

Emily Balivet · *The Solstice Queen* · **United States 2009** The artist explores the mystical feminine symbolism of ancient goddess mythologies from many cultures. In her contemporary vision, the winter pagan goddess sits in the elements, on the longest night of the year.

IMBOLC

Fanning the Creative Flame

SAINT BRIGID'S DAY · CANDLEMAS
JANUARY 31 — FEBRUARY 2

Imbolc is celebrated on February 1, but rituals may start the night before on Brigid Eve. This sabbat corresponds to the midpoint between the winter solstice and the spring equinox. Its name derives from Irish Gaelic and is translated as "in the belly," usually interpreted as indicating pregnant ewes. Another name for the sabbat, Oimelc, also derives from Irish Gaelic and is translated as "ewe's milk" or "butter bag." The roots of this sabbat lie in an ancient Celtic fire festival that evolved into one associated with the lambing season. Celebrated in Ireland for hundreds of years, Imbolc is not a universal witches' sabbat but is most likely to be commemorated by those who identify with Celtic traditions.

Brigid presides over Imbolc. It is her primary annual feast, and some devotees may celebrate her to the exclusion of other aspects of Imbolc. An ancient deity who ranks among the most popular modern goddesses, Brigid's origins are now mysterious. Currently associated with Ireland and the Scottish Highlands, she may once have been venerated throughout the British Isles. Her name means "fiery arrow," and she is a goddess of fire and water, associated with numerous healing wells. Brigid herself is a great healer with dominion over midwifery, poetry, crafts, brewing, iron-working, and technology.

Brigid visits devotees, offering blessings and responding to pleas. Many inaugurate Brigid Eve, the gateway to Imbolc, by placing cotton handkerchiefs outside on a ledge at nightfall. Brought inside in the morning, the hand-kerchief is believed to radiate the essence of the goddess and will not be laundered but preserved as a lucky talisman.

Some modern practitioners celebrate Imbolc as a harbinger of spring with no associations with lambs, Brigid, or Ireland. It is considered an ideal time for candle magick.

Kris Waldherr · *Brigit* · United States · 1995
Waldherr presents Brigit, who is honored at Imbolc, in *The Book of Goddesses*. As goddess representing fertility, poetry, prophecy, and crafts, her skill is sought by many.

OSTARA

Rebirth and Renewal

SPRING EQUINOX

MARCH 21 — 22

Ostara is the Wiccan sabbat corresponding to the spring equinox. The date varies annually but will be on or near March 21. The power of the vernal equinox is recognized worldwide by many religious traditions, but only Wiccans and pagans celebrate it under the name Ostara. Coinciding with the sun's entry into the astrological sign Aries, it is the start of the zodiacal year. Other holidays celebrated on or near the vernal equinox include Passover, Easter, and Nowruz (Persian New Year). In the Northern Hemisphere, the vernal equinox marks the beginning of spring, the awakening of the earth, and the victory of light.

Ostara is named for a Germanic goddess of spring, whose name is also spelled Astara, Eastra, or Easter. The name is etymologically related to words such as *estrus* or its variant, *estrum*, indicating her associations with fertility. Ostara is envisioned as a beautiful young woman crowned with flowers and bearing a basket of eggs. She is accompanied by a rabbit or hare, though its nature may vary — sometimes appearing as a cute bunny and other times as a lascivious, human-sized upright hare. Ostara is the ideal time to request her blessings of enhanced fertility and new beginnings.

Pagan traditions that have been absorbed into Easter, such as decorating eggs or hunting for them, are part of Ostara festivities too. Rain falling on Ostara is believed to be imbued with special magick. Personal benefits may be accrued by simply standing in the rain, but rain may also be collected and preserved in order to serve as a kind of pagan holy water. Ostara water is used to spiritually cleanse magickal tools, such as wands, crystals, or runes. It is also sprinkled over people or added to baths to enhance personal magickal power and to remove curses and hexes. Although it must be collected on Ostara's feast day, it may be used at any time.

Esao Andrews · *Black Eyed Susie* · United States 2015 The surreal style of Andrews enlivens the posing horned goat, a symbol of fertility and generative abundance, sacred to Greek and Sumerian goddesses.

BELTANE

Blossoms and Blazing

MAY DAY

APRIL 30 — MAY 1

Beltane, also known as May Eve, begins April 30 and continues through May Day. The date is intended to mark the midpoint between the vernal equinox and the summer solstice, although this is not always astronomically accurate. Beltane, derived from the Gaelic *Bealtaine*, is typically translated as "bright fire." Other names for this beloved sabbat include *Walpurgisnacht* and *Heksennacht*, literally "Witches' Night" in Dutch. The first of what the Welsh call the Three Spirit Nights (Beltane, Midsummer, and Samhain), it is among the dates most closely identified with witchcraft by witches and non-witches alike. The veil separating the realms of the living, the dead, and the spirits is especially permeable, making it perfect for magick. It is classified among the faerie festivals and considered an ideal time to attempt contact with them.

Metaphysically understood as the point in time when Earth's generative and sexual powers are at their peak, Beltane is a water *and* a fire festival, celebrated with bonfires *and* water magick. Candle magick is believed to be especially effective, as are love spells and sex magick. Beltane is famed as a night of revelry. Witches have long been rumored to gather on sacred peaks, traveling on broomsticks or magickally transported by flying ointments. Numerous sites are associated with these conventicles, but none more so than the Brocken, the highest peak in Germany's Harz Mountains. Johann Wolfgang von Goethe's epic *Faust* associates Brocken revels with witch goddess Lilith. Freya, another goddess of witches and magick, also presides over witchcraft gatherings on this night.

Daytime Beltane celebrations include dancing around a Maypole, crowning a May Queen, and drinking May wine, typically white wine infused with sweet woodruff (*Galium odoratum*). Spring flowers, which should be in full bloom on this date, are incorporated into flower crowns and garlands, as well as enchanted baths and other magick spells.

Susan Cavaliere · *Beltane* · England · 2016
A dancing, ghostly, surreal spring queen emerges from fertile vegetation in a sabbat ceremonial vision. A flowing energy emits from the earth flora as fresh growth, possibilities, and new life, while the mystical Glastonbury Tor ascends in the background.

MIDSUMMER (LITHA)

Solar Spirits

MIDSUMMER · SUMMER SOLSTICE
JUNE 21

Midsummer, or Litha, is the Wiccan sabbat corresponding to the summer solstice in the Northern Hemisphere, the longest day of the year. The date varies annually but is on or near June 21. The sun is at the peak of its power but will soon begin to wane and diminish. Festivities begin the prior evening. Midsummer rivals Samhain as the most magickally powerful time of the year. It is the second of the Three Spirit Nights. Faeries and spirits of all kinds are reveling too. Faeries emerge from their mounds, and Midsummer is among the ideal times to observe them or request their favors.

The origin of the name Litha is now mysterious, but it is believed to reference an ancient Germanic calendar. The name Midsummer may be used as a synonym for Litha, but it may also be another name for the feast of John the Baptist, a fixed-date holiday celebrated annually on June 24. John is the saint most associated with magick and considered a patron by many practitioners of witchcraft. As the solstice likely occurs before his feast, many will celebrate continuously for several days.

Midsummer is dedicated to fire, water, and botanical magick. Herbs and other plants harvested on this day are believed to be at their absolute peak of power. Rain that falls during the sabbat is believed to have exceptional healing powers and may be preserved to use as needed. Bonfires are lit and rituals held beside living water, such as lakes, springs, and rivers. The date is considered advantageous for any kind of spell, whether cast by an individual or a coven. For the solitary practitioner: Position candles around herb-infused or floral baths to better enhance your own personal magickal power.

Edward Robert Hughes · *Midsummer Eve* · England 1908 A faerie with a musical instrument under her arm calls upon multitudes of smaller forest inhabitants to celebrate, by firefly light, the delightful eve of Midsummer.

LUGHNASADH (LAMMAS)

First Harvest

This sabbat, celebrated on August 1 and its eve, marks the midpoint between the summer solstice and the autumnal equinox. Many modern pagans consider Lughnasadh and Lammas to be synonymous, but the meanings of their names are quite different. They may initially have been two distinct festivals, though some scholars believe that they may share prehistoric roots. Regardless of origin, both holidays celebrate the mysteries of grain.

Lughnasadh, pronounced *loo-nah-sah*, is an ancient Irish fire festival. Its name means "the marriage of Lugh," referencing the once very popular Celtic solar deity. At least 14 European cities are believed to be named in his honor, including Leyden and Lyon. Now restricted to one day, Lughnasadh once lasted for weeks. Celebrations include bonfires and harvesting herbs and other plants. The name Lammas derives from the Old English words *hlaf* (loaf) and *maesse* (mass). Originally called Loaf Mass Day, Lammas is an early English Christian harvest festival. Bread baked on this

day is believed to be especially blessed and magickally powerful.

Regardless of the name, for the Wicca, this sabbat is beloved and associated with romance and gratitude. It is considered especially beneficial for any kind of love magick. Today is also another opportunity to harvest magickal herbs. A botanical amulet known as the 9 Herbs of August must be crafted on August Eve, the final night of July. The entire ritual, from gathering the herbs to completing the amulet, must be done in total silence. The August herbs — arnica, calendula, dill, lovage, mugwort, sage, tansy, valerian, and yarrow — must be picked by hand or with a crystal, wood, or stone knife. No metal implements may be used. Once gathered, a stalk of millet, rye, wheat, or other grain is slipped into the center of the herbal bouquet. It is then tied with a ribbon and hung within the home. If properly crafted, the amulet will radiate protection and attract love, romance, safe childbirth, and other blessings.

Lawrence Alma-Tadema · *A Harvest Festival* Netherlands/Germany · 1880 Topped with a flower crown and wrapped in a goat skin, the harvest queen dances. The harvest is considered a time to give thanks to the spirits and deities for promoting the growth and ripening of crops. Modern celebrations include the crowning of a goat as king.

MABON

Abundant Thanks

AUTUMNAL EQUINOX · HARVEST HOME
SEPTEMBER 21 — 24

This Wiccan sabbat coincides with the autumnal equinox. Pronounced *MAY-bon*, it is named after a Celtic deity who appears in the Welsh epic "Culhwch and Olwen" and whose name means "son." Born on the equinox, Mabon is kidnapped three days later, and held captive in the Otherworld. Mabon is the Child of Light, and his disappearance coincides with the waning sun. King Arthur eventually rescues him, liberating Mabon on the winter solstice, thus allowing light to increase. Despite the antiquity of this myth, the deity's association with this sabbat is recent and associated with Gardnerian Wicca, rather than earlier traditions.

However, celebrations of the equinox are truly ancient. Because of its associations with equilibrium, the equinox is connected with those sacred spirits who hold scales, such as Lord Thoth, Archangel Michael, Themis, and Lady Justice. This is considered an ideal time for spells and rituals devoted to justice and for restoring harmony to families and communities.

Mabon is currently among the most beloved sabbats. For many pagans, it substitutes for Thanksgiving. A harvest holiday, its themes include gratitude for blessings, friends, and family, as well as Earth's bounty. It is also increasingly dedicated to activism on behalf of Earth and natural resources. The symbol of Mabon is the cornucopia. Activities associated with this sabbat include harvesting botanicals and crafting magickal tools and talismans derived from them.

Léon Bakst · Costume Design for a Bacchante in *Narcisse et Echo* by Nikolay Tcherepnin · Russia 1911 This pencil and ink rendering provided the initial inspirations for the mythological-character costumes created for the Balletts Russes ensemble's performance of *Narcisse et Echo*.

SAMHAIN

Honoring the Ancestors

PAGAN NEW YEAR · HALLOWEEN · ALL HALLOW'S EVE
OCT 31 — FIRST WEEK OF NOVEMBER

No night is more associated with witchcraft than November Eve, the last night of October. Of all the witches' sabbats, this is the one most familiar to non-witches, who may enjoy it as a secular holiday dedicated to candy and costuming, or fear it as a time of occult forces from which they must hide. For witches, it is a holy day, potentially the most significant of the year.

The most famous name for November Eve, Hallowe'en or All Hallows' Eve, is a synonym for All Saints' Eve, as *hallow* is an archaic word for *saint*. The Catholic Church created a fixed-date commemoration on October 31. However, in the context of the witch's year, this sabbat marks the midpoint between the fall equinox and the winter solstice; many witches celebrate the precise astronomical date, instead of or in addition to October 31.

Samhain, the name favored by many witches, is pronounced *SOW-en.* Emphasis is on the first syllable, which rhymes with "cow." It is also the start of the dark half of the ancient Celtic year. The veil between the worlds is at its most sheer. Witches of a shamanic orientation will avail themselves of this energy to travel between the realms of the dead and the spirits to return with messages and information from beyond the veil. It is believed that the dead return to visit the living at this time, whether as nurturing ancestors or vengeful ghosts. For many, this is a time to honor the dead, to build altars or make offerings to appease them. It is considered especially beneficial for séances and other necromantic rituals.

Samhain is the third and last of the Three Spirit Nights — a time to celebrate with the spirits. Spirits of all kinds are active, especially fairies. It is the feast day of Nicnevin, a Scottish fairy queen, who grants wishes on this night. It is also a holy night dedicated to Hekate, a goddess of witches and witchcraft, who presides over the dead. Hekate may be requested to facilitate contact between the living and the dead or to remove unwanted ghosts. Samhain is the perfect time for any kind of spellcasting, whether solitary or with a coven, for divination, and for honoring one's ancestors.

Anonymous · *The Dance of Death* · Germany · 16th Century How vain the grandeur of earthly life! In death, we all unite. One of many portrayals of the death dance, the artwork shows all walks of life joining together in equality consciousness, joyfully acknowledging life's impermanence.

SHADOWS
AND LIGHT

The Witch & The Moon

The season of the witch ascends again, and the moon has always been our emblem: since Hathor's crown, since Sappho's lyrics, since the first stone temples were built to worship Hecate's sorcery. Witch on broom, flying across a full moon. Cauldron in a clearing, night shadows dancing, potion charged for healing. Because she is here to remind us that everything sacred returns.

— SARAH FAITH GOTTESDIENER, *The Moon Book: Lunar Magic to Change Your Life*, 2020

The witch and the moon have been close companions and coconspirators for thousands of years. Both cast spells, unveil truths, and make folks uncomfortable. Witchcraft has even been referred to as a "lunar cult." As our planet's only (natural) satellite, the moon connects us to the sparkling web of the infinite that we exist within. The moon, with its correlation to the seasons, assures us that change is constant.

Witches, like the moon, cannot be controlled – but as symbols, they exert power. The moon correlates to water and all bodily fluids: rivers, blood, amniotic fluid, the ocean, tears. While many witches are not women – and many women do not menstruate – there has long been a correlation between menstrual cycles and the moon. Witches and the moon both push the boundaries of what dominant

civilization tells us certain bodies *should* do, especially as they become more powerful as they age. Witches exist in service to all forms of magick, not to men. The priestess is often thought of as a timekeeper, and the moon, a reliable clock. Magick has been traditionally enacted in the cloak of night, under the gaze of the "Queen of the Night." Both the witch and the moon are fundamentally mysterious, anchored in the realms of felt sense. They refuse succinct definitions and continue to inspire awe.

Over the centuries, both have been subject to much misalignment. The way the patriarchy views women and femmes affects the way these emblems of wildness are interpreted. The moon has been blamed for mental illness by scholars since classical antiquity. England's 19th-century Lunacy Act contained

Albert Aublet · *Selene* · France · 1880 The moon is personified as a triple goddess, symbolizing the stages of womanhood and the cycles of the moon. An Impressionist painting of the goddess radiates cool lunar forces. Her celestial luminosity transmits pure majesty.

verbiage linking abnormal behavior with a full moon. Contemporary astrologers caution folks not to do anything around a full moon. The word *witch* has been frequently used as a slur. Attributes of the feminine are often discounted, discarded, or destroyed. Silvia Federici, in the 1998 book *Caliban and the Witch*, posits that the witch embodied all "that capitalism had to destroy: the heretic, the healer, the disobedient wife, the woman who dared to live alone..." What threatens power stirs up fear. As witches reconnect to our intuition, we continue to rise.

The connection between the witch and the moon is tied to the wisdom of the earth. Along with the tides, the moon's gravitational pull throughout its cycle influences the moisture in plants, soil, and the water table. Farmers throughout history have practiced lunar gardening. Centuries ago in Europe, women traditionally were the planters, harvesters, and herbalists who knew the effects of the moon intimately. Women were the first brewers, birth workers, diviners, nurses, and healers. One of the ways their vital roles were usurped over time — by the Church, then industry and corporations — was by painting them as witches: evil, incompetent, dangerous. Yet witches, healers, herbalists, and diviners still persisted, utilizing the cycles of the moon. Some herbalists steep their brews for one entire lunation before disseminating. In this political climate, herbal abortion recipes still circulate.

Witches adore the moon because of all the permission slips we are granted through our relationship with her. The moon allows us to *be* and *feel* and *morph* through our own identities and phases as she moves through her own: crone, destroyer, empress, creator, mother.

Maximilian Pirner · *Hekate* · Bohemia · 1901
A voluminous and chaotic vision of a flying Hekate — goddess of sorcery, necromancy, and magick — shows her holding her classic key. She flies entangled with other beings who hold her other totems, the mystic torch, and an ankh.

Catherine Zarip · *Night* · Estonia · 2012 The children's-book illustrator depicts the goddess of night as both daughter of chaos and loving mother to sleep and darkness. In soft blue hues and her flowing veil, she guides us into dream states.

Marjorie Cameron · *Danse, Songs for the Witch Woman*
United States · Date Unknown Cameron illustrated a book of poetry, a fierce love story, by her
lover, Jack Parsons. The nude and dancing sorceress
decorates a poem about an ape, werewolf, and vampire that dance and sing by the light of the moon.

Glyn Smyth · *Savage Mistress* · Northern Ireland
2013 A modern sorceress balances the crescent
moon on the tip of her finger with an inverted cross
in the other hand. Her hair streams downward over
the alchemical symbol of lead, a metal of transformation and redemption.

After all, the moon dies every month, only to rebirth herself anew.

The myriad qualities of the moon are reflected in the many deities associated with her. Hekate is the ancient goddess of magick, crossroads, and liminal spaces, both young and ancient. Artemis is the Greek goddess of the hunt, the wild, and animals. Chang'e, the Chinese moon goddess of immortality, is still prayed to for safety and fortune at the Mid-Autumn Festival. Chandra, the Hindu god associated with the moon, rules over the mind, emotions, vegetation, and fertility.

In many magickal traditions, the light of the moon itself is the power of the moon – not a symbol, but an actual magickal substance. Practitioners "draw down the moon": standing under the moon, they draw its energy inside of them, and become the moon, or a lunar goddess. Sometimes they channel messages from that space, but they almost always cast spells. In Wiccan tradition, esbats, or celebrations of the full moon, are considered holy days.

The lunar phases provide us witches with a supportive structure that helps us navigate

Betye Saar · *Lo, The Mystique City* · United States 1965 A phenomenal etching teems with celestial detail, highlighting the contrast of darkness and light. Various beasts populate the mysterious cosmological story by the legendary assemblage artist Betye Saar.

Alméry Lobel-Riche · *Salammbô* · France · 1935 From the third chapter of Gustave Flaubert's work, the priestess Salammbô invokes her moon goddess, Tanit, on the palace terrace. The beauty of her veneration of the full moon is captured in a stunning spectrum of color, darkness, and shadow.

energy and consciousness. The basics of lunar magick are simple. When the moon is new, we rest, recharge, and regenerate. We call in the energy that we need to plant the seed of our next cycle. As the moon waxes, light and energy accumulate. Our actions and attention do as well — which is what we focus on with discernment and precision. The full moon is the site of alchemy and harvest. It is the space where we gather with others, practice gratitude, and make any and all kinds of magick. The time of the waning moon supports clearing work, subconscious reprogramming, and tying up loose ends. At the dark moon, we surrender, find closure, rest, and envision the seeds of new worlds. Once the lunation (or series of lunations) is complete, we embody — and reflect — the light and vitality of our source, inside and out.

In a world where confusion and chaos continue, the moon nudges us toward that which is real — our desires and intuition. Witchcraft is a crossroads of the past, present, and future. In a world where everything is fleeting — seen through filters, contrived curation, and screens — a glowing moon never disappoints. These timeless qualities are why the witch and the moon remain sites of exploration in art and culture. They have endured, and are having a renaissance as a new era dawns. Whether you identify as a witch or not, the moon continues to enchant us enough to make its way into subcultures and pop culture alike. Whether or not you believe in magick, all things witchy stay circulating in our collective consciousness.

These days, it isn't hard to find a full-moon circle on social media, or to join any number of new-moon intention-setting workshops online. Now we have apps that remind us to go look at a full moon. Technology helps us time our spells to the exact minute. Popular culture has begun to see the value in cyclical living, rituals, and introspection. Even after all this time, humans still find themselves drawn to the moon. Eventually, some will come to find what witches already know: Lunar magick is incredibly potent. Maybe that is why the two are best friends: Witches are after results, and the moon always delivers. Why mess with a perfect cosmic algorithm?

The moon is our companion shape-shifter in the spiral of the Milky Way. The witch follows suit here on Earth. *As above, so below.* The witch and the moon are mirrors of each other.

Agnes Pelton · *Spring Moon* · United States · 1942
Inspired by mysticism, Theosophy, and her practice
of Agni Yoga, Pelton translated her meditative experiences into luminous works of spiritual wonder.

Jodie Muir · *Moon* · England · 2016 The goddess
of the moon is exquisitely portrayed with a lunar
diadem, symbolizing inner vision, covering her eyes.
Seven stars around her head form a halo, or septa-
gram, a sacred representation of magickal power
in witchcraft.

Jean Léon Gérôme · *Night* · France · ca. 1850 A woman in a midnight-blue robe is suspended in the still and quiet sky on a dark-moon night. She drops red poppies to cast the spell of sleep on those below, while holding the mystic torch of eternal wisdom.

Jules Joseph Lefebvre · *Diana* · France · 1902 The artist created a delicate spectacle of the moon goddess, twin sister of Apollo, the sun god. With strawberry hair and holding her lunar diadem against a clouded-sky background, Diana hovers in radiance.

I am a witch. A witch engages in magickal practices to take destiny into their own hands without needing an intermediary on their behalf. The witch is the spiritual other living by their own spiritual rules and ethical codes that are based upon their own experience and sovereignty. All of this being taken into account, a witch defines themself, and each witch will uniquely answer this question, since each witch has their own connection to witchcraft. For me, witchcraft is about connecting with the seen and unseen world, and a particular way of orienting myself with it. It's touching the core of Earth and drawing down the energies of the stars. It's syncing with the phasing of the moon and aligning with elemental forces. It's building relationships with nature itself and the spirits and deities residing within and beyond it. Witches often define magick as being both "a science and an art." That art aspect is all about connecting and expressing your magick on a personal spiritual level. Since witchcraft deals with the energy of interconnection and embracing symbolic action to create change in the external world, how you approach everyday life begins to become magickal. You stop practicing magick — you start becoming the magick through alignment.

— MAT AURYN, Witch, Psychic, Author, & Scholar, 2020

Meagan Donegan · *Moon* · United States · 2018
Blending the element of spirit, ancestry, and the
process of intuitive creativity, Donegan channels
the divine into her stunning work. In her graphite
image, the moon goddess frames a body of water
over which she has gentle command.

ELEMENTAL PROTECTION

The Pentagram in Witchcraft

Symbols are oracular forms—mysterious patterns creating vortices in the substances of the invisible world. They are centers of a mighty force, figures pregnant with an awful power, which, when properly fashioned, loose fiery whirlwinds upon the earth.

— MANLY P. HALL, from *Lectures on Ancient Philosophy,* 1970

A pentagram is an equilateral, five-pointed star that symbolizes to many practitioners of witchcraft the unity and balance of five elemental forces: most often, in Western witchcraft practice, air, fire, water, earth, and spirit or the self. Although ancient and timeless in its pleasing geometry and the metaphorical resonance of the number five (fingers, senses, etc.), the symbol was popularized in magickal circles through its prominence in *The Key of Solomon the King*, a pseudo-ancient text that purports to be the grimoire of the biblical King Solomon, but more likely dates back to Renaissance-era Western Europe. In modern witchcraft the pentagram is believed to represent integration of the elements, a harmonious geometry that allows for the five elements to remain in balance.

In the same way that the cross has come to represent Christianity and the six-pointed star is a symbol for Judaism, the pentagram has been viewed as the emblem of witchcraft in its many forms. The inverted pentagram, on the other hand, symbolizes Satanism to some, but to others when inverted, the symbol represents spirit matter or (in some

Sara Hannant · **Skull Used in Ritual Magic** England · 2014 Once belonging to a wise witch who called it her "friend" and kept it hidden in England's Easdon Tor, the human skull is har- nessed by iron to a pentagram. Now archived in the Museum of Witchcraft and Magic in Cornwall, England, Hannant photographed it and other relics for her show *Of Shadows*.

Wiccan practices), the face of the Horned God. Inverted crosses and other inverted symbols of spiritual significance have similarly been used by Satanists. The 1960s occultist Anton LaVey, founder of the Church of Satan, chose the sigil of Baphomet – an inverted pentagram inscribed with the face of a goat and encircled with Hebrew letters – as the symbol of his church. Hence, it has mistakenly entered popular culture as a symbol of all blasphemy.

Among witches, however, this star formation is often enclosed within a circle, transforming the pentagram into a pentacle, a more ambiguous term that was originally used to refer to any shape of magickal symbol inscribed on paper or any natural material. Such is the case with the Pentacles suit in the Tarot, which most often depicts encircled pentagrams as gleaming coins, representations of physicality, material manifestation, and the gains of hard work. Due perhaps to

the dominance of Tarot interpretation in the modern occult imagination, many modern witches use the words *pentagram* and *pentacle* interchangeably, if somewhat inaccurately.

During rituals, witches employ the pentagram in myriad ways. They often draw the shape of an invoking, or point-upright, pentagram (whether the form is made by a gesture of the hand, wand, chalice, cauldron, or blade) in the ground or air, or on an altar, to attract positive energy and protection. Some inscribe an upright pentagram to open a ritual circle and an inverted pentagram to close it, while others use an inverted, or banishing, pentagram when performing a ritual cleansing, attempting to shed what isn't useful. An encircled pentagram is often found among the items on a witch's altar, even among those who would not consider themselves Wiccan or affiliated with any particular tradition.

Anna Biller · Film Still from *The Love Witch* United States · 2016 A scene from the black comedy by director Biller shows curses being cast on unsuspecting men. Samantha Robinson stars as the witch Elaine, who believes that her spells will bring her true love.

Fay Avnisan Nowitz (Nyxturna) · *Ritual I* · United States · 2018 A series by Nowitz reinterpreting magick, queerness, and sexuality in vintage and historic occult cinema, pulp magazines, and popular culture through a Sapphic lens. The set was hand-painted by the artist as part of the ritual, creating a multidimensional work in collaboration with model Carol Naisanga and makeup artist Arpita Brahmbhatt, with styling, set design, and photography by Nowitz.

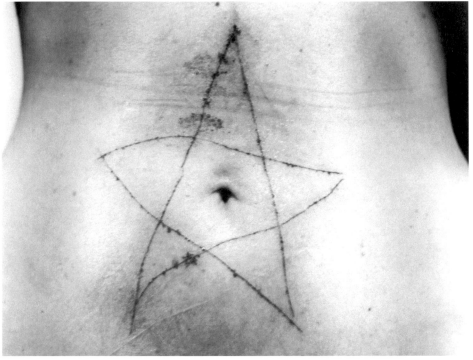

(opposite) **Marina Abramović · *Lips of Thomas*
Yugoslavia · 1975** Images from a piece by the artist
exploring psychic energy. For the performance,
Abramović consumed a kilo of honey, drank a liter
of wine, and carved a pentagram on her stomach,
among other acts of endurance.

(above) A recursive geometric structure governed
by the golden ratio; a larger pentagram can be
subdivided into smaller pentagrams, as illustrated
above. Representing the sacred feminine and
divine goddess, it is one of the oldest symbols on
Earth and was used as early as 4000 years BCE.

Witchcraft is outside of the time-space cube, as it is techniques used to come into relation with spirit and so it becomes a perennial philosophy valuable in all times. The usefulness and pragmatism of witchcraft is a coming into being with spirit as we progress through our fleshy existence. Is there anything more useful than a practice which allows us to include our spirit in the physical, natural world? This is our greatest human destiny to achieve. The modern world attempts to dissociate us from our nature, condemning, shaming, and punishing our bestial realities, resulting only in an amplification of shadow and a scapegoating that reinforces what the brave new world seeks to eradicate through emotional manipulation. INCLUSION of all regardless of personal judgment of good and evil is the constant shouted recommendation of the goddess of wisdom Sophia. The modern world NEEDS witchcraft in order to assimilate, integrate, evolve, and empower our instincts to rise into the shape-shifting form of the true human. There is no teacher greater than nature. For people (of all genders/identities) gaining desire towards the craft, please disregard the voices of others and attempt to focus on your inner voice, your guiding sentience. Focus on spirit, focus on your connection to spirit. Disregard your influences, needs, power and turn your inward gaze instead to crafting your spirit, your supernatural being, and coming into communion with your spirit. Once you make the connection to spirit you come into knowing and that knowing is your teacher that gives you gifts of revelation every day that you may use to grow yourself as a tree stretching towards infinity.

— MAJA D'AOUST, Author, Artist, Scholar, & Witch of the Dawn, 2020

Éliphas Lévi · *Tetragrammaton Pentagram* · France 19th Century A famous illustration contains the microcosm of man as the image of God. The five-pointed star represents the five elements, and within it are the seven planets, alchemical symbols, and the Hebrew four-lettered name of God.

PART IV

---

*Calling in
the Elements*

THE SPELL
IS CAST

Types of Magick

Not only are magical texts among the oldest surviving pieces of literature, but many scholars and anthropologists suggest that it was the need to record spells and divination results that stimulated the very birth of writing.

— JUDIKA ILLES, *Encyclopedia of 5,000 Spells*, 2004

A magick spell is a conscious, focused attempt to obtain a goal. Though "attempt," while true, may be too tentative a word. A magick spell is a determined effort to control life, rather than to simply allow fate to take its course. When a spell is cast, it is as if an arrow of magickal energy is released and directed toward a target, to avert it, ensure it, or alter it.

Magick spells take many forms, from the most spontaneous and minimalistic to elaborate, multi-day rituals. They involve candles, crystals, herbs, flowers, perfume, and spices, as well as words of power. Specialized tools are incorporated, such as wands and chalices,

and household items, like pins and needles. Spells exist from all documented eras and from all over the globe. No single culture has a monopoly on spellcasting.

While spells are the brainchildren of human beings, magickal energy exists naturally and independently. There are words for this energy in many different languages: *baraka* in Moroccan Arabic, *qi* in Chinese, *mana* in Polynesian languages, and *ashé* in Yoruba. These words refer to an intangible energy coursing through everything — living beings, objects, colors, numbers, sounds, and anything else you can imagine. For things to go well, this energy must flow harmoniously and

(previous) Sarah Sheil · *Ophiolatreia* · Ireland · 2020 Surreal and mesmerizing, a woman communes with a serpent, a phallic symbol, in rapt worship. A single candle dimly unveils this ancient veneration, conjuring sexual and creative energy and power.

Josephine Close · *Hand of Mysteries* · United States · 2021 Close creates at the intersection of art and magick, channeling into her expressions true spellwork. The symbol of apotheosis, man becoming God as the key to divinity, awakens the nature of the human mystery in the ritual paper altar.

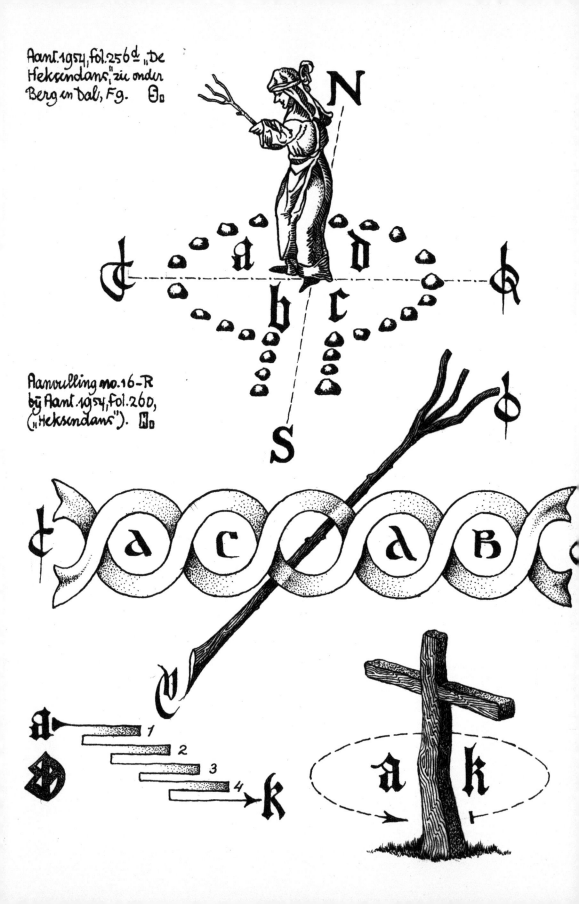

Aant. 1954, fol. 256ᵈ „De Heksendans" zie onder Berg en Dal, F9.

Aanvulling no. 16-R by Aant. 1954, fol. 260, („Heksendans").

provide power. This energy can be depleted, generated, replenished, and transmitted. It is contagious. Surrounding yourself with objects, animals, and people possessing powerful energy automatically increases your own and makes your magick more likely to succeed.

A creation tale describes the birth of *heka*, the ancient Egyptian name for magickal energy: Having completed creation, the creator gazed out upon it and realized that all was not good and that humans would suffer heartbreak and sorrow. As an antidote, the creator's final act of creation was to produce *heka*, an energy that, if used correctly, would ward off the harsh blows of fate. Magickal theory suggests that in order to live a happy, harmonious, productive life, one should avail oneself of this energy, manipulating it so that it produces the desired results, including prosperity, safety, autonomy, and the attainment of one's desires. Magick spells are concerted efforts to accomplish this.

Every spell has two things in common: a goal – the spellcaster's desired result – and the spellcaster's own personal magickal energy. These two components are crucial. Spells exist for every possible desire, for anything you can imagine. As they derive from so many cultures, eras, and spiritual outlooks, there are innumerable styles of spellcasting. People can rely on ancient spells or create new ones tailored to them. Different schools of spellcasting exist. Here is a sampling:

Ceremonial magick features complex, formal rituals devoted to Hermeticism and Western esotericism, often rooted in medieval grimoire traditions. Chaos magick is a modern magickal practice that focuses on the spellcasters' independence and personal needs. Folk magick, traditionally the province of the marginalized, typically incorporates accessible, inexpensive ingredients and reflects the cultures of its practitioners. Green witchery, or botanical magick, focuses on the mysteries of the natural world, whether for practical purposes, such as healing, or for esoteric intent, as with working with plant spirits. Hedge-witchery is an ecstatic, shamanistic school of magick that emphasizes interaction with the spirit world: The proverbial "hedge" serves as the boundary between civilization and wild nature. Kitchen witchery taps into the magick power of the home, incorporating items easily found on kitchen shelves. Spells may be cast by cooking, baking, and concocting potions. A wooden spoon or ice pick may serve as a wand. Wicca and other magicktolerant religions may use spells in ceremonies and rituals.

Although spells may be cast for anything, common desires include protection, love, prosperity, and justice. Reflecting these desires, spells are traditionally classified into categories that are not mutually exclusive. Elements of each may find their way into spells.

Unknown · Drawing from the Richel Collection
England · 20th Century Housed at the Museum
of Witchcraft and Magic in Cornwall, England, this
collection consists of more than 2,000 drawings
related to the occult.

APOTROPAIC
MAGICK

The word *apotropaic* derives from the Greek root *apotrépein*, and is generally translated as "to ward off" or "prevent." Apotropaic magick is protection magic, intended to provide safety and deflect danger. It also serves as magickal maintenance — preserving what is valuable and preventing loss. Apotropaic magick often takes the form of amulets: objects and images that are expected to radiate protective power, though objects are not essential. A spontaneous apotropaic spell may be cast by visualizing oneself within a bubble of protection, similar to Glinda's pink bubble in *The Wizard of Oz*. This bubble deflects curses and malicious spells, and provides safety.

The most common apotropaic objects include images of fierce deities and stylized human anatomical parts. Prehistoric eye images, such as the Eye of Ra or the Neolithic eye goddess, ward off evil; their modern descendants, evil eye beads, continue to provide personal protection from unseen forces.

Amulets shaped liked genitalia, such as Roman penis amulets, are believed to ward off dangers emanating from the afterlife by virtue of their profound life force, while hand-shaped amulets serve as magickal stop signs, arresting whatever evil approaches. Favored hand-shaped amulets that depict magickal hand gestures include the hamsa, the mano figa (fig hand), and the mano cornuta (horned hand). One can form the gestures as needed, but because danger is omnipresent, an amulet provides a constant force, allowing one's hands to be otherwise occupied.

In the ancient world, images of fierce deities were used to ward off danger. The gorgon Medusa famously transformed all who looked upon her face into stone, stopping them in their tracks; her image is expected to reproduce that effect upon spiritual and magickal danger. The gorgoneion that depicts Medusa's face was posted on homes and temples in the Mediterranean world. Likewise, in New Kingdom Egypt, images

Unknown · Scrimshaw Wand · United States ca. 1800 A magickal wand made of carved bone bears the name Amasarac, a demon that possesses the power of transformation. The piece is part of the Stephen Romano Collection.

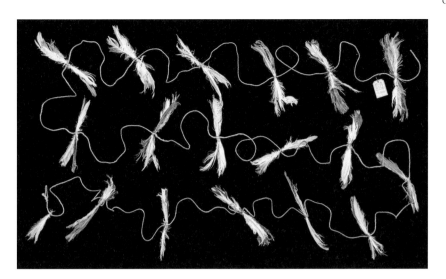

of the Egyptian god Bes were tattooed onto women's thighs — not dissimilar to the modern practice of tattooing images of Santa Muerte (Saint Death), a Mexican folk saint, on the backs of devotees. Religious medals serve a similar purpose — images of protective saints ward off trouble and provide protection. The Egyptians carved images of Bes and Taweret, the hippopotamus goddess, onto beds to avert the dangers of the night.

Other apotropaic objects include witch balls and spirit traps — both believed to be able to lure and entrap negative energy, low-level demonic entities, and perhaps even the intrusive souls of malefic practitioners. Witch bottles — ceramic jugs or glass bottles filled with magickally protective items such as iron nails, pins, and urine, then capped and buried beneath doorsteps or fireplaces to radiate constant vigilance — were expected to protect against malevolent witchcraft.

Witches' marks are another form of apotropaic magick, consisting of ritualized geometric markings etched into wood or stone, so as to protect inhabitants of a building. Found within barns, homes, and even churches, they are typically placed near openings — doors, fireplaces, and windows — so that no danger may enter. A "daisy wheel," the folk name for the most popular type of mark, also known as a hexafoil, resembles a six-petal flower and appears innocuous, compared to the fierce visages of Medusa or Bes, but these symbols are trusted to exert apotropaic power just the same.

Unknown · Female Bes · Middle Kingdom ca. 1981–1640 BCE Found in an ancient Egyptian cemetery, this statue of the goddess Bes is thought to have been worshipped as a guardian of mothers and childbirth.

Unknown · "Witches' Ladder" · England · 19th Century Bird feathers tied on a knotted cord were found and labeled "Witches' ladder" in an attic where a supposed witch once lived. At each knotted interval a cursed incantation is embedded.

ATTRACTION MAGICK

"Come to Me, Lover" names a standard magickal-formula oil that, whether worn as perfume or rubbed on a candle, reputedly draws a desired lover into your arms. It is a prime example of attraction magick – spells intended to produce a magnetic effect. Attraction magick is fueled by the desire for life's joys: love, romance, offspring, health, prosperity, money, and success. Attraction magick is based on the metaphysical Law of Attraction, the concept that like attracts like.

Such spells rely on things that share an essence to magnetically attract each other, similar to the concept of wealth attracting wealth. Magnets, iron filings, and lodestones are popular spell items when seeking to draw something toward you, as is sugar, which is believed to have magickal attraction powers. One must only approach the open door of a bakery to feel – or rather, smell – its magnetic pull. A folk-magick tip for attracting good company, customers, and auspicious people is to sprinkle a sugary path from the street to your door.

Talismanic objects also are important in attraction magick, as they are believed to magnetically attract whatever their owner seeks, although the right charm must

be chosen. Famous lucky charms include horseshoes, four-leaf clovers, wishbones, and dice. Depictions of lucky creatures also bring good fortune, such as white elephants, ladybugs, fish, and spiders, which supposedly capture good luck in their webs and prevent its departure.

The maneki-neko, Japan's beckoning cat, is a visual depiction of attraction magick in the form of a front-facing feline holding its paw up in the air. In Japanese culture, that upraised paw signals "Come here!", literally beckoning the viewer closer. An upraised right paw beckons cash, while the left attracts business. A red maneki-neko invites love, while a leopard-spotted one encourages political success. Maneki-nekos are available in various sizes and price ranges – from inexpensive figurines and phone charms to priceless antiques and precious porcelain. The figure's mythology explains its power. Legends vary, but all involve a cat who wishes to provide for its human. The amulet attracts not only the desired result, but also the spirit of that benevolent mystical cat.

Metaphysical author Annie Besant compared the Law of Attraction to gravitation, the phenomenon by which all things with mass

(following, top) Unknown · **Apotropaic Wand** Egypt · **12th Dynasty** Used to ward off evil magick toward women during childbirth, the wands were made of hippopotamus tusk to symbolize Taweret, the hippo goddess of childbirth.

Neil Daftary · *Spider Web at Storm King* · United States · **2020** The allure and attraction of the spider's silken web is captured in this photograph taken at the Storm King Art Center in New York.

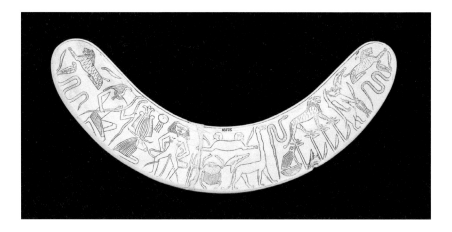

Unknown
Shell Amulet in Box
Netherlands · 1909
A painted amulet on
an oyster shell serves
as protection against
the dangers of fire. The
oyster symbolizes defen-
sive strength in general,
with its tightly closed
musculature shielding
the treasures inside,
making it a perfect
totem for security.
The relic is preserved
in the Museum of
Witchcraft and Magic
in Cornwall, England.

gravitate to each other. For example, the moon's gravitational effect causes ocean tides. Magickal theory would extend this – if the moon controls the tides, does it not also affect other bodies of water, including the water contained in human bodies? Coordinating spells with lunar phases enables successful magick. Spells to increase what needs to grow (money, love, safety) are best synchronized with the waxing (growing)

moon, while spells intended to shrink that which should decrease (trouble, debts, bad luck) should be cast with the waning moon. Similarly, spells for weight gain or hair growth are best coordinated with the waxing moon, and for weight loss and hair reduction, with the waning moon. The dark moon is best for spells that require secrecy or discretion: especially malefic magick.

Meagan Boyd
Patron Saint · United States · 2020 Creating work that aims to heal and reveal the interconnectivity of all things, Boyd depicts Mary, Gaia, and Venus in Scorpio as love manifest. Her art embodies the elements of nature and the cosmos.

MALEFIC MAGICK

Witchcraft has historically been the province of the marginalized, disenfranchised, victimized, and oppressed — those most frequently denied protection or justice. Malefic spells are a magickal arsenal for those who lack any other. The components of malefic spells tend to be accessible, inexpensive, and discreet: fabric, wax, twine, or other binding material; thorns, pins, and other sharp objects, as well as dirt. Malefic magick is typically performed secretly, not only to prevent the person targeted from being alerted — thus avoiding possible countermeasures — but also because, outside the realm of magick, that individual might possess control over the spellcaster.

The most notorious form of malefic magick involves dolls. They may be crafted from the target's clothing and stuffed with their hair, and may also be made to resemble the victim, but the presence of items intimately associated with them should suffice. Poppets may also be formed of wax, using the same principles. A Roman-period Egyptian wax doll, now in the collection of the British Museum, features human hair stuffed into its navel. What happens to the poppet depends upon the spellcaster: It may be bound with twine, stuck with pins, left in a dark closet, or buried in a cemetery.

Dirt also can transmit magickal energy and the spellcaster's will, but not just any dirt. Dirt from a crossroads or a cemetery is typically most potent. Gathered from ancestral graves, it provides protection for descendants and may be used to seek vengeance. It's sufficient for the target to step over the dirt or have contact with it for the spell to work. Graveyard dirt is a primary component of goofer dust, a powder intended to wreak mental havoc or worse.

A person's own footsteps can even be used against them. Popularly known as "foot-track magick," it is ancient and international. The ancient Greek philosopher Pythagoras forbade his followers from piercing footprints with knives or nails. Footprints are believed to contain a person's lingering essence, providing a direct connection between spellcaster and target. The most common procedure is to carefully gather up the entire footprint and combine it with other spell ingredients to provide a destructive effect. Foot-track magick is thought to be especially effective because of the idea that no one can escape their own tracks, but there may be exceptions: Russian witch goddess Baba Yaga famously swept away all her traces with her broom, preventing others from harming her or knowing her business.

Unknown · Wax Figure with Papyrus · Egypt 1–3 CE Housed in the British Museum, the ancient wax effigy has the hair, perhaps of the intended victim, stuffed in the navel and a spell written on a papyrus scroll adhered to its back. Such vehicles for cursing were created for harm or love spells.

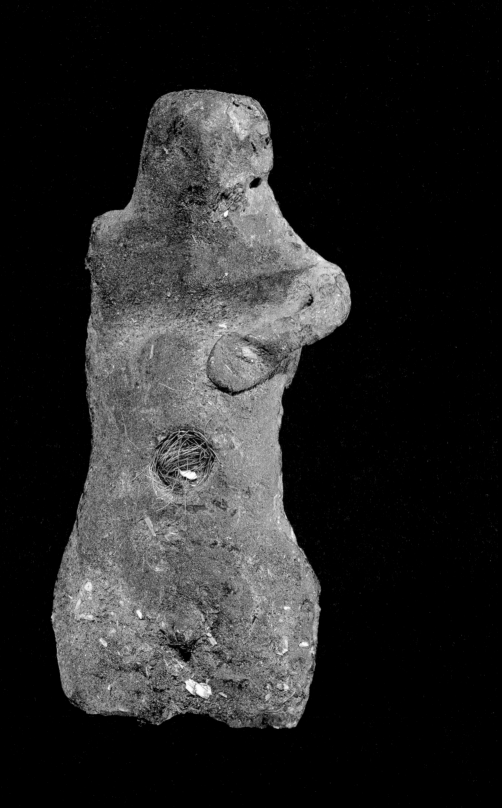

Unknown · Witchcraft Poppet · England · 1953
The doll with a spike through its face was made to
defeat the influence of an evil Nazi wife in Bavaria.
To complete the spell, it was secretly shipped through
Switzerland to arrive in the United Kingdom.

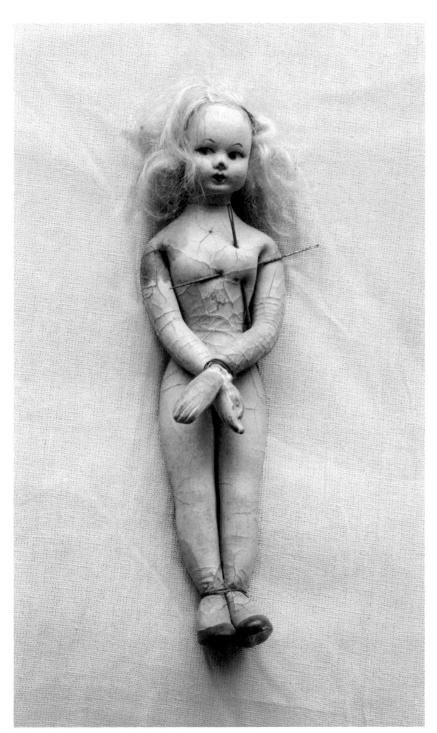

Unknown · Witchcraft
Poppet · England
1950s This commer-
cially produced doll has
the victim's name writ-
ten on the leg, Norma
Keys. Norma was hav-
ing an affair with the
maker's husband. The
aggrieved wife resorted
to this age-old method
of revenge. Wrists and
ankles are bound with
wire and the heart is
pierced by two needles.

REPULSION MAGICK

Repulsion or repelling magick is the opposite of attraction magick. Sometimes things or people must go. They need to be removed from a person's life or at least their vicinity. While apotropaic magick seeks to ward off trouble and prevent it from happening, repulsion magick counteracts and repels danger that is already present, and includes banishing and cleansing spells.

Innumerable things might require banishing, including bad neighbors, toxic relations, or people who prey upon the spellcaster or their loved ones. There's also poverty, danger, and even illness, whose cause is frequently associated with harmful beings, whether viral or spiritual. Many rituals designed to remove diseases are essentially banishing spells. Oppressive thoughts, phobias, ghosts, and demons, whether personal or literal, may also be candidates for banishment.

Banishing spells take many forms: from the mild to the wrathful, from simple to elaborate. Florida Water is believed to have begun as a homemade magickal potion that was eventually packaged and marketed commercially, although recipes abound, and many practitioners still craft their own. This citrus-scented cologne is believed to repel negative entities and harmful vibrations. Hot-foot powder is directed toward troublesome humans — made from black pepper, salt, sulfur, and habaneros or other spicy chili peppers, it is administered by sprinkling in shoes or on a chair, and is intended to make your enemy hotfoot it out of town.

Four Thieves vinegar, an herbal concoction, first emerged as a European health tonic, its formula provided by four legendary thieves who used it so that they could burgle locked-down, infectious, quarantined homes at will. When the potion arrived in plague-ridden 19th-century New Orleans, practitioners understood it as banishing illness. The traditional formula was then transformed into one intended for external use only, as additional ingredients were added to expel other kinds of danger too.

Unknown · A Witch Mark in a Herefordshire House · England · 16th Century This apotropaic mark was discovered carved into a home's wooden beams. The daisy-shaped wheel design was thought to protect the house from evil.

Terence Spencer · *Mrs. Ray Bone* · England
1964 In ceremony at her altar, the matriarch of
British witchcraft, Eleanor "Ray" Bone, consecrates
a ritual bowl of water and salt. The smoke eerily
mirrors the lit candle as she immerses herself in
mystic awareness.

Fiona Pardington · *Still Life with Mussel Spat,
My Name Sigil Crystals and Wolf Moon Holy Water,
Ripiro* New Zealand · 2013 Using tabletops
as ritual platforms for concentration, Pardington
creates altars of sacred objects and elements.

While serious hauntings may require professional help, many negative entities are kept at bay via botanical repulsion methods. Smoke cleansing via sage is most famous, but smoke generated by plants such as lavender, rosemary, frankincense, and myrrh is also effective. The mere presence of wormwood, whether a living plant or its dried root, may be sufficient to repel unwanted spirits.

Cleansing spells fittingly remove and repel unhealthy attachments, eliminating the spiritual debris absorbed during daily life. This debris resembles household dust that continually accumulates on furniture and must be removed on a regular basis. A tiny bit of this debris may cause no harm, but significant quantities can prevent an individual from achieving success. Cleansing spells often serve as a preliminary to any kind of spellcasting, removing anything that may block the spellcaster's personal power. They encourage healing from trauma or humiliation, serving to repel lingering traces of defilement. The simplest cleansing spells involve bathing. Adding vinegar, lemon slices, crystals, rose petals, and especially salt to a bath will automatically cleanse the aura. More intensive cleansing spells may require immersion in the ocean or another living body of water.

Vera Petruk · *Still Life with Witch Books, Scrolls, Herb and Candle* · Russia · 2016 Potion-making recipes and ingredients are prepped for magickal arts. The apothecary photo by Petruk comes from a series of modern visuals that breathe new life into the sacred art of altar, spell, and ceremony making.

SYMPATHETIC MAGICK

Sympathetic magick relies upon the theory of correspondences: Things that resemble each other will naturally and magickally impact each other, sharing an essence that creates an unbreakable connection. The philosopher and mystic Emanuel Swedenborg was one of the first to introduce the theory of correspondences, which claimed there were relationships between different levels of existence – for instance, body corresponded with spirit, and intention with action.

In sympathetic magick, objects or rituals are used that are symbolically linked to the focus of intent – the subject, person, or event one hopes to influence. Often elements such as dolls or poppets are used. Elements of sympathetic magick are integral to spellcasting, in general. A doll used for either attraction or malefic magick and intended to represent a specific individual is crafted to resemble that person or will contain some other sort of connection to them. Otherwise, it is just a doll. Inserting the target's fingernail clippings or hair strands forms a link, for example, so that what happens to the doll will also befall the person.

Sympathetic magick also serves as the basis for much folk medicine. Plants perceived as resembling a body part – a heart or kidney, for instance – are believed to have the capacity to heal that part. The phallic-shaped daikon radish reputedly counteracts impotence, while hibiscus flowers encourage healthy menstruation, especially when steeped in water and served as a crimson beverage. Many anthropologists believe that the depictions of animals in ancient cave paintings, such as those of Lascaux in France, are prehistoric examples of sympathetic magick.

Magickal practitioners would enter the cave and envision the animals they wished to hunt, painting these visions as an act of manifestation and visualization. By creating and controlling the imagery, hunting success is ensured.

Sympathetic magick enables one to create one's own destiny. By utilizing the power of correspondences, one is able to manifest the object of one's desire.

Georges Merle · *The Sorceress* · France · 1883
In the midst of a spell, a witch sits in a ritual symbol circle with a vodou doll comfortably resting upon a pillow over a magickal diagram. The exquisite detail of her dark eyes draws one into the mystery of her seemingly sympathetic act.

GEORGES MERLE

Table of Correspondences

PLANET	Sun	Moon	Mars	Mercury	Jupiter	Venus	Saturn
SYMBOL	☉	☽	♂	☿	♃	♀	♄
METAL	Gold	Silver	Iron	Quicksilver (Mercury)	Tin	Copper	Lead
COLORS	Yellow Orange Gold	White Silver	Red	Gray Indigo Violet	Blue Purple Violet	Blue Green	Black Brown Gray
BOTANICALS	Citrus Heliotrope Sunflower	Lily Moonflower Mugwort	Garlic Nettles Onion	Cinquefoil Dill Dog's Mercury	Borage Hydrangea Walnut	Jasmine Myrtle Rose	Blackthorn Night Shades Tobacco
DEITIES	Apollo Helios Sol Invictus	Artemis Diana Hekate Lilith Selene	Ares Mars Ogun Tyr	Hermes Mercury Odin	Jupiter Thor Zeus	Aphrodite Freya Oshun Venus	Kronos Saturn
DAY	Sunday	Monday	Tuesday	Wednesday	Thursday	Friday	Saturday
GEMSTONES	Diamond Topaz	Moonstone Pearl	Ruby	Opal	Amethyst Lapis Lazuli	Emerald	Onyx

Austin Osman Spare · *Ritual and Ceremony* England · 1952 Working with his friends Kenneth and Steffi Grant, Spare was inspired by the British witchcraft revival of the 1950s. Together they produced text and images that explored the rituals of the witches' sabbath.

RESURGTIM

AOS ISOV

F.S.CHURCH.
N.Y. 1881.
COPYRIGHT.

ELEMENT

AIR

I

INDICATION

Thought · Breath
Language · Truth
Travel · The Mind

SYMBOLS

Flight · Feathers
Brooms · Blades
Birds
Grimoires
Magic Words · Sigils

MANIFESTATION

New Beginnings
Discernment · Clarity · Levity
Adventure · Rebirth

Breath of Life

In witchcraft we are connecting to source and the energies that be, by using different ancient and modern modalities. The biggest way I integrate my craft into my own life is by singing my spells. All of my songs are spells. Energy, frequency, and vibration are all the components of music. When I began to educate myself more on soundwaves and the physics of it all, it was undeniable that music and sound is witchcraft.

— **BROOKLYNN,** Artist, Musician, & Sonic Spellcaster, 2020

When casting a magick circle, a witch traditionally begins by facing east and welcoming the spirits of air. Associated with breath and wind, air is the subtlest of the four material elements, for it is by and large invisible to the human eye. It fills lungs and cells, circulating around and through us. It may come in the form of a soft breeze or a terrific gale, and it can lift us up or bring us to our knees. A shift in the air portends a change in one's life, and can deliver important messages or point one in an entirely new direction. Air is a fresh start, a perpetual beginning.

It also moves in currents, so air is a carrier. Birds and other winged beings use it to travel, and witches are said to ride it using brooms or their own magickally enhanced bodies. The feather is a sacred symbol, whether avian or angelic — a gift from an aerial guide. "Light as a feather, stiff as a board," chant young witches as they lift their sister up to the sky. Air is all floating, flight, levity. It transports planes of paper and aluminum, pirate ships and rocket ships. It is what gets people where they want to go.

Air brings information and ideas, thus it is the element linked with thought, the mind, the head. One may invoke air when in need of discernment and clear thinking, hence its association with blades, daggers, swords. Air cuts through the unnecessary. It sharpens our focus and helps us visualize more vividly.

The voice is made of air, as is language. This is why communication dwells in the realm of air. It transmits secret knowledge through words and whispers. Air entrances through incantation, sound waves, song. It speaks to us quietly or howls in our bones. Air tells us precisely who we are and what we need to know.

(previous) Frederick Stuart Church · *The Witch's Daughter* · United States · 1881 Known for his illustrations in an edition of Aesop's Fables, Church brings his whimsical touch to a scene of the daughter of a witch sitting with her mother's familiar.

Francisco de Goya · *Witches' Flight* · Spain · 1798 Considered the most beautiful of Goya's witch paintings, the treasured work expresses the ignorance (symbolized by the donkey) of the Inquisition, with witches wearing conical hats denoting power.

Miguel Opazo · *Witches' Sabbath* · Chile · 2014
A witch rides a goat to the summit to meet the Devil
on May Eve. Her right-hand fingers point up to
express half of the principle "as above, so below."

Jan de Bisschop · Untitled · Netherlands · 17th
Century Mischievous magick abounds as a witch
flies on a dragon holding her opened grimoire in
its mouth. By way of incantation, she lays waste to
a village below.

FLYING

Henbane's Voyage

Night flights are said to be a frequent activity of witches, allowing them to gather and revel under a full moon – or wreak havoc on a local village, depending on who's doing the telling. They may fly together in a cackling pack, filling the air with their lunar laughter. Or a witch might take a solo flight for some clandestine purpose, a secret kept between herself and the sky.

Brooms or cooking forks might be their most typical mode of aerial transportation, though there are depictions of witches riding flying goats or other winged beasts. A witch may also use her shape-shifting abilities and fly using her own enchanted wings. A commonly mentioned tool in a witch's arsenal is flying ointment, a mythical unguent said to be created out of everything from baby fat to magickal plants. In Giambattista della Porta's *Magia Naturalis* of 1558, he writes that these ointments were in fact real, though made of psychotropic botanicals such as belladonna, which made the witches merely *believe* they were flying.

But whether witches' flights were literal or phantasmagorical hallucinations, the notion of flying is one that spans history and region. In his 2002 *Cauldron* essay, "Cultus Sabbati: Provenance, Dream, and Magistry," Andrew D. Chumbley writes, "An important dimension of magical and folk religiosity was the oneiric or dream realm. Peripheral areas of European folklore retain vestigial myths which relate the oneiric location of witch-meetings, fairie convocations, and the nocturnal flight of the Wild Hunt." These gatherings as described are happening "between worlds," in the space of sleep and dreams.

When she flies, is a witch actually relocating, eventually arriving at some faraway spell space – the Brocken of Germany, Blockula in Sweden, or the ancient balete tree in the Philippines? Or is she merely tripping, in a trance, or astral-projecting? No matter. The experience of being sky-bound, of levitating, of projecting oneself upward and forward has meaning in itself. A witch can defy gravity and break the rules of nature. In flight, the witch is truly free.

Kiki Smith · *Sky* · United States · 2012 The third work of a triptych by Smith, alongside *Earth* and *Underworld*, *Sky* weaves themes of cosmology and femininity, animal nature and celestial consciousness, into her creative work.

Edward Robert Hughes · *Dream Idyll (A Valkyrie)*
England · 1902 A supernatural female being
from Norse mythology surveys a city below before
making her grand descent to choose which slain
warriors are to be guided into Valhalla.

Hieronymus Bosch · *The Temptation of St. Anthony*
(detail) · Netherlands · 1501 The virtuous and
celibate lifestyle of St. Anthony is fervently tested in
the storytelling triptych. This portion of the painting
shows the Devil's forceful offer of the gift of flight
to the witches' sabbath.

Carlos Luis de Ribera *A Witch Heading to Witches' Sabbath on Back of a Winged Fanciful Animal* · Spain · 1875 A sky-clad witch maiden rides with a striking determination, clutching the horns of the beast. The horned beast clutches her back, and as one they soar to their unholy destination.

Max Klinger · *Finis, from A Life* · Germany 1884 Inspired by the works of Goya, Klinger's drawings bear dark, arcane, and grotesque themes. His series tells a visual story of a woman rejected by society, resulting in a life of destitution.

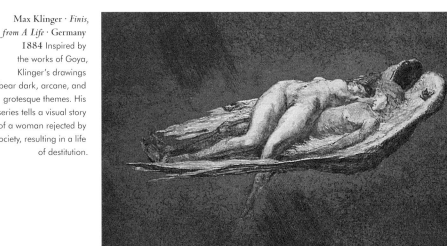

People have turned to healers, mystics, and witches for cures and wisdom for all of human history. We have not embraced empirical science and mechanical philosophy because of an evolved intellectual capacity — we were forced to adopt our current healing, spiritual, scientific, and philosophical systems upon pain of death for the profit of a few. As a witch I am proud to belong to a world that capitalism is anxious to destroy: a world where nurturance is valued above competition, a world rooted in local communities and knowledge, a world alive with magickal possibilities, a world that respects the earth, water, air, fire, plants, and animals that sustain it, a world where people are connected to their own healing process, a world deep in the process of renewal. Magic is a living energy that can be harnessed by anyone at any time — you do not need advanced degrees, expensive tools, or permission to proceed. What interests me in magic is the wild way that harnessing the mystery of desire produces a quantum array of possibility — not just for the witch — it opens new dimensions within everything they touch. Art at its center is magick — art changes, defines, shapes, and nourishes the spirit of the collective imagination which is the engine of our communal will. Imagination combined with will changes everything.

— ELIZA SWANN, Founder of Golden Dome School,
Artist, Writer, & Scholar, 2020

Anthony 'Bones' Johnson · *Lilith* · England/Ibiza 2018 In his last series, "The Gathering," Johnson painted scenes that honor the alchemical forces of nature and the power of women. A flying female and other fierce women wear a blend of Spanish and Romani attire.

(previous, right) Denis Forkas · *Celaeno's Pledge* Russia · 2012 In Greek mythology, Celaeno was one of the Pleiades, the seven sisters who became a cluster of stars. She was a winged spirit in the flesh with a somewhat darker wrath, and has numerous tales attributed to her.

BROOMS

Mounting the Staff

Flying witches are most often shown riding broomsticks, and besides a pointed hat, the presence of a broom is an obvious signifier that a mysterious woman may be a witch. There are many theories as to the derivation of this symbol, the most popular one being that it is a remnant of an ancient pagan practice to help crops be more abundant. As Raymond Buckland writes in his 2002 tome, *Buckland's Complete Book of Witchcraft*, "An old ritual act for fertility was for the villagers to go to the fields in the light of the full moon and to dance around the field astride pitchforks, poles, and broomsticks, riding them like hobby-horses. They would leap high in the air as they danced, to show the crops how high to grow…"

The earliest known depiction of witches on broomsticks is found in the 1451 edition of French poet Martin Le Franc's work *Le Champion des Dames* (*The Defender of Ladies*).

These two painted ladies are shown as marginal illustrations, one riding a broom with a twig end (known as a besom), and one on a bare stick. They have been identified as Waldensians, members of a religious group that the Catholic Church deemed heretical and often framed as diabolical witches (as it did with many other "threatening" outsiders).

Later witch pictures show them riding everything from distaffs to cooking forks. As with the broom, these are all domestic implements that are traditionally associated with women's work, and thus are hidden in plain sight. For a witch to then use these objects to temporarily free herself from the home — and to place them between her legs, at that — can be read as an act of subversion or liberation. The phallic shape of these tools is another marker of transgressive behavior, for witches ride their broomsticks for their own pleasure and without apology.

Leonor Fini · *La sorcière* · Argentina/France · 1935
Eccentric feminist icon Fini painted wild women – androgynous and sexually liberated. She confidently overcame the misogyny of her contemporaries, as a Surrealist artist who rarely conformed.

Cornelis Saftleven
A Witches' Sabbath
Netherlands · 1650
Depicting a chaotic
sabbath scene, this
piece explores the
myth of demons
cavorting with witches
in heretical rituals.

(top) William Mortensen · *Flight of Fancy...Off for the Sabbot* · United States · 1927 A gleeful young witch dances her way out of the chimney and into the sky, excited and delighted with what may be her first flight. Silver-printed and whimsically dark, the depiction of her journey is thrilling.

Auguste Rodin · *Witch's Sabbath* · France · ca. 1890 A late example of the sculptor's work depicts an abstract, broom-riding witch in the naturalist style Rodin was known for. The pastel colors bring a feminine grace to the wide-legged sabbath ride.

sabbat

Aug Rodin

Laduersaire vng peu restour
Respondy. tu feras sa avir
Quant tu auras le cas ouy
Vray est ouy say je men avis
Que les vielles ne .vij. ne trois
Ne vingt, mais plus de m. milliers
Vont ensemble en aucuns destrois
Veoir leurs dyables familliers
Ce nest pas truffe non ne gale
Garde mai je de menterye
Ne cuide pas que je te gale
En parlant de leur sorcerie
Quant tu sauras leur puterie
Toutes les vouldroies vir arses
Et nest au monde flaterie
Qui leur fait plus toner a farses
Je te dy avoir veu en chartre
Vielle la quelle confessoit
Apres quescript estoit en chartre
Comment des le temps quelle estoit
De vij Ans ou roy sen aloit
Certaines nuis de la vil pute
Sur vng bastonnet sen aloit
Veoir la Synagogue pute
Dix mille vielles en vng touch
Auoit il comunement
En fourme de chat ou de bouch
Veans le dyable proprement
Au quel faisoient franchement
Le cul en signe dobeissance
Remune Dieu tout plainement
Et toute sa haulte puissance
La faisoient choses diuerses
Les vnes du dyable aprenoient
Arts et sorceries peruerses
Dont plusieurs maulx elles faisoient
A vng aultres les danses plaisoient
Et aux plusieurs menguer et boire
La en habondance trouuoient
De tout plus quon ne pourroit croire
Le dyable souuent les preschoit
Et qui se vouloit repentir
Trop durement il le tenchoit
Ou le batoit sans alentir
Mais a tous ceulx qui consentir
Vouloient a tous ses plaisirs

Il promettoit sans rien mentir
Le comble de tous leurs desirs
Cellui dyable en fourme de Cat
Parmy le monde tournoioit
Et come iuge ou aduocat
Toutes requestes escoutoit
Et hun tel honneur luy faisoit
Come a Dieu: aussy le faulx traire
Vnes et aultres resiouissoit
Par paroles et par retraire
Et sachiez quen la departe
Chun sa chascune prenoit
Et saulaine nestoit lotre
Lhome vng dyable luy souruenoit
Puis vng chascun sen reuenoit
Come vent sur son bastonchel
Telle puissance luy donnoit
Sathan ce mauuais larronchel
Item la vielle nous conta
Que quant hoemaige au dyable
Vnif ouliement luy aporta
De diuerses poisons confit
Dont elle maint home deffit
Depuis encores plus de Cent
Et affola et contrefit
Maint bel et plaisant innocent
Item redit la male teste
Que par pouldre quelle souffloit
Il faisoit foudre et leuer tempeste
Qui blez et vignoble siffloit
Entes et arbres essiffloit
Et en estoit vint puys gaste
Et sauain contre elle ronfloit
Il estoit tantost tempeste
Plus de vij. ont depose
Sans quilz fussent mis a torture
Quilz ont le gresil compose
Par dessus tous les mone dest
Et pluie et vent contre nature
Fait trebucher ou ilz vouloient
Et mainte aultre male auenture
Les dyables faire leur faisoient
Encor pluffort elle disoit
Dont le me domme trand hideur
Que le dyable home se faisoit
Et auec luy prenoit saueur

Martin Le Franc · Witches Going to Sabbath from *Le Champion des Dames* · France · 1451 These illustrations from the epic book-length poem are thought to be the first depiction of a witch riding a broom.

Albert Joseph Pénot · *Départ pour le Sabbat* · France 1910 A mischievous yet delightful young witch travels sky-clad on a broom to sabbath. The hazy, macabre portrayal of the classic flight is a striking example of a sensually depicted witch maiden.

Witchcraft is the guiding light of my entire life. It touches upon everything I do. I work as a psychic medium, professional witch, and writer, authoring articles about Tarot and witchcraft and manifestation. I lead my life by the principles of our universal connection. I seek the support of the allies of plants, animals, guides, and ancestors. I practice paganism and celebrate the sabbats of the wheel of the year. I have a devotional practice that I engage in throughout my entire day, every day. I have morning and evening rituals to open and close my day. Having a devotional practice helps me stay grounded and connected to my intuition, so I can be of service to the best of my abilities. There is so much outside noise and chaos! Witchcraft brings in balance and gets us back to center. Remember to trust your power and innate wisdom. We must believe in ourselves, honor ourselves, and celebrate our own self-possessed power. And we can put that power into action. Treat others with kindness, love, and respect. What we do has an effect on everyone (and everything!) else. A witch is connected to their intuition, living life in tune with the cycles of nature, and aware of the deep connection between themselves and the greater universe, which includes the elements, other living beings, ancestors, and those of the spiritual realm.

— SARAH POTTER, Witch, Tarot Reader, Author, & Scholar, 2020

Salvador Dalí · *Faust Suite: Witches with Broom* · Spain
ca. 1968 On Walpurgis Night in the fifth act of
the opera, witches on brooms swarm Faust and
Mephistopheles. Dalí reimagines the scene with soft
and seductive sorceresses gliding on a golden breeze.

Jean Veber · *Witches*
France · 1900
A lighthearted car-
icature from Veber
shows witches riding
double on a broom
in his cartoonish style.
More comic than black
magick, the driver
seems carefree, as if
to mock the normative
travel style on the
ground below. The pas-
senger, however, holds
on for dear life.

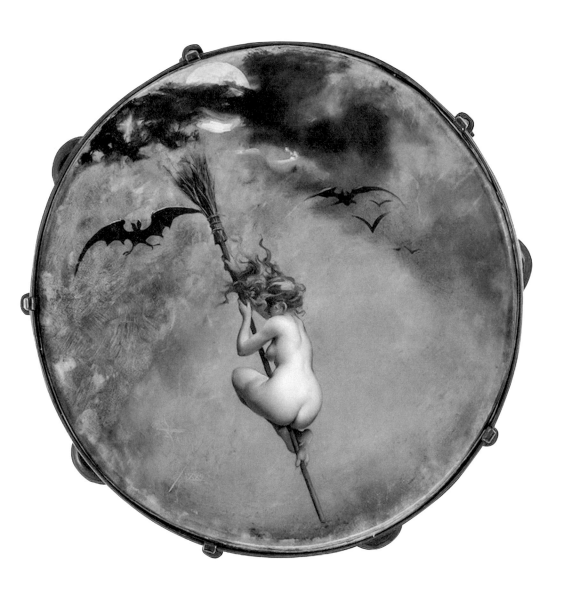

(opposite, top) William Holbrook Beard · *The Witches' Ride* · United States · 1870 Often drawn clothed, the decrepit old crones fly with a familiar in tow, and one of them has lost a shoe in a wonderful charcoal drawing of broom transport on a full-moon night.

Luis Ricardo Falero · *The Witch* · Spain/England 1882 Painted on a ceremonial tambourine, a cherubic young witch brooms backward to sabbath beneath bats and a big moon.

BLADES

Cleaving the Veil

Daggers, bolines, swords, and other blades have long been used for spellcraft. An athame is a consecrated ritual knife. Gerald Gardner popularized its ceremonial use as he was developing the modern religion that came to be called Wicca, but magickal blades have been believed in and utilized across the globe throughout history.

In witchcraft, the athame's primary application is for drawing a magick circle on the ground or in the air. It is a banishing tool that "defends from hostile forces," as Doreen Valiente writes in her 1978 book, *Witchcraft for Tomorrow*. Undesired entities are kept outside the circle so that the caster may do their work within an unencumbered space. Descriptions of ritual knives are found in the medieval grimoire *The Key of Solomon the King*, and the Roman Pliny the Elder wrote about them in the 1st century CE as a means for protecting the body from various forms of *maleficium*. His *Naturalis Historia* states:

"As touching the use of iron and steel, in physic it serveth otherwise than for to lance, cut, and dismember withal: for take a knife or dagger, and make an imaginary circle two or three times with the point thereof, upon a child or an elder body, and then go round withal about the party as often, it is a singular preservative against all poisons, sorceries, or enchantments."

Iron and steel are still considered to be conductors of magickal energy, though a blade may be made from other metals as well.

Blades have other symbolic meanings. They are related to the Tarot suit of swords, and thus are linked to discernment, thought, and cutting away excess to get to the core of a situation. A blade can also be an avatar of masculine energy, and one is plunged into a feminine chalice during some versions of the Wiccan Great Rite to represent the balance of creative opposites.

Frank Frazetta · *Sun Goddess* · United States · 1970
The horror-drama comic *Vampirella* featured the Frazetta oil painting on the cover of the seventh issue. As the daughter of Lilith, the vampire heroine had the ability to shape-shift and hypnotize, but refrained from going on a rampage to quell her blood needs.

Stewart Farrar
Alex Sanders: King of the Witches · England 1971 In the photo, Sanders consecrates a magick circle with his coven and ritual sword. Farrar archived the growing Wiccan tradition through photos and books, after being initiated into Alexandrian Wicca by Maxine Sanders.

Rowan E. Cassidy · *Circulus Maledicti* · Australia 2017 Archaic symbols form a circle around the sorcery, with a snake and an athame empowering the incantation in a severe and foreboding curse-casting. The modern, ink-drawn witch practices by the light of the waning moon.

(top) Raymond Buckland · *High Priestess & Sword* England/United States ·1968 Wiccan High Priestess Lady Rowan holding her coven sword, gifted to her by Gerald Gardner. This photograph is one of many in the Buckland Museum collection.

Growing up in a very religious mixed Romani and Polish home, every moment was an opportunity to connect to our God and the ancestors through prayer. For me, the way that I as a witch interact with this life force determines my relationship with magick. I am a folk practitioner, a hedge witch, and a practitioner of traditional magick. Traditional magick is practical, everyday magick. It is an invitation to ritualize even our most mundane relationships and apply our resources for the betterment of our communities. Traditional magick enacts a worldview that is culturally specific and allows us to be in a deep relationship with our lives. I believe that when we practice magick in a way that aligns us to our cultures of origin, our ancestors empower us to ritualize our relationship with magick in ways that are beneficial to not just our wants and needs but those of our communities. Every moment is a sacred opportunity to ritualize our relationship to life in ways that contribute to the world in meaningful ways. Magick effects change in the worlds around us and those correlating realms and realities within us. In order to make sense of these changes we must also make sense of ourselves, pushing gently against our comfort and capacity. The work of the witch is to disrupt. To disrupt systems of oppression outside of ourselves, within ourselves, and with our ancestors. As modern witches, we take this knowledge and our privileges and make principled action in the world to steward the earth, advocate for one another, stay silent when our voices will not further action or empathy, speak up when necessary, and do what is just, kind, and right.

— YLVADROMA MARZANNA RADZISZEWSKI, Founder of
The School of Traditional Magic, Author, Scholar, & Witch, 2020

Terence Spencer · *Mrs. Eleanor Bone Practicing Witchcraft* · **England** · 1964 A prominent figure in Wiccan history, Bone uses the ritual items of magick. She stands in front of a painting of the goddess Isis of Egyptian mythology.

BIRDS

The Witch Takes Wing

Avian creatures are frequent witch companions, for they can traverse between sky and earth. The ancient Greeks believed that some birds were psychopomps – spirit creatures who would escort newly deceased souls into the underworld. If a witch is a liminal being, it's only fitting that she would choose other boundary crossers to accompany her.

The word *auspicious* is derived from the practice of augury, a Roman style of divination that involved the interpretation of the behavior of birds. Winged beings are still seen as omens today, and those from the corvid family in particular, such as ravens and crows, are linked to magick, witchcraft, and the afterlife. These glossy black birds are often depicted as witch assistants, both bringers and bearers of otherworldly messages.

Owls and witches have deep associations that harken back to centuries-old beliefs that witches could shape-shift into nocturnal birds. The witchy night demoness Lilith is actually hardly in the Hebrew Bible, and the one mention of her in Isaiah 34:14 is often interpreted to mean "screech owl." This term roots back to a class of Mesopotamian storm demons called *lilitu*. As with the Roman *strix*, the words for witches and owls are often interchangeable. *Cailleach-oidhche* is a Scottish Gaelic word that refers to both an owl and an old hag, and La Lechuza is an owl witch in Mexican folklore (*lechuza* is also the Spanish word for barn owl).

Even when witches aren't changing into owls themselves, they are still connected to them. Stories from J. K. Rowling's Harry Potter novels to Rudolfo Anaya's *Bless Me, Ultima* feature owls that protect or otherwise help their magickal comrades. They represent wisdom, keen vision, and nocturnal flight, and so they are the perfect occult accomplices.

Edgar Bundy · *A Witch* · **England** · **1896** Poisonous mushrooms, and ravens frame a cackling witch in a burning forest. Bundy produced the painting when frequent headlines detailed abhorrent witch killings. He may have painted it in response, as his character has a look of revenge.

Manisha Parekh
Witchcraft · India · 2006
A murder of crows in
a chaotic commotion
is always an ominous
sign of sorcery. The
paper-layered abstract
work invokes the
deathly disquiet one
feels when witnessing
this phenomenon.
Some of the birds look
partially dismembered.

(opposite, top) Julien Champagne · Frontispiece
for *Le mystère des cathédrales* · France · 1926
Champagne's illustration for Fulcanelli's manuscript on alchemical symbolism in architecture
features a raven, commonly used for their assistance in spellcasting.

Juanita Guccione · *Three Women and Three Owls*
United States · 1948 Overtones of the occult
imbue this scene from Guccione as three women
dance in a magickal circle and owl familiars guard
the celebrations of the coven.

Our society has long had the idea that a witch is a person on the edge of society, part of it but not quite fully "socialized" to the norms. Therefore the witch is both endangered and dangerous, no matter how benign the ideas they espouse. Witchcraft is my religion. I was made a priestess and a witch when I was 26 years old, through my initiation. I had applied to be a member of a coven, a group of priests and priestesses who themselves had been initiated and who stayed together, year on year, to work the rituals and honor the old gods in the way they had been taught to. In the Gardnerian tradition, the group mind is a strong element; it is believed that the group only functions magickally if the members feel a sense of kinship with one another. It was the Gardnerian tradition which dedicated itself, back in the 1940s and 1950s, to bringing about a revival of the Goddess into the world, and to work to elevate the position of women in society, freeing them from the shackles of patriarchy. It was the first Western religion in 2,000 years to formally have priestesses, and not only that, priestesses as leaders carrying real religious authority. It was the Gardnerians who wrote extensively in the 1960s and 1970s those books which gave us the wider revival of witchcraft which is flowering today — while it is a private, mystery tradition, it always had a wider mission to help people find a spirituality which was at once woman-friendly and joyous.

— CHRISTINA OAKLEY HARRINGTON,
Author, Scholar, & Priestess, 2020

Tino Rodríguez · *Owl Shaman Moon Goddess (Spring Eternal Quartet)* · United States · 2018 Promoting the equality of polar opposites, Rodríguez synthesizes nature's elements, animals, humans, and deities into a complete narrative. Owl and goddess merge in a pleasant depiction of spring being poured forth from winter's gestated egg.

MAGICK WORDS

Books, Shadows, & Sigils

Abracadabra has been translated to mean "I create like the word." Writing and speech have long been believed to be magickal activities, and knowing just the right combination of syllables can unlock a secret door or manifest a desired outcome. A witch's incantation may be uttered or sung, and a spell may be inscribed on a piece of paper to be buried, burned, or placed under a pillow. Language is power, for it can alter consciousness, shift perception, bring about change, and invoke the divine.

Some spells are passed down through oral traditions, and some are improvised in the moment, delivered straight from a witch's intuition. Many have been recorded in books, a literary legacy inherited by modern practitioners after generations of secrecy. These tomes are sometimes called grimoires, from the Old French *gramaire*, which meant any work written in Latin (as many magickal publications originally were), and which is now related to the English word *grammar*. In 2010's *Grimoires: A History of Magic Books*, author Owen Davies describes a grimoire as a book "of conjurations and charms, providing instructions on how to make magical objects such as protective amulets and talismans." Grimoires typically focus on supernatural content involving contact with spirits or the employment of ceremonies

meant to harness cosmic or chthonic energies (or some combination thereof).

Other magick books may contain recipes and spells that engage the natural world, including plants, minerals, and the elements. For this reason they are considered works of "low magick" (as opposed to the "high magick" of grimoires), but in truth, today these distinctions have become blurred as styles of practice have cross-pollinated and mutated. Magick is always in flux.

Gerald Gardner's own book of rituals was passed down and adapted by other initiates in the Wiccan tradition, though parts of it were derived from the writings of other occultists, including A. E. Waite, S. L. MacGregor Mathers, and Aleister Crowley. Gardner first called his manuscript "Ye Bok of Ye Art Magical" in the late 1940s, but its eventual name, *Book of Shadows*, has since become synonymous with any witch's private diary of magickal practice.

One of the most powerful ways to work with magick words is through the creation of a sigil. This is a symbol that is charged with the magick-maker's intentions and energy. Sigils have been used in ceremonial magick traditions for centuries in the form of seals or magick squares meant to invoke angels,

Jean Delville · *Portrait of Mrs. Stuart Merrill* Belgium · 1892 A medium in a trance is draped over a book inscribed with the alchemical symbol for air – or, as the artist describes it, the mark of knowledge achieved through magick.

demons, or planetary currents. Today, a more common method of sigil crafting is to come up with a short phrase that expresses a specific desire, and then arrange the single consonants into one aesthetically pleasing emblem. HAPPY NEW HOME, say, would become HPYNWM, and then the symbol would be constructed using elements of those letters. This sigil may then be drawn, painted, carved, or traced onto a surface, and then activated through visualization, anointment, sex magick, or any other method of enchanted enhancement. Though this technique was developed by the 20th-century English occult draftsman Austin Osman Spare, artists from Leonora Carrington to Brion Gysin have embedded sigils into their work, and witches and chaos magicians of all stripes now incorporate them into their magickal practice. A hybrid of artistry and witchcraft, a sigil is an elegant tool that blends – and bends – language into spellbinding new forms.

John Belham-Payne · Gardner's Spellbooks England · 2009 Wicca founder Gerald Gardner's books contained rituals, spells, and other collected magickal info. Doreen Valiente rewrote and reinterpreted a modern version of these books that are still in use today.

Eduard Fuchs after Félicien Rops · *A Witch Reading Her Magic Book* · Belgium · 1909 From a book of erotic art, a voluptuous witch is shown perusing her grimoire while gripping her broom between her legs. Her wide-eyed simian familiar below appears titillated.

ELEMENT

FIRE

II

INDICATION
Spirit · Inspiration · Will
Energy · Desire · Sex

SYMBOLS
Wands
Candles · Bonfires
Flames
Cauldrons
Demons · Devils

MANIFESTATION
Passion · Attraction · Animation
Illumination · Creative Spark

Harnessing the Inferno

Let my worship be within the heart that rejoiceth, for behold: all acts of love and pleasure are my rituals. And therefore let there be beauty and strength, power and compassion, honour and humility, mirth and reverence within you.

— DOREEN VALIENTE, from *The Charge of the Goddess*, ca. 1950s

In its magickal function as a sensory metaphor, fire serves to represent passion and motivation, decisive action and bold deeds. Astrologically speaking, the element fire is most often associated with the planet Mars and the Sun. The fire signs in astrology (Aries, Leo, and Sagittarius) are thought to embody the elemental qualities of warmth, kinetic energy, spontaneity, and the desire to be seen. In the Tarot, the suit of wands represents fire, and the cards indicate various states and stages of taking action. Along these same lines of thought, the wand itself has come to be commonly employed among the tools on the Wiccan altar in the same representative function.

The element of fire is of particular interest and utility to witches because fire is so spectacularly transformative. The other elements — water, air, and earth — undoubtedly transform their subjects, but unlike fire, they tend to do so in a more gradually perceptible way over time; fire is immediate in every instance. Fire is the process that transforms matter's dense units of stored life energy into heat and light. This energetic transformation, as it dances before our eyes and permeates our bodies with invisible warmth, naturally entrances and inspires awe in nearly everyone. But for witches, observing the process of fire confirms physically and visually the suspicion that many mystic traditions and practitioners take as the basis of their faith: that we as mortal beings are also just bundles of stored life energy engaged in a gradual process of dispersal. Witches revere the purificatory quality of fire, how it scours things to their essences.

In many witches' rituals, a fire is the central feature of the magick circle for reasons both magickal and practical. The very act of a group of people gathering around fire was an essential step in our evolution as a species, so it's no wonder that people would ascribe to it an essential magickal and spiritual significance in addition to reverence for its life-sustaining properties.

(previous) Marjorie Cameron · *Lion's Path* · United States · Date Unknown The abstract watercolor is from a series of the artist's paintings based on a past psychedelic experience. Cameron conveys an elemental vibration of intrinsic occult understanding in her artwork, as she did in her life.

Lucien Shapiro · Raven from the Film *Thank You Darkness, Thank You Light* · United States · 2018 Dark, gothic, raw, and meticulous, the sculpture grants the observer a glimpse into the artist's compulsory ritual. Shapiro elaborately sublimates his identity into awe-inspiring relics.

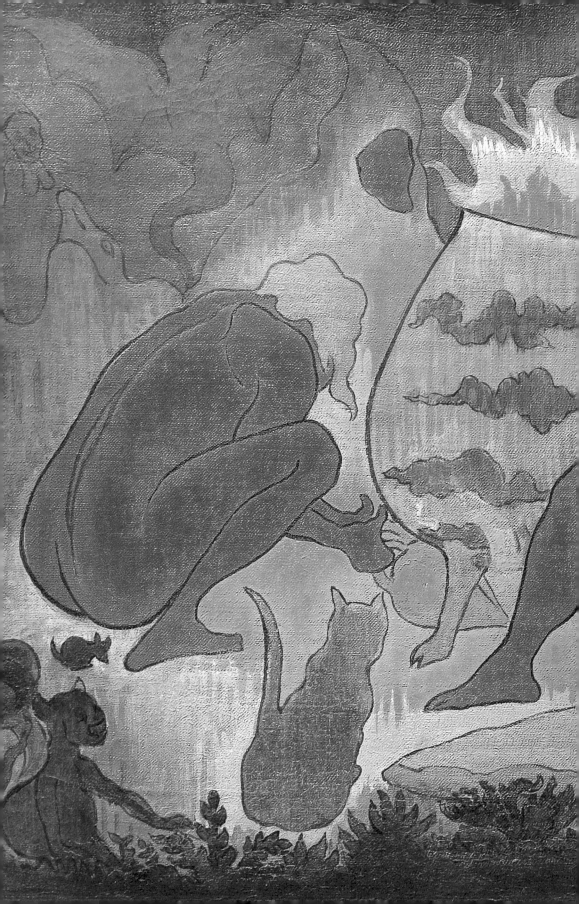

Unknown · A scene
from the opera
Der Freischütz by
Carl Maria von Weber
Germany · ca. 1830
From a German
folktale of a marksman
who sells his soul for
magick bullets that
never miss their aim.

A witch is a priestess/priest of the god or goddess they serve, a servant of the divine in whatever form it takes in their culture. This is the role I fill. Witch is a useful word to describe what I do, and the function I perform in my own culture, but other cultures may call me other things. Being a witch is about what you do, and not about defining yourself with a label. Witchcraft is not judgmental of race, sexuality, gender or culture. In fact, it tends to be more accepting of diversity than the orthodox religions, with many witches being actively involved in these issues in their local communities. It teaches that you don't need to follow dogma to connect with the divine, and that ultimately such connection can be healing for the individual and for society; witches strongly believe in the old adage "heal one person and you heal the world." Those that are drawn to witchcraft are drawn to the mystery of it, something that is lacking with a more science-based and rational society. But witches believe that science and rationality are just as important as mysticism. Science deals with the physical world, but in witchcraft we deal with the spiritual and psychic. We do not believe that belief in one excludes belief in the other, as we need both in our lives. When I came into the craft in the early 1970s, it was a lot more underground. There were no contact networks, so you joined whatever coven or group you could find. So much has changed. Anyone interested in the craft now has a choice of so many books and so much material on the net compared with what we had. My advice to seekers: don't join the coven you first find. Join an open group, work solitary for a while, and then find a coven or magickal group that suits what you practice. Read as much as you can, but be critical of what you read. Stick to your original vision of what the craft is, and don't be swayed by those who try to shoehorn you into their form of practice. Most of all, be true to yourself and what you believe.

— JANET FARRAR, Author, Teacher, & Priestess, 2020

(opposite, top) Vic Oh · *XV* · France/Mexico · 2019
A highly symbolically decorated witch by Oh is based on the Devil Tarot card. The pineal gland, represented by the pine cone, tops her scepter, expressing her connection to divinity. She wears the sacred ceremonial jaguar mask, to suggest her great power.

(previous) Paul Ranson · *Witches around the Fire*
France · 1891 Nude witches surround a cauldron in a modernist scene that brims with color and feeling. As a founding member of the Les Nabis art movement, Ronson was interested in magick, Theosophy, and occultism.

WANDS

Implements of Manifestation

As it is so famously depicted in the Major Arcana Magician card in the Tarot, the wand is an extension of the magician's will and a symbol of their ability to make their will manifest through action. Phallic in shape and symbolism, the wand is considered a tool of vigorous manifestation. In the Minor Arcana of the Tarot, suit of wands is also often associated with the element of Fire, and represents passion, action, sexuality, and the spark of creativity. In witchcraft, the wand holds similar symbolic power, often representing power and expression.

The use of the wand as a magic tool goes back to the ancient Greek myths of Homer, who wrote of rods (or wands) being used by the goddesses Circe and Athena. The wand was later referenced as essential among the magician's tools in the Éliphas Lévi's widely influential grimoire of early-20th-century European magick, *The Key of Solomon* the King. The practice of using wands in ritual was subsequently embraced by the 19th occult society, the Hermetic Order of the Golden Dawn, whom were greatly influenced by Lévi's occult writings. Wands were considered an important element of many of the Golden Dawn's elaborate, prescribed rituals. In the 20th century wands were later embraced by Wiccan practitioners as well. In Wicca, the wand is most often associated with the element of Air rather than Fire.

The wand has since become a popular symbol of magick and witchcraft and is referenced frequently in modern culture from Glinda the Good Witch transforming Dorothy's shoes into ruby slippers, in the *The Wizard of Oz* to the wand as central trope in the *Harry Potter* books.

The wand is a rod often composed of natural material, carved from woods like oak or hazel or sometimes constructed of various metals. A classic wand is generally no more than a foot long and depending on types of materials used, each wand is thought to be able to conduct various energies. Crystals and stones can be added as ornamentation and special symbols can be inscribed for specific uses and spells. Witches have long embraced the wand in ritual, using the wand in a symbolic manner of wielding unseen power.

George Romney · *Emma Lady Hamilton* · England 1782 Romney's muse, the mistress of Lord Nelson, is painted in the guise of the goddess Circe with a wand. As an actress and model, Hamilton easily portrayed many Greco-Roman mythological women for Romney's works.

Remedios Varo
Embroidering the Earth's Mantle · Mexico · 1961
Women in a high tower, above a male-dominated, indoctrinating society, embroider the fabric of the world in the middle section of a triptych. Varo is among many feminist artists who surmounted the misogyny of the Surrealist scene through art and the occult.

CANDLES
AND BONFIRES

Catharsis in the Flame

Candle magick is a contained and focused way to employ fire's power in enclosed spaces. As in all things, the best, most powerful tools are the ones that are accessible, and candles are a readily available source of illumination in both the practical and the metaphysical sense — and have been an essential element of magickal practice across cultures. The simple act of lighting a candle is considered an act of devotion to the very concept of light amid darkness. In witchcraft, often the work of a candle spell is to serve as a vehicle for one's intention. The color and size of the candle, as well as any symbols that might be inscribed (carved into the wax with an athame, boline, or other carving tool) on its surface, or oils with which it's anointed, can be specified to incorporate different magickally resonant materials into a single item to further a particular intention. A witch's honed attention and intention are made physical in the tangible, flammable form of the spell candle.

Candles are particularly important to the midwinter holiday, Imbolc, a celebration of the quickening or return to life that begins as winter's hold on the world begins to relax in February. It has since come to be syncretized with the Christian holiday of Candlemas. In some traditions, adherents make a crown of candles to be worn by a child as a reminder of youth and regeneration.

Bonfires are particularly important to witchcraft and magickal traditions as well. Many pagan traditions incorporate the fire at the center of ceremony and celebration. In modern witchcraft practices, sabbat observances are similarly rooted in both Celtic and Central European folk traditions, many that include celebration around ritual fires and the burning of effigies to celebrate the peak and/or the changing of the seasons.

Unknown · Film Still from *Legend of the Witches* **England · 1970** Maxine and Alex Sanders, founders of Alexandrian Wicca and outspoken about their personal practice of witchcraft, appeared in the dramatic visual documentary of the origins of witchcraft in the United Kingdom.

Sara Hannant · *Baphomet* · England · 2014 A taxi-dermy animal as the Devil or goat of Mendes is full of symbolism and occult meaning. The photo is from the artist's exhibit *Of Shadows: One Hundred Objects* at the Museum of Witchcraft and Magic in Cornwall, England, and is one of the popular items on display.

(opposite, top) Meagan Donegan · *Altar Candle for the Full Moon in Taurus* · United States · 2020 A carved candle used for a moon ritual to honor and give blessing to ancestors. Shaped in the form of the goddess Hathor, who moves between realms to help those who have transitioned to the great beyond.

Alexandre-Gabriel
Decamps
The Witches in Macbeth
France · ca. 1841
The rough-brushstroke
style of Decamps lends
drama to the three
witches gathering in
conjuration over a caul-
dron. Dropping in one
last ingredient, a toad,
they invoke Macbeth's
fated prophecy.

My father's from Pakistan and my mum's English, so I've always been straddling these two cultural legacies, two different religions, two different landscapes. I think the way I've dealt with that is to create my own sort of tradition. I wouldn't say that I follow any particular witchcraft practice, but I think in the music I do and in all areas of my life, I developed this folklore or this archetype of my own. And I would call that archetype "the witch muse." From seeing my parents being so conflicted and estranged by this idea of a "God", that it has to be one thing or another, I went in another direction. All these stories, all these myths and legends and religions and meditations and access points, they're all taking us to this universal unconscious. And it's ironic that we believe that our version is the most important or the best way. We all want to get to a place that's greater than ourselves and to be connected universally to something that's nourishing and uplifting. When I'm singing onstage, I feel like I reach that place. When I did the Sexwitch record, I took all these Iranian and African and Indian folk songs, songs by strong sensual women. And in taking those women's poetry and then transmuting that into my own way of singing and being—that has been one of the ways I follow a witchcraft practice. I feel like I tap into the swirling cosmos of ancestors and witch archetypes and all these women that have gone before. I read Tarot regularly and give readings and I've read so much about unexplained phenomena and symbols and fairy tales. I've done a course in myth and fairytale and a writing course in mythology and archetypes. I feel like the witch crops up in all of these things because, to me, the witch is the repressed power of the female. I know there are male witches as well, but I think over the years, people have feared a woman that's so in tune with her connection to nature, her connection to plants, her connection to creativity, childbirth. The wildness of women has been maligned and repressed. I think that the story of women is for me the story of the witch.

— NATASHA KHAN/BAT FOR LASHES,
Musician, Artist, & Performer, 2020

Louis Chalon · *Circe* · France · **1888** Circe sits on a throne in a lotus pond, beaming forth her glowing magick wand amid golden statuary. In the foreground, the turned-to-swine crew of Ulysses root around in filth.

(following) Georg Jerzy Merkel · *The Flame* · Austria **20th Century** Control of the elements is a natural and basic form of sorcery in which air, fire, earth, and water are manipulated at will. From within a ritual circle, the witches call forth a bonfire from an earthen crevice to heighten their invocation.

I am a multiracial, interdimensional, and hereditary medium. My draw to witchcraft, magick, healing arts, sacred sites, extraterrestrials, and the esoteric started from as early as I could walk. My great Italian aunt first introduced me to more folk Italian magick and strega traditions as a young girl. However, my first reclamation of magick came in my teens as I followed a more traditional path of worshiping the Goddess as Isis. In my adulthood, I reconnected (after being adopted out) with my Irish, Filipino (Visayan), West African (Yoruba and Mali), and Indigenous (Wampanoag Tribe) bloodlines. I started to understand the connection to my magick was much more Earth-based than I had known previously. My paternal grandmother is a medium, as was her mother, and there were many folk magicians on both sides, maternal and paternal. I connect deeply to the understanding of the reclamation of power when it comes to magick. Witchcraft in the form of public ritual and divination is very much part of my creative process. As it is in this space, I can merge with the divine and channel a connection to Creator, and bring it into physical form.

— MARCELLA KROLL,
Artist, Creator, Performer, & Psychic Medium, 2020

Salvator Rosa · *The Witch* · Italy · 1646 Sitting with her feet in a circle of candles over a magickal diagram, the witch reads her spell in the dark night.

CAULDRONS

The Iron Womb

Used throughout the centuries and across cultures for cooking, the cauldron is an ancient tool, usually a large cast-iron pot suitable for boiling on an open fire. Symbolically, the cauldron is often associated with the feminine and the power of creation. In many mythologies, the cauldron was associated with rebirth and the womb, a vessel which held the power to create life and resurrect the dead. In Arthurian legends of the grail, the latter was sometimes referenced as a cauldron, the Celtic traditions, it is most readily associated with the goddess Ceridwen, from whose cauldron issues the essence of poetic and magickal inspiration.

Thought to be used by witches as a vessel for magick spells, the cauldron has become inextricably linked with witchcraft. The three sisters of Shakespeare's *Macbeth*, famously hover over their heated cauldron, casting their infamous spell, "double double/toil and trouble/fire burn and cauldron bubble."

Witches might utilize their cauldrons to combine elements for a spell or potions. But most often, modern witches use a cauldron as a safe and convenient way to burn loose or powdered incense and resins that require a burning coal to release their scent. A small cauldron is ideal for this purpose because cast iron can take the considerable heat of coals. It has a handle to protect the hands, and is often fashioned with three legs to keep the hot bottom from burning the surface it rests on. A cauldron is also a convenient receptacle for any magickal petition letters, or other written spells and symbols that one might burn in order to release their intention and power.

In witchcraft, the cauldron's primary symbolic purpose is to serve as a vessel of transformation, a womb-shaped place for mixing disparate elements together into something greater than the sum of their parts. Like the broom, the cauldron is also a tool of the hearth, a method for making magic hidden in plain sight under the veil of domesticity.

Daniel Gardner · *The Three Witches from Macbeth* England · 1775 Interest in the supernatural led to frequent renditions of *Macbeth*'s cauldron scene. Possibly commissioned, Gardner portrays the Weird Sisters as three upper-crust English socialites: Elizabeth Lamb, Viscountess Melbourne; Georgiana Cavendish, Duchess of Devonshire; and the sculptor Anne Seymour Damer.

Gino D'Achille · *SHE* · Italy/England · 1978
"She" stands before her cauldron in the 1970s
cover art for the fantasy novel *The Vengeance
of She* by Peter Tremayne.

(opposite, top) George Cattermole · *Scene of Three
Witches from Shakespeare's Macbeth* · England · 1840
A watercolor rendition of the famed three witches as
they summon the fate of the future king of Scotland.

John Dixon
The Witches' Cauldron
England · 1772
A ghostly etched
hidden-cave scene
depicts two sorceresses,
a crone with her wand
and an awestruck
maiden, firing up the
cauldron. Magickal
symbolism marks the
ground and a skeleton
assists as a grimoire
page holder.

PART IV

Essay by
MYA SPALTER

WITCHES, DEVILS, AND DEMONS

A Union with Darkness

In most belief systems, malefic spirits serve in the necessary role of scapegoat for the inevitable misfortunes that can befall a community. By extension, witches, in their anarchic spiritual independence, have been historically and often inaccurately assumed to be aligned with devils and demons. There are beliefs that witches are joined heretical partnerships with devils, signing pacts to do a demon's bidding, engaging in orgiastic unions — all accusations popularized by persecutors like Christian clergyman Heinrich Kramer, who penned the witch hunt manual *Malleus Maleficarum* in 1486. Historically, anyone who fails to conform to the prevailing religious hegemony has been assumed — again, inaccurately — to be a witch!

In this way, devils, like witches, have come to embody in the popular imagination the antithesis of dominant value systems. It seems to be the conceptual work of devils, demons, and witches to carry the shadow that is inevitably cast by the sources of light

and warmth that sustain a people. Members of The Satanic Temple, some of whom consider themselves witches, embrace this contrarian spiritual position as a place from which to highlight religious hypocrisy and encourage compassion for all people.

While the popular concept of devils and demons is largely based in Christian theology, a broader, more classical definition of the term *demon* simply refers to a powerful spirit, and does not ascribe any particular morality to that spirit. In the foundational magickal text, or grimoire, *The Lesser Key of Solomon*, alternatively referred to as *Lemegeton*, is an accounting of certain demons or spirits and the symbols and rituals by which these demons can be summoned to aid in a witch's magickal workings. Although the original provenance and antiquity of these symbols and rituals is a murky historical matter, this magickal text informs a great many modern Western witchcraft practices.

(previous) **Jacques de Gheyn II** · *Witches' Sabbath*
Netherlands · Late 16th to Early 17th Century
Called the master of witchcraft art, Gheyn depicts the sabbath with a pen-and-ink drawing of a swirling cauldron. The artist had a macabre fascination with the fictional tales of infanticide.

Ian Howard · *Isobel Gowdie Meets a Devil* · **France 2018** A contemporary painting depicts the queen of the Scottish witches, who was accused of and convicted of witchcraft in 1662. She vividly confessed to all manner of sorcery, service to the Devil, and carnal activities at sabbath.

Paul Klee · *Wald-hexen* · Germany · 1938 Two forest witches are hidden among the shapes, colors, and thick black lines in Klee's late-oeuvre style. One witch is nude; the other wears a dress. Klee painted the impressive work just two years before his death.

Giovanni Fontana · *The Fire Witch* · Italy · 1420–30 A fire-breathing robot witch that moves on rails appears in the technological manual *Bellicorum instrumentorum liber*, drawn by physician and artist Fontana, who thought himself a magician.

Der Neid:

Unknown · *Compendium of Demonology and Magic*
Unknown · 18th Century From a series of illustrations accompanying essays on magick and witchcraft, whose author and illustrator remain a mystery.

Gustave Doré · *La Danse du Sabbat* · France · 1884
An illustration from the famous book *Histoire de
la magie* by Paul Christian features a frenzied
nocturnal dance of witches and beasts. An aged
sorceress sits next to a cauldron with her wand
and a human skull.

SEX MAGICK
The Temple of Venus

The witch lives with an awareness of the subtle and the unseen. The witch exists in the liminal, and one of their most ancient secrets is the use of erotic energy, of the flesh and the sensual. The witch has always been, and will always be, connected to the sexual. It was one of the occult's most (in)famous figures, Aleister Crowley, who brought Eastern tantra to the West through his system of sex magick. Tantra, a school of Eastern thought present in both Hinduism and Buddhism, works with the taboo and the subversive as means of enlightenment; it also works with the idea of nonduality, of true union, as a means of transformation. Through tantra, energy is raised through the body, with the intention of union with your partner as a representation of the union of god and goddess.

Sex magick, in its simplest form, is coupling visualization and intention-setting with the raising of sexual energy. This can be done solo, through masturbation, or with a partner or partners. Sexual energy is life energy; it is the energy of all creation because all life comes through sex. Witches don't turn their heads away from this ancient ritual, but honor it as a reflection of the divine power of nature.

The witch stands in the temple of the god/dess of love and sex, peeling back the veil and calling forth an ancient song of songs, beckoning the erotic to be made manifest through the flesh. The power and magick of the witch doesn't reside outside of them; it doesn't belong to anyone else, or to any tool. It is because of this that sexual energy is so powerful; it is not reliant on any outside circumstances, but is something that the witch can conjure up, strengthen, and share.

Crowley coupled his own definition of magick – "the science and art of causing change to occur in conformity with the Will" – with Eastern practices, sexual energy, intentional use of mind-altering substances, and altered states of consciousness, to share his current of sex magick with the world. One such mind-altering substance, so-called flying ointment, goes back to the 14th century, when it was said that groups of European witches would gather and indulge in ritual with the Devil. These witches would allegedly anoint themselves with herbal preparations to be possessed by the magickal and erotic current, which would also allow them to fly. The herbs used in the hallucinogenic or flying ointment often were poisonous, such as hemlock, deadly nightshade, datura, and others. It is said that witches would apply the ointment to the mucous membrane of their vaginas by using the handle of a broomstick, which is part of the reason witches believed they could fly, and came to often be depicted as riding on broomsticks.

Vali Myers · *Sydney Sheliah* · Australia · 1980 Erotic humans and animal synthesis are frequent themes in Vali Myers's art. As an untamed radical, this gem of an artist truly embodied the beingness she portrayed in her drawings – liberation, oneness with nature, and subversive sexuality.

Flying ointment is still used by witches today, though the method of application is usually external. Herbal preparations have always been staples in the magick of the witch, and the connection of witches to love potions also holds truth. The ancient Egyptians used the flowers of the blue lotus to reach altered states of consciousness and perhaps to perform sexual rites. This aphrodisiac is still adopted by modern herbalists and witches who want to enhance their own erotic energy.

Aphrodisiacs like damiana, passionflower, ginger, rose, and jasmine are one ancient form of magick available to those who want to connect to their own sacred sexuality. The earth is reeling with fertility and fecundity, all her plants and flowers beckoning forth magick and

Unknown · *Love Spell* · Germany · ca. 1470 With a beguiling gaze, a young bare witch dashes some enchanted potion upon a human heart. Her familiar lies still and silent.

Shimon Okshteyn · *Satisfaction* · United States 1984 There is a certain victim/voyeur vice when viewing the seductive prowess in the modern siren paintings of Okshteyn. Their relationship to the element of fire is signified in cigarette smoke, and in *Satisfaction*, a look of gratified glam and gloat.

abundance, and this is one way that the witch finds inspiration for their own carnal magick.

Alongside plant magick, glamour is also a part of the erotic esoteric milieu, as it has the power to transform, as well as the power to amplify. Casting a glamour on the self casts a glamour on the other, as it changes the seen and the seer, and glamour is one way a witch may embody their erotic essence. Many sex workers, like the hierodules or temple priestesses of the ancient past, are aware of the power of sexual energy that can be raised by creating an altered state of self. The power of red lipstick to transform, to mimic the vulva and the red petals of the rose, is another ancient form of sensual magick, dating back to ancient Mesopotamia, where insects, gemstones, and pigments were crushed and applied to the lips. Lingerie and fetish wear, color magick, perfume, and makeup are all aspects of glamour magick that may be used to enhance a sex magick ritual, or the energy of the one veiling themselves.

Another way that modern witches are working with sex magick is through the guise of talismans, which can be paired with glamour by being worn or kept on the body. A talisman is an object charged with an intention to attract something (as opposed to an amulet, which is charged to banish or repel something). To charge a talisman, you raise energy that you then infuse into the talisman. You can do so through sex or masturbation, two of the most potent ways to imbue talismans with power. Smearing the talisman with sexual fluid once you're finished with your rite further empowers this object.

While sexual energy can act as a means of raising energy for anything ranging from getting a job to healing the self, to attracting love or lovers, sexual energy by itself can be a form of magick. Having sex with a partner or with yourself as an act of devotion can be a dynamic offering. In Wicca tradition, the Great Rite is a representation of the union of the divine feminine and the divine masculine energies, which can be done through joining in sacred sexual union, or through the symbolic action of piercing a filled chalice with an athame, or ritual blade. The act of sacred sex is a powerful one and can act as a bridge to the divine.

Drawing down the power of the god/ dess through sex can be done in numerous ways, including by ingesting sexual fluids, whether that is vaginal secretions, semen, or a combination of both, after performing sex magick. Because menstrual blood is intimately connected to the sexual cycles of those who bleed, it can also be incorporated into sex magick, and like other sexual secretions, it can be worked with through ingestion or by being used to anoint a talisman or a grimoire, to draw sigils or glyphs on skin, or even to anoint objects like candles.

Through sex magick, whether solo or partnered, the witch is drawing from the ancient well of sexual energy that is available to all. But because the witch is familiar with how this works, how it feels, and its volatile and alchemical qualities, they are able to use this to fuel their spells, strengthen their confidence, draw forth new opportunities, and embody their true self.

Jean Delville · *The Treasures of Satan* (detail) · Belgium 1895 A muscular Devil with tentacle-shaped wings drags the souls of the damned through flowing flames in an orgiastic composition. The fire element here, although hellish, seems to connote sexual energy, the inner fire.

ELEMENT

WATER

III

INDICATION
Emotion · Intuition
Dreams · The Unconscious
Primordial Forces

SYMBOLS
Rivers · Wells
Lakes · Baths
Mirrors
The Chalice
Potions · Elixirs
The Ocean

MANIFESTATION
Cleansing · Blessing
Completion · Ending
Radiance · Release

Cleansing through Immersion

My relationship to witchcraft is all-encompassing. There is a ritual, spell, or intention for just about everything that I do. When bathing I infuse the water with energy, minerals, or charged stones and ask anything not helpful to be washed away. Observing and practicing witchcraft leads me further and further into an intimacy with Nature, with Spirit(s), with the Universe.

— LIZA FENSTER/CROW MOTHER, Healer, Scholar, & Witch, 2020

Water is related to the west, the direction of sunsets and twilight and saying "so long." It washes away all that no longer serves us, allowing us to dissolve and shed the shells we have outgrown. It is also shapeless, and can fill any container, taking its form all the while. It can change states from solid to liquid to vapor, and thus represents adaptability and transformation. Water moves, even when it appears still. It is always in the midst of becoming.

A cleanser and purifier, water is a common ingredient of spellcraft. Physically it removes debris, swirling in corners and cracks to dissolve cobwebs, dirt, dust. In doing so it also spiritually replenishes, allowing our spaces and selves to gleam anew. It is the prime component of a potion or witch's brew, and may be magickally ingested or externally applied. As an anointing element, water transfers blessings from the divine, whether poured over one's head or immersing the entire body. When we arise from the water in a ritualized manner, we are reborn.

Our bodies are mostly made of water, and it flows through and from us as blood, sweat, saliva, tears. Water is also associated with the emotions, so its magick is connected to what we feel, sense, and intuit. It is said that dreams and archetypal imagery come from the realm of water, which is why witches may use a bowl of it for scrying, or seeing divinatory visions. It speaks in liquid language, and after a time, one may become fluent in its fluidity.

Baths, wells, rivers, and lakes each have their own water magick — and some say they also have nymphs to guard them. But the mightiest aquatic sorcery comes from the ocean herself. Sea witches honor her for her sparkling surface and dark depths. They work with her rhythms and tides, which are tied to the movements of the moon. Salted droplets coat their hair, their chanting tongues. Her holy water crashes at their feet in silver waves.

(previous) **Harry Clarke** · *The Little Mermaid* **Ireland** · ca. 1916 The sea witch offers a dangerous deal to the little mermaid: a human body to pursue the prince, in exchange for her melodic voice. She cuts out her tongue and transforms her fins into feet in the fairy tale from Hans Christian Andersen.

Gilles Grimoin · *Dame blanche et étang noir* · **France 2019** Highlighting the delicate balance between darkness and light in his gothic style, Grimoin portrays a "white lady," supernatural spirits similar to faeries who serve as guardian goddesses in medieval folklore.

Rik Garrett · *Untitled (from Earth Magic)* · United States · 2012 Liberated from public opinion and using the water's restorative power, a woman freely immerses herself in the depths. Garrett's photo series tells a tale of how women connect to and use earth's primitive energy.

Hernan Bas · *The New Witch* · United States · 2006 Having grown up with a fervent appreciation for the paranormal, Bas infuses this neophyte witch scene with a bizarre chaos of colors.

Leonor Fini · *The Veil*
Argentina/France
1956 The masterful
Surrealist Fini explores
mysticism, the occult,
and other esoteric
subjects in many of
her artworks and
costumed photographic
self-portraits.

(top) Asli Baykal & Princess Nokia · Still from
the Music Video "Brujas" · United States · 2017
A coven in the water honors Yemayá Orisha, the
protective mother spirit and patron saint of rivers,
in a scene from "Brujas," by rapper Princess Nokia.

Paul Delaroche · *The Young Martyr* · France · 1855
The bound and haloed female victim of Delaroche's
dark painting was drowned.

SACRED WATERS

Magickal Seas, Lakes, Rivers, & Springs

The beloved baths of Mother Nature abound in mythology, folklore, and the beautified realms of our tangible existence. From rivers and lakes to springs and wells, the most life-giving element overflows with properties of magick. Many mythical creatures of lore live in or around bodies of water, as do animals, plants, and people. We are drawn to this source of spiritual soaking for healing, rebirth, purification, and burial. Water *moves* and is associated with the fluidity of our emotions, connected to and carried by the moon cycles. The moon pulls on oceans, rivers, lakes, and streams, and stirs the abundant water in our bodies. We are intimately allied with this sublime substance.

The mighty seas entice witches to call upon the power of ocean wind and the force of the tides. The immense energy is harnessed and focused in some of the darker forms of sorcery. Rivers are feminine flows that originate from a divine source and are connected to goddesses and nymphs, like the Ganges, considered a goddess who cleanses one of sin. Around the globe, springs pulse from the depths onto fertile ground in the vernal season, often collected for spells and curative potions. Springs form at grottos known for miraculous events or magickal healing, like the pilgrimage site of Lourdes. Hot springs in volcanic mountain terrains deliver mineral-rich nourishment and rejuvenation. Holy wells and fountains are enchanted sources of immortality.

The ancient Roman philosopher Seneca decreed: "We worship the sources of mighty rivers; we erect altars at places where great streams burst suddenly from hidden sources; we adore springs of hot water as divine, and consecrate certain pools because of their dark waters or their immeasurable depth." Although Earth's beauty has been mishandled and exploited, respect for and worship of her bounty is indeed necessary. Water is life.

Hermann Hendrich · *The Norns* · Germany · 1906
Appearing at the time of birth, the Norse version of the Fates determine one's destiny. As weavers of the world wheel, the Fates are considered all-powerful.

(following)
Frank Frazetta
Sea Witch · United
States · 1966 In the
cover art for *Eerie*
magazine issue number
seven, fantasy artist
Frazetta depicts a sea
sorceress creating a
wild storm across the
ocean waves.

Maria Giulia Alemanno · *Yemayá asesu* · Italy · 2006
Mother of the oceans and their contents, the particular avatar of Yemayá from the Yoruba tradition is
the patron saint of ducks and geese. She frequents
the swampy waterways and is often depicted as a
mermaid and associated with the moon.

Jos. A. Smith · *Witches and Eggshells* · United States
1981 Commandeering empty eggshells, witches
sail in them to sea, wreaking havoc on ships and
stirring the forcible winds into destructive storms.
Smith donated these paintings to the Museum of
Witchcraft and Magic in Cornwall, England.

Charles Turner · *A Witch Sailing to Aleppo in a Sieve*
England · 1807 In many myths and folktales the
witch is depicted as crossing the sea on boats
made of eggshells or cauldrons. Turner renders his
witch magickally atop the waves, floating in a sieve
without sinking.

(opposite, top) Walter Edwin · Mary Fuller in
The Witch Girl · England · 1914 The actress Mary
Fuller plays a sorceress, bathing in a magickal
scene from the early cinematic esoteric experiment
The Witch Girl.

Jean-Francis Auburtin
Chants sur l'eau
France · 1912
Known for his con-
templative, symbolic
landscape scenes
in twilight, Auburtin
departs from his typical
subject matter to
depict water nymphs,
renowned for their
beauty and singing,
in *Songs of the Water*.
One strums a harp
as they croon to the
cosmos.

MAGICKAL BATHS

Bathing as Ritual

Taking a bath is a relatively accessible form of magick, because one need not leave their home to cast this submergence spell — provided there is a tub, of course. Going on a pilgrimage to visit a sacred body of water can be powerful, indeed, but a witch need not look any further than her own bathroom or backyard to engage in aquatic rites.

The bathtub is its own chalice — a sacred vessel that holds life-giving fluid that simultaneously purifies and nourishes. It is a watery womb, a place to seek refuge and replenishment. It is a cauldron, brewing and bewitching one's body. It is a distillation chamber, vaporizing the unnecessary and leaving behind only the most concentrated, consecrated self.

Like any good potion, a magickal bath often involves adding specific ingredients, such as herbs, flowers, oils, salts, or crystals. Sometimes a bar of soap with certain botanical properties or carved sigils is incorporated into the ritual as well. A witch may bathe in the dark or surrounded by candles, but the atmosphere should provide a sense of solace. As Herman Melville writes, "Yes, as everyone knows, meditation and water are wedded forever."

Some plan their ceremonial baths to coincide with certain phases of the moon, while others may choose to simply take one on an as-needed basis. A soaking spell can be used for healing, protection, or manifestation. Water carries the intention with which it is infused. But whatever its purpose, magickal bathing is a practice that is elegant and intimate. One enters this liquid cocoon naked, and emerges even more pure.

There are some witches who insist on draining the tub fully before rising, and some even go as far as insisting that they must air-dry rather than using a towel, so that the magick is fully absorbed in the skin. Regardless, a bath may be either a cleansing preparation for more elaborate spellcraft to follow, or a self-contained act of soluble sorcery.

Penny Slinger · *Sue in the Bath* · England/United States · 1969 The artist describes the bathtub as one of her favorite canvases. Slinger's ability to crack open the feminine soul and reveal the sexuality of creativity highly influenced many later feminist artists.

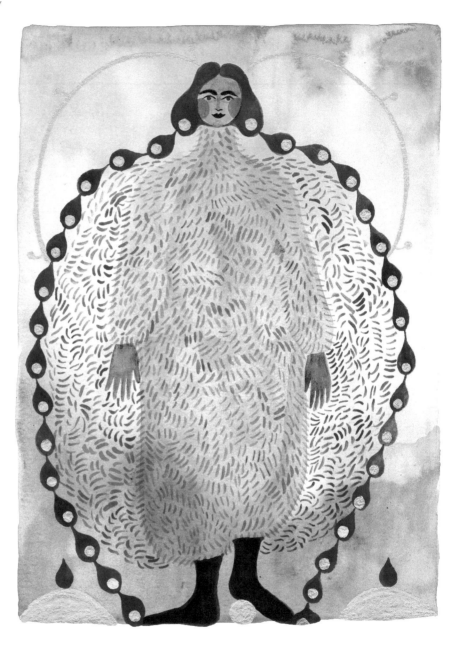

Malwine Stauss · *Water Witch* · Germany · 2019
Women reclaiming their power and natural sorcery
are the subjects of Stauss's watercolors. This witch
has hair of raindrops and a supernatural, elemental
bodysuit of water. Stauss's work boldly defies the
male criticism she received in her fine-arts education.

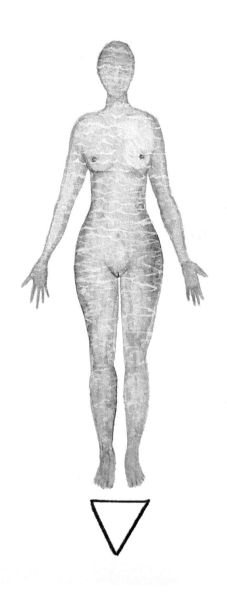

Susan Jamison · *I Am Water* · United States · 2017
Using the antiquated egg-tempera-and-pigment
method, Jamison imbues each of her visionary
works with alchemy, powerful feminine archetypes,
nature, and mythological allegory.

CHALICE

Cup of the Goddess

The chalice is among the richest of symbolic tools in witchcraft. Used as a receptacle in ceremony, a silver chalice holds ritual contents to be shared for the communing of coven members, or from which to offer a potion. Sometimes set upon altars as an offering cup or to request fulfillment, the chalice serves to hold elements for gestation and to then bestow the alchemical result. The circular base symbolizes the mundane world; the stem is a symbol of connection between humanity and spirit; and the open rim is a vessel for receiving divine attainment as depicted in religious, alchemical, and occult art.

The Holy Grail is the chalice used by Christ in the Last Supper, the supposed hidden relic of great speculation. Esoterically, the holy chalice symbolized the womb of Mary Magdalene, who carried the seed of Christ. The chalice is a key magickal tool used by many Wiccans in the Great Rite, a ceremony in which the phallic athame, or ritual knife, is plunged into the symbolically feminine cup.

The proto-sorceress Circe of the Greek epic poem *The Odyssey* is an early example of a witch who relied heavily on the chalice as a delivery device for poison. Her exquisite beauty and seductive charm could compel any man to partake of the offering that would cause his ultimate demise. A "poisoned chalice" became a common term for something that appears alluring at first, but signals eventual ruin.

The chalice remains a sacred container from which all creations are born. It represents a holy container, the fertile, creative womb of the goddess or the feminine principle.

Chalices also symbolize the element of water, one of the four elements used in witchcraft, Tarot, and other spiritual practices. Water is associated with emotions, creativity, joy, and receptivity. Chalice imagery as a life-giving source permeates art and literature from time immemorial.

John William Waterhouse · *Circe Invidiosa* · England 1892 In this pre-Raphaelite exquisiteness, an enthralling vision of Circe poisons the waters in which Scylla bathes. The water is so lavish one forgets the goddess is vindictively violating the clear blue bath. The menacing woodland behind hints at her devious bewitchery.

Ithell Colquhoun · Abstract Artwork · England 1931 Occult, Surrealist painter and poet Colquhoun, who created her own Tarot deck, portrays its four suits framing the five elements. This fluid arrangement displays her connection to the revelations of the dream state.

Stewart Farrar · Consecration of Wine · England 1971 Janet, the wife of Stewart, appears as the high priestess. She places the symbolically masculine athame into the chalice, which represents the feminine. The ritual is meant to invoke the sacred union of male and female – the alchemical wedding.

Jean Jules Badin · *Circe* · France · 1875 A powerful portrait of Circe depicted holding her chalice and magick wand. Calm and confident of her exploits of sorcery, she imparts fierce femininity with a stoic gaze.

Beatrice Offor · *Circe* · England · 1911 Known for her rich, esoteric feminine portraits, Offor paints a young, fresh-faced, and smiling version of the witch goddess Circe.

For me, witchcraft is a way of life. It is my way of living, through which I sustain my spirituality. By having a magickal spiritual practice, I have a foundation, which carries me through the ups and downs, joys and sorrows of life. Always remember the occult is knowledge that lies in the hands of the universe. Though we may seek others to find it, no one owns it. I am deeply attuned to powerful women, goddesses, and witches who have gone before me. Although I do not belong to any one tradition, I bow my head to Marie Laveau, Doreen Valiente, and Tituba. Marie Laveau was an exceptional, powerful woman of color. It is through my love for her, and my practice of African American folk magick, known as hoodoo, I found my way into the religion of vodou. Doreen Valiente, she is Mother Witch. Without Doreen Valiente, the modern witchcraft movement would have no legs to stand upon. Without Tituba, there would be no Salem witch trial history to look back upon. She is the integral piece that formed and shaped the American landscape of how we view witches. There is little documented history about her actual life because of who she was and the times she lived in, yet she calls to me across the ethers, and I acknowledge and embrace her for the powerful witch woman of color she was. I identify as a witch and reclaim the word as a powerful label for women. It is a word that has been used to malign and disparage women for centuries, simply because others didn't understand or appreciate their power, natural intuitive abilities, or deep connection to the natural world.

— NAJAH LIGHTFOOT, Witch, Author, & Scholar, 2020

Marjorie Cameron · *Holy Guardian Angel According to Aleister Crowley* · United States · 1966 Cameron was a major occult artist and scholar, and a charismatic figure within the early Pop Art scenes in Los Angeles. Her own art was imbued with themes of magick, sexuality, and feminine power.

POTIONS

The Witch's Apothecary

Known to all as enchanted elixirs concocted in cauldrons, potions invoke witchcraft like nothing else. A mere utterance of the word and our minds immediately fill with wonder. Who but a maker of magick could brew a stew with otherworldly ingredients and supernatural consequences? Potions are known for both their curative capability and their spellcasting significance. Whether it's stomach sickness or loss of love, immortality or hexing an ex – liquid bewitchery can be either a coveted cure or a vengeful venom when all else fails.

From the Latin term *potio*, meaning "poisonous draft" or "magick potion," these elixirs burst into European apothecaries during the Middle Ages. Originally medicinally intentioned, the makers of these tinctures and tonics used locally available herbs and flowers. But as knowledge of the plant kingdom advanced, more efficacious ingredients were added to the milder herbs – some had sedative effects, others were stimulating. When potions began to function fully, their makers became known as healers. Once psychoactive plants were discovered and added for further fixing, minds were altered. Some

healers became considered witches, accelerating the flawed beliefs about and subsequent persecution of women with healing skills.

Potions became synonymous with witchcraft. However, occult interest, curiosity, and desperation led to demand for enchanted elixirs of love. Called philters, these specific potions were said to encourage an unwilling victim to fall head over heels for the devious defrauder. An example of the classic witch-made medley is mentioned in Girolamo Folengo's 1519 volume *Maccaronea*: "concoction of Philtres/ Black dust of tomb, venom of toad, flesh of brigand/lung of ass, corpses from graves and bile of ox." With a wave of a wand, putrid particles became potions of purpose. In addition to the classic vials of venom, teas, soups, and stews were also delivery devices for the spells.

Be they bizarre or benevolent, early apothecary discovery paved a plant-based path for modern herbal therapy. From compounds that cure to potions that elicit mind-opening adventures, today's witches, Wiccans, and neo-pagans have a plethora of prescriptions with which to practice and perform.

Natalya Kuzmina · *Witches* · Canada · 2001
Decanters and poppies are used in potions for love spells and fertility. The sedative influence of the white poppy seems to emit an ethereal reality to this surreal spellcasting scene.

Frederick Stuart Church · *Circe* · United States
1910 A dreamy depiction of Circe and her animal
companions shows them at the water's edge.

John William Waterhouse · *The Sorceress* · England
ca. 1911 *The Sorceress* is the third in Waterhouse's
series of Circe paintings.

Franz von Stuck
Tilla Durieux as Circe
Germany · 1913
Inspired by a film still,
this image features
Austrian actress Tilla
Durieux playing Circe
in the movie *Calderon*.
The 1912 film is
based on a play of
the same name, first
written and staged in
the 17th century.

Hans Weiditz
Witches' Sabbath
Germany
16th Century
A woodcut shows
witches seemingly
preflight to a sabbath,
compounding their
ointment. Their urn
bursts with a fiery
fume as they prepare
to rub the mixture
on their bodies and
ascend into the air.

SCRYING
AND VISIONS

Between Worlds

Our dreams can take us to the watery psyche, the plane of consciousness in which we may access libraries of divine knowledge, where wisdom resides in the form of etheric and symbolic information. From the old and obsolete English word *descry*, or "to reveal," to scry is to enter mysterious realms with keen awareness and intention. Ancient Egyptians were the first known practitioners of this, which they treated as an act of ceremonial magick. Scrying was also considered a sacred art form of prophetic divination in ancient Greece and Mesopotamia.

For those seeking to access these realms, deliberate intention and a method of achieving a deeply meditative state is required. To achieve access to a visionary state or what might call consider a divine consciousness, requires commitment and focus. Sometimes various tools are used to assist in the practice of scrying. The famous Elizabethan magician and astrologer John Dee, for instance, was known to possess both a rock crystal ball and a "shew stone", a black obsidian mirror which he was said to have used to connect with spirit world. The mirror, which is today

in the collection of the British Library, was originally made in Mexico, where volcanic glass mirrors of the same kind were used by Aztec priests for summoning visions.

In many cultures around the world, those who were considered shamans, witches, and sorcerers were believed to be able to consciously enter visionary states where they could experience vivid revelations. Water, oil, mirror, obsidian, crystal, and other instruments of a glassy or reflective surface are also means by which to acutely enter this state of altered consciousness. Chinese adepts used cracked-open eggs, pre-Hispanic civilizations used grains of corn, and other cultures use chalices of wine or oiled fingernails.

In Greek myth, the Graeae Witches shared one eye (symbolic of the third eye), which they passed between them to see the future. Enchanted, fate-revealing mirrors served as spellbound companions to several evil fairy-tale witches. Crystal balls are perhaps the most well-known symbols of conscious gazing, used by oracle, witch, or fortune-teller.

Charlotte Edey · *Rain* · England · 2018 The artist explores the mystical intersection of identity and spirituality, sharing a magnificent expanse cleansed by rainwater yet shielded by salted air.

I am Native Hawaiian and have been a practitioner of earth-based spirituality all my life. I first came to know the practice of witch-craft through the entrance into motherhood, learning more about the connection between the moon, wombyn, and the cycles of being female and Goddess/Her/She of 10,000 Names. I was drawn to the power of the sacred feminine and moon magick. I adore the Dianic female-centered practice of witchcraft, the sacredness of our blood, the changes of the seasons, the Wheel of the Year, and the embodiment of maiden, mother, and crone as we women move through our lives. Weaving magick and ceremony together is one of the biggest parts of my life. I also love the interrelationship between my Hawaiian roots and path as a Hawaiian kahuna/healer. They intertwine powerfully and lovingly. My advice to others interested in witchcraft? Don't be afraid of the power of magick and follow your soul's calling.

— LEILANI BIRELY, Author, Kahuna, Healer, & Priestess, 2020

John William Waterhouse · *The Crystal Ball* · England 1902 A sorceress is at work in Waterhouse's striking and vivid painting. She enters astral trance through the crystal ball with her magickal text, wand, and a skull.

Paul Lehr · *Occult* · United States · 1972 The prolific science-fiction artist depicts the witch as a mysterious woman deeply focused on a floating crystal ball. She glimpses her vision, reflected in the background of the eerie print featured on the cover of *Occult* magazine.

(opposite, top) Marjorie Cameron · *Night Tide* United States · Date Unknown Occult artist Cameron starred alongside Dennis Hopper in a movie called *Night Tide*, in which she played a siren sea witch.

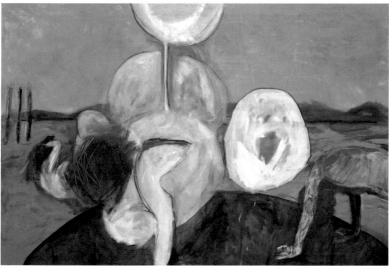

Karen Strang · *The Drowning* · Scotland · 2018
Following her research about the brutal Scottish
witch killings that began in 1403, Strang based
a series of impressionist oil paintings on the slaugh-
ter of more than 4,000 victims.

(following) John William Waterhouse · *The Lady
of Shalott* · England · 1888 Waterhouse's ethereal
painting depicts the recluse of Tennyson's poem, who
floats unknowingly towards her demise.

ELEMENT

EARTH

IV

INDICATION

The Body · Land · Medicine
Materiality · The Home

SYMBOLS

Trees · Plants
The Forest
Stones · Crystals · Salt
Dirt
Animals · Familiars

MANIFESTATION

Healing · Abundance · Sensuality
Grounding · Sanctuary

Roots of the Mother

Witchcraft is all about connecting with the Earth, and our living spirits, both of which desperately need each others' love and connection to thrive. Witchcraft is an ancient practice of living in communion with nature and being embedded in the cosmos.

— CASEY ZABALA, Founder of Modern Witches Confluence, Scholar, & Tarot Witch, 2020

And so we call upon earth in the north. This is the element that grounds us and grows us. It makes up the land we live on, and some believe that humankind was originally created from animated clay. Earth is home and body. It offers shelter and is a sacred place for our souls to occupy. We are born from a mother's womb and we are buried in the Great Mother's tomb, and so we are part of her, and she is part of us for the duration of our lives and beyond. The words *matter*, *matrix*, and *mother* are all derived from the same etymological root, and many cultures believe that the earth is a source of the divine feminine and fertility in all its forms.

Earth magick is also associated with vitality and healing. The 12th-century German mystic Hildegard von Bingen believed that the natural world was vibrating with a green energy she called *viriditas*. According to her, this electric greenness flows through all living beings who are both physically and spiritually healthy. It is linked to universal forces of growth, lushness, and fecundity.

Plants are strong carriers of this power, each with its own distinct signature and specific applications. Though it must be said that while green witchery is primarily a fortifying practice, it can also be used to poison or expel unwanted entities. This is why witches are often depicted with deadly flowers growing in their gardens, for they know that creation *and* destruction are both necessary for a balanced planet. A witch's apothecary cabinet may be filled with spices, herbs, tinctures, salves, and balms. Witches make medicine from the forest or their kitchen shelves. Their spells may be made from rare ingredients, but more often than not, they use whatever bewitching weeds are growing in their own backyard. The magick of earth is plentiful, accessible, and, if used respectfully, available for all.

Ultimately, earth teaches us that nothing is static, even that which seems most still. Stones, bones, and seeds all dwell in dirt, buried treasures that may decay or metamorphose into blossoming. And on the earth's surface are creatures great and minuscule, a myriad of messengers who aid the witch's work, and teach us all what it means to be alert and aware of the majesty that surrounds us always.

(previous) David Teniers the Younger · *Witches Scene* · Flanders · 1640–50 Mushrooms, berries, and other plant magick encircle a witch over her cauldron and a candle-holding familiar.

George Wilson · *Spring Witch* · Scotland · 1880 Wilson's painting depicts the myth of Persephone and explores themes of the persistence of life, fertility, and regeneration.

Josephine Close · *Nature Ritual No. 4* · United States · 2021 Art intersects with intention in these medicinal altars. Close connects to her clients through artistic, sacred containers of woodland elements, crystals, and other ritual items.

(opposite, top) Josh Sessoms · *So Tonight That You May See* · United States/Guyana · 2018 In a contemporary artwork, signifiers and symbols of both earth and moon are transformed into a mythological portrait of feminine power.

Ian Rorke · Garden Pentagram · England 1981 The Farrar coven forms a human pentagram in front of their garden altar. A symbol of the five elements, the pentagram is commonly used in Wicca as natural invocation and protection.

Essay by
MICHELLE MAE

ENCHANTED WOODS

Sacred Groves, Trees, & Forests

There is nothing more undeniably magickal than the vibrations one senses when among a sacred grove of trees, a cluster of beautiful vegetation that mysteriously emits an observable power and energy. Witchcraft has always been able to thrive in secrecy within these hidden, deep woodland wombs. In literature and fairy tales, witches are often depicted as living in deep thick forests, the iconography of witchcraft forever linked with stories of the dark and silent woods.

In many cultural mythologies, the forest serves as a gateway to the spirit world; trees often form a natural circle or parcel of earth energy that concentrates the beauty of the locality and the force of elemental nature. These wonderlands contain an inexplicable force field — a well-known phenomenon all over the world, from the earliest history to the present. Ancient Greeks believed them to be portals that connect the sacred realms of the gods with the mundane world of humans, filling one with such compelling power that animals were (and are) sacrificed as offerings to this higher source. The trees are also considered divine entities or ancestors, able to hold this space and contain the charge of these landscapes.

Possibly due to ley lines in the earth, those who are energy-sensitive can feel a centralized magnetism when entering these dynamic vortices. Ley lines are the earth's underground veins of life force, similar to the acupuncture meridians in Chinese medicine, or the nadis in yogic philosophy. A network of channels flows through the body, housing chi or prana, life-force energy. Being invisible, this system is philosophical, but it similarly resides in the earth. These lines of energy are said to lie beneath all folkloric forests and enchanted groves. Like the stone circles of Druidic legend, these places of potency are often visited for rituals, ceremonies, magick, and solstice and equinox celebrations.

Magickal creatures and mythical beings are also said to make these sacred spots their home. Elders of villages, witches, sorcerers, healers, and shamans perhaps discovered these places in the distant past, sensing the force, realizing opportunity for mystical activity. Hallowed ground was then established, allowing seekers to channel the divine power for various purposes. Some say spells enchant an area where magick is said to thrive.

Vivienne Shanley · *Lammas* · England · 1997–98
This watercolor depicts a witch at Lammas. One of the eight seasonal sabbats, this magickal day is celebrated and ritualized by decorative altars and the gathering of herbs for protection and romance.

Paul Sérusier · *The Incantation or The Holy Wood*
France · 1891 Huelgoat women practice ceremony
in the enchanted Brocéliande forest, known for
faeries, magick, and curiously shaped rocks.
The French artist Sérusier visited and painted the
legendary locale of Arthurian folklore.

Sir Edward Burne-Jones · Witch's Tree from *The
Flower Book* · England · 1905 In one tale from a
book of flower paintings, Merlin is being enchanted
by Nimue. She uses her powers to tempt him, gaining his trust and luring him to the forest.

My relationship to witchcraft is open, nonhierarchical, and green, based in Earth connection. It is ecofeminist in perspective. Witchcraft is essentially a practice and way of living that helps you to connect with the animating force that runs through everything. Caring and compassion are natural outgrowths of true witchcraft and counter the pathological disconnection we are suffering from. We need this awakening, this recognition of interconnection. We also need to awaken to our power as people who can unite to achieve change in our world. Real witchcraft is about coming into a co-creative relationship with the universe (God-Goddess-All-That-Is), discovering who you are, gathering your personal power, and using it in service of creating the most beautiful, authentic life possible for yourself, and for everyone else too. The archetype conjures the image of woman as magick, of birthing life out of her body as the Earth does, of woman as creative/destructive goddess. We can update this archetype to include gender fluidity in the metaphor, yet the message is the same. We need this wisdom, which is also indigenous wisdom, of accepting death as part of life, especially now as we let go of the structures of domination that are falling to pieces all around us. The witch can help us embrace the reality of co-creation and of the ongoing cycles of regeneration and rebirth that follow death. This will give us the courage and hope to move through the difficult times that are unfolding, as we will continue to face the consequences of how we have lived, letting the greed of the few dominate the needs of the many. The witch can help us find our way through what I call "the evolutionary chaos of the now."

— ROBIN ROSE BENNETT, Author, Scholar, & Green Witch, 2020

Valera Lutfullina · *Witch* · Russia · 2019 A dark and evocative work features a witch in a natural and liberated scene with a herd of goats. Lutfullina illustrates in pure fantasy style and captures the whimsical nature of a free woman in beautiful grandeur.

(previous) Maria Torres · *The Witches* · Spain · 2017 A mystical merging of nature and feminism, the piece features three witches gazing into a realm-revealing scry mirror, with ritual implements surrounding the natural setting.

MAGICKAL PLANTS

Spells of the Green Witch

Plant magick is one of the oldest and most primary expressions of witchcraft. Having a deep connection to nature and its botanical language served early humans well, especially those attuned to the spirit world. Wisdom about the profound properties contained in the plant kingdom has been catalogued and cultivated by people since ancient times, to ensure all aspects of vegetation were properly proliferated. In addition to being used for food and medicine, plants are utilized for building, art, weaving, ritual, and protection. Common benefits are ample, but magickal properties and enigmatic energies are also attributed to the earth's flora.

Trees, flowers, and herbs are the domain of "green witches" — botanical alchemists and healers who integrate the power of plant life into their magickal practice. Their wildcrafting ways are a result of deep communion with the spirits of plants to glean esoteric information for concocting potent oils, elixirs, incense, and charms. Rituals of incantation and compounding ingredients produce blends for any desire. Peony protects from hexes and jinxes. Myrrh can enhance psychic ability. Licorice can attract a lover. Black pepper can banish negativity and evil spirits. Grape seed promotes fertility.

Medicinal properties of plants also inspired psychedelic magick. Medieval folk healers often used psychoactive herbs, which contributed to the stereotypical claims of witchcraft poisoning. Witches' ointments were infamous for provoking dreamlike, hallucinogenic reactions for the purpose of flying, conjuring spirits, and shape-shifting. Manuscripts from early civilizations abound with recipes that include entheogens such as peyote, salvia, changa, henbane, belladonna, psilocybin, agaric mushroom, mandrake, and the blue water lily. Whether utilized as a form of healing, to aid in spellwork, or to open the mind and gain entrance into alternate realms, the magickal plant world offers humans numerous benefits and profound connection.

L · *Spell for Fae Portal Access* · **United States** · 2020
The glass receptacle filled with oil and objects produces a magickal energy gateway and provides assistance to the recipient. Los Angeles artist L's alchemical knowledge infuses their magickal creations to facilitate states of consciousness for seekers.

MAIN DE GLOIRE

I never considered myself a witch. I consider myself the descendant of healers — the granddaughter of medicine people. My grandfather and grandmother knew spirit, plants, and how to heal, and they passed this on to me. I was born into this, so I guess that was my first initiation at my birth. I realize now that many would call me a witch because of my knowledge of intangible and not-always-seen things. The witches of Africa were and are powerful, and influence change in significant ways. All African religious traditions are significant to me. It's my origin — Ifa, vodou, Obeah, Kumina, etcetera. I work with plants. Plants are energetic beings just as we are, and their energy matches ours to create healing. A plant healer matches the energy of the plant with the energy of the person; this can feel like witchery. I lean heavily on plant medicine to heal and nourish joy and resilience. I practice primarily in my community of spiritual herbalists at Sacred Vibes. Our values revolve around honoring our ancestors, the land, and spirit. We connect deeply to valuing the voices of Indigenous peoples in our healing practices, and continue to do the work to decolonize the practice of herbalism. We are a community of more than 400 people who identify as spiritual herbalists. My mentors are the healers who practice out of sight in my community, the ones you have to know to work with: seers, vodou practitioners, etcetera. Research your ancestral lineage. Know that you are being called back, and somewhere in your lineage, this existed before you. Get to know that and start from there. The practice of witchcraft is self-determination and autonomy. Witch to me means freedom, freedom from a colonized mind and an oppressive reality, freedom to choose to envision my life and my community's future outcomes beyond this current reality, and invoking nature and spirit to get there.

— EMPRESS KAREN ROSE, Healer, & Spiritual Herbalist, 2020

Unknown · Mandrake Man · England · 20th
Century An illustration from the Museum of
Witchcraft and Magic in Cornwall, England,
depicts the anthropomorphized mandrake root,
which is commonly used in plant-magick potions
for its hypnotic and hallucinogenic properties.

Niki de Saint Phalle
The Witches' Tea Party
France/United States
1972 The phenom-
enally radical artist
had a long series of
nanas. She believed all
women are goddesses,
and through sculpture
and painting depicted
their dynamism, energy,
and strength. From the
series *Nana Power*,
her colorful, surreal
garden party unites
some powerful beings.

THE witches tea party

N. de St. Phalle

SACRED ROCKS

Standing Stones, Crystals, & Magickal Minerals

Stones are a natural source of magickal potency. These earth formations, as abundant and varied as plant and animal life, contain structures that harness, configure, and emit energy. From mysterious, megalithic wonders to pocket charms, the potent contents in stones have been primary sources of ritual in witchcraft, mysticism, and other cultural customs. For millennia, crystalline forms have been employed in the healing of every kind of mental, emotional, physical, and spiritual health concern, due to their fluid ability to resonate, move, and remove information, and amplify frequencies.

Beginning in the Neolithic period, standing stones have been erected, typically in circles or other grid patterns, for ceremony, initiation, burial grounds, and as portals that hold and magnify celestial energies. They lay scattered around the British Isles, Europe, Africa, and the Middle East. Modern megaliths have popped up everywhere in the world. The ancient architecture of such massive boulder installations is often found at the crossing of

ley lines, to contain and intensify energy. A magickal matrix is generated. It thins the veil between the spirit world and our physical reality, providing a dynamic and sacred laboratory for magick.

Smaller and concentrated versions of the colossal energy enhancers are crystals and minerals. Crystals provide a more focused and undiluted capacity. With their diverse frequencies and organized structures, they can be used as transmitters of any kind of intention. They can pull and trap negative debris, malaise, or malformed thought from a place or a person. In turn they can transmit that collected dross. When formed into a polished ball they become scrying devices; as wands, they serve as healing tools.

Using the Earth's gifts of rock to channel and direct energy has been crucial to witchcraft, and has recently been embraced in an unprecedented manner, by mainstream and fringe communities alike, as metaphysical practices continue to flourish and evolve.

Lucien Shapiro · *Quartz with Iron Inclusions Protector* United States · 2017 From a collection of works examining, as the artist explains, "the relationship between modern waste and memories of ancient cultural artifacts. Discarded materials are transformed into objects analogous with self-protection."

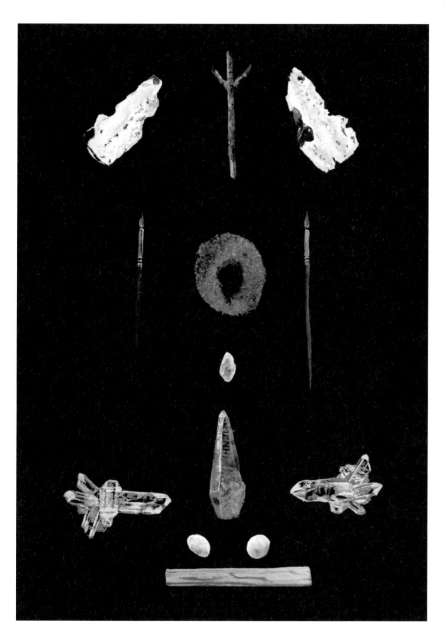

Steve Speller · *Long Meg* · England · 2017
A Neolithic standing stone, *Long Meg* stands tall in
a circle with her stone "daughters." Legend has it
that Meg and her daughters were a coven of
witches who were turned to stone by a warlock.

Josephine Close · *Art as Magic Paper Altar* · United
States · 2020 Showcasing imagery of quartz crystal,
moss, and other grounding elements, the artist
created this illustration for the purpose of creating
a ceremonial altar for earth worship.

KITCHEN WITCHERY

Magick in Hearth & Home

Hearth and homestyle witchcraft certainly delight the senses: Imagine the sights and scents of a kitchen heaped with herbs, plants, broths, and brews, all over a cozy fire. This style of sorcery appeals to those who prefer the sympathetic, medicinal, and nurturing types of magick. While some witches have a propensity for fire, water, or air activity, some are more naturally connected to the earth and its abundant cornucopia of plants and animals. Blending all of these elements together in one's own dwelling promotes feelings of accomplishment and purpose. The kitchen becomes an extension of the person who runs it, infusing every creation with their essence, intention, and vibrational signature.

Kitchens are traditionally feminine territory. In many cultures, knowledge of edibles and their combined efficacy, preparation of nutrients for nourishment, and culinary flair has been perceived as handed down among or natural to women for millennia. Eventually this became an expected form of domesticity, with forced routines. Women being relegated to the kitchen diminished cooking to be a mere necessity or chore. As fun decor (or

possibly as an antidote to this oppression), the European kitchen-witch poppet, or handmade doll, was created. As a popular good-luck charm, it kept dishes from burning and evil spirits out, and unintentionally served to empower women to consider themselves as sorceresses instead of servants.

In historic imagery, depictions of witches are often shown in the kitchen or at the hearth. Today, for contemporary practitioners, kitchen witchery is about accessibility, the ability to utilize magickal ingredients that are easily on hand in the pantry. Modern witches use herbs and spices as ingredients for spells or teas and fresh flowers for ritual and celebration. Certain foods can be used to heal or to bewitch.

As witchcraft regenerates into a modern source of curating the wellness and vibrancy of oneself and others, the kitchen has once again become a place of alchemy. Fresh herbs are hung, stoves become altars, tools of the trade are collected, and recipes transform into spellwork. For the modern witch, the kitchen is a space for magickal creation.

Cornelis Saftleven · *A Witch's Tavern* · Netherlands 1650 A horde of sorcerers, demonic animals, and half humans appear at a chaotic sabbath soiree. Like much of Europe, sophisticated collectors in the Netherlands coveted these early witchcraft themes in art.

Roger Frugardi · *Medieval Apothecary Shop* · France
14th Century Long before we were inundated with
synthetic chemistry, plant medicine treated ailments.
Herbal and botanical formulas were potent, and
due to their efficacy, pharmacists were often accused
of being witches.

(following) Jacques de Gheyn II · *A Witch's Kitchen*
Netherlands · ca. 1600 This portrayal of the
kitchen witch, shows them concocting magickal
remedies, oils, and healing foods for cleansing and
clearing.

(top) Benjamin Christensen · Film Still from
Häxan: Witchcraft Through the Ages · Denmark · 1922
A witch brews her stew in the banned silent Danish
documentary, which set out to expose the imagined
horrors of witchcraft.

(bottom) Fiona Pardington · *Amanita Muscaria*
New Zealand · 2011 The *Amanita muscaria* is the
hallucinogenic mushroom of fairy tales, legends,
and witchcraft.

FAMILIARS

Guardians of the Supernatural

The animal companions of witches are known as familiars. They can take the form of animals such as dogs, birds, toads, hares, and most notably, cats; felines are particularly favored by witches in literature and myth. The witch Circe, for instance, is said to have lived among tame lions and wolves. Bonds are believed to develop between witches and their familiars in which a single consciousness is established. This unified relationship grants the familiars the ability to perform tasks or retrieve objects. Some have healing powers or harming potential, depending on their magickal master's request. A familiar may simply serve as a guardian or spy, and may be capable of shape-shifting when needed.

In folkloric, shamanic, and magickal traditions, supernatural assistants abound throughout history, everywhere in the world. Various spirit encounters arose according to specific customs and traditions. In ancient Greece, people believed they were protected and aided by unseen or animal spirits in their daily matters. The Romans thought that protective spirits called *genius loci* inhabited and guarded specific areas. Spirit alliances formed in magickal circles when witches gifted other witches their familiars, or familiars were said to come from the Devil himself. Some witches were said to conjure their allies through spellwork, using their charms to turn wild animals into tame companions.

Beasts have always accompanied witches. During the frenzied witch trials, if an accused witch had a pet, she was more likely to face the torture of being pricked by inquisitors searching for what were known as witches' marks, places on the body that were believed to serve as nipples for familiars to suckle or where the Devil had stamped his seal. A mole, scar, or skin tag was considered evidence and means for conviction. Black cats were singled out for being the most notorious witch accomplices due to their nocturnal behavior and color, and were similarly killed for their supposed association. Witches were also believed to shape-shift into black cats for ease of travel and camouflage, reinforcing the necessity for extermination. As early as the 1400s, witchcraft art has depicted supernatural women with ebony felines, maligning them in history as evil. They were so frequently characterized as bad omens that we still think of them as harbingers of misfortune.

For those who are sensitive to elusive realms or drawn to the supernatural, a familiar may merely show up unexpectedly. Any living thing with whom we share an irresistible affinity could be a spirit companion. Familiars may also be fleeting and appear in the guise of imaginary creatures — mentors offering guidance, support, or a symbolic message if one is receptive and observant enough to notice.

Lucien Lévy-Dhurmer · *The Sorceress* · France · 1897
With a psychic connection and supernatural bond to their mistress, these servant spirits assist in her sorcery. This witch is surrounded by her familiars, the cat, lizard, and snake that coils around her wand.

John Collier · *The Witch*
England · 1893 Which
is the witch? One of
many of Collier's works
of mythological female
figures, *The Witch* hints
at the phenomenon
of sleep paralysis,
from which the word
nightmare originated.
A cat, demon, or
witch's familiar sits
on a sleeping victim,
who becomes immobile
but awake.

(opposite, top) Paula Modersohn-Becker · *The Fairytale Witch* · Germany · 1901 A pleasant-seeming plant witch sits in quiet repose surrounded by her familiars. Her floral dress matches her roses, all symbolizing her dominion over natural life and resonance with Mother Earth.

Lionel Lindsay · *The Witch* · Australia · 1924 A black cat, a favorite feline familiar, is rendered in intricate pen and ink by the well-known Australian illustrator.

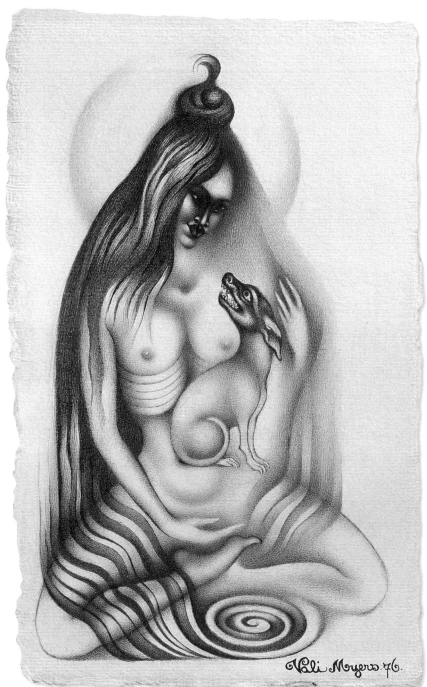

Vali Myers · *Kukuripa*
Australia · 1976 The
Witch of Positano called
her art "spirit drawings."
Myers included her pet
fox, Foxy, in the vibrant
self-portrait.

(opposite)
Penny Slinger · *Cats'
Eyes* · England/United
States · 1974 The artist
explores the representa-
tion of cats as signifiers
of magick, clarity, and
intuition in one of
Slinger's series of col-
laged artworks.

*I'm an Indigenous bruja, so witchcraft has been part of my entire
life. Both my parents and throughout their lineages are brujas and
healers. We are a mix of practices because we are indigenous to Cuba,
where there was colonization, so African practices are intertwined
into our native ones. I practice natural magick, a more native practice
that involves the cycles of the moon, the journey of the sun, as well
as plants, trees, animals, all of nature, especially the water and earth.
It has influences of Santeria. My key mentors are my family. My
mother's side is pure native Taíno, indigenous to the Caribbean practice
that is earth-based, and our gods and goddesses are nature — the moon,
the sun, the oceans, and so on. My father's side is also native and
African. So, I merge Santeria into my practice as well. I believe each
individual should create their own — merge or mold whatever they do
and/or believe in to fit their unique selves. Magick is special to each
person and works differently for each person. The more personal it is,
the more powerful it will be. It is useful in all areas of our lives, from
healing the inner self and deprogramming our minds to connecting to
divinity. Today, more than ever, we need to find the divine within and
acknowledge the sacredness that runs through our bones and veins; it
keeps us grounded, powerful, and in charge of our realities. A witch is
an embodiment of your truth in all its power. In my lineage, the bruja
was sacred, powerful. Once the colonizers came, they tried to erase our
practices, so we hid them in their forced religion. My ancestors were
brave, and did not let anyone stop them from practicing and believing.
They taught me that you can't take the WILL of a witch away from
her, nor can you take her magick.*

— JULIET DIAZ, Author, Scholar, & Indigenous Bruja, 2020

Arthur Rackham · *By Day She Made Herself into
a Cat* · England · 1909 In the Brothers Grimm tale
"Jorinde and Joringel," a shape-shifting witch disguises
herself as a sinister feline. In Rackham's beloved
Grimm's Fairy Tales book, she is perched to lure and
capture birds and other small animals for food.

(previous) Jean-François Portaels · *The Witch*
Belgium · 19th Century This highly sought-after
painter of biblical scenes gives a startling vision
of a tensely fisted sorceress. Her black cat familiar
lurks, obscured in her shadow, compelling the
viewer to contemplate her wide-eyed fervor.

ELEMENT

SPIRIT

V

INDICATION
Guides · Lineage
The Liminal · Death
Mystery · Source

SYMBOLS
Altars
Snakes · Bones
Smoke
Curtains · Crossroads
The All-Seeing Eye
The Veil

MANIFESTATION
Omens · Messages
Guidance · Protection · Shadow
Work · Transformation

Through the Veil

Witchcraft is a state of being. Our choices, thoughts, and actions are spells that we weave throughout all our days and lives. The craft for me primarily is about being able to intentionally focus those energies. Magick is our essence, and lives in everything.

— ALIA WALSTON, Scholar, Healer, & Witch, 2020

Conventional Western wisdom suggests that there are four elements, but many alchemists, occultists, and witches disagree, positing the existence of a fifth element, variously named ether, spirit, and quintessence. This esoteric belief derives from ancient Greek philosophy. Ether is simultaneously a distinct element and the product of the union of the four traditional elements (air, earth, fire, water). In the 2021 book *The Four Elements of the Wise: Working with the Magickal Powers of Earth, Air, Water, Fire*, Ivo Dominguez, Jr., describes the fifth element as "the fascia, mycelial network, the web, and the weft and warp of creation." Medieval magicians defined quintessence as the material that permeates the universe.

According to the axiom attributed to Aristotle, nature abhors a vacuum. Thus, there is no such thing as empty space. Until the 19th century, ether was thought to permeate space, though scientists now disagree. The ancient Greeks believed that celestial beings breathed a different substance than that required by humans. They named this substance ether.

Although the words *ether* and *spirit* are frequently used interchangeably, some occultists perceive subtle differences, defining ether as the product of the four elements, the result of their highest union. Spirit is defined as the sacred material from which the four elements are formed and which serves as their foundation. Quintessence, literally the "fifth element," encompasses ether and spirit and is thus their fullest expression.

Unifying all the elemental powers, the fifth element is a sacred vehicle for magickal power. It is believed to be the material that enables communication between the realms of the living, the dead, and the spirits. The alchemically oriented might suggest that, while magickal practices may contain components of other elements, they depend upon ether to be effective.

(previous) Robert Venosa · *Buddha Sphinx* · United States · 1979 Visionary artist Venosa studied under Mati Klarwein, and employed a similar technique in his quest to interpret the relationship between spirit and matter. Mythology and spirituality converge in Venosa's conception of divine consciousness.

Helen Duncan · *Ectoplasm* · Scotland · 1939 Thought to flow forth from the mouth during séances, ectoplasm became a popular subject of early photography. Duncan was the last woman prosecuted under the Witchcraft Act of 1735, after having contacted the specter of a dead sailor.

ALTARS

A Space for Ritual

At its most basic, an altar is a tableau — an array of objects. Nothing is placed upon an altar randomly. Altars may be plain or elaborate, permanent or temporary. Serving many purposes, creating altars is a versatile magickal art. Altars serve as an expression of one's spirituality and magick. They honor ancestors, spirits, and the dead. They also serve as communication devices — vehicles that enable the witch to communicate with spirits of all kinds and where gratitude may be offered or favors requested.

The simplest altar beckons the dead and features one lit candle and an uncovered vessel of pure water. A splash of anisette added to the water creates a stronger lure. Although these items attract the dead, it is ether that connects the living and the dead.

Altars to deities display statues and sacred imagery, as well as items believed to share the essence of that deity, intended to serve

as sympathetic magick. An altar dedicated to Athena may display owls, for example, while one dedicated to the Orisha Oshun might feature river stones, oranges, and cinnamon, items in which Oshun will recognize herself and thus be drawn closer.

Ether may be represented by a tableau of objects representing the four elements, brought together on an altar. This is displayed in the Magician card of the Tarot, especially the version created by artist Pamela Colman Smith. The magician stands before a table upon which are a pentacle (earth), a chalice (water), a wand (fire), and a sword (air). The magician's right hand is raised, while the left points down, illustrating the hermetic axiom "as above, so below." This image may be interpreted as representing complete mastery of the elements, including ether. The card is numbered I, indicating unification of the elements and the magician's capacity to perform any magick.

(previous) John Martin · *Macbeth* · England · 1820
The three witches who deliver Macbeth's prophecy wildly emerge from pure cosmic transcendence. A limitless landscape paralyzes the men, who sense the shuddering truth in the fabric of reality.

Cecil Williamson · *Double Cubic Altar* · England ca. 1950 A model of the magician's altar by Williamson, this finely detailed piece integrates the symbolism of a secret alphabet developed by John Dee, the famous astrologer and magician of the Elizabethan courts.

Georg Pencz · *Afgoderij van Salomo* · Germany 1529–33 In this engraving by the German printmaker, King Solomon of the Old Testament is depicted worshipping idols, calling on the Witch of Endor to tell his fortune.

Henry Fuseli · *Conjuration Scene with a Witch at the Altar* · England · ca. 1779 A witch sits at the base of her altar, wand in hand and spellbook open, using her power to conjure up magickal acts of flight and divination.

Unknown · *Samhain Ritual* · England/United
States · 1968 The high priestess places the horned
helmet onto the high priest, signifying the turn of
the wheel and ushering in the dark half of the year.
All of the artifacts of which are on display at the
Buckland Museum.

(following, left) Fay Avnisan Nowitz (Nyxturna)
Altar IV from the Ceremony Series · United States
2020 Featuring styling, set design, and photography
by Nowitz, this work aims to conceive ritual as part of
an artist's practice. Crafting the work and documenting the ceremony were part of the artistic process.

(top) Edward Collier · *Vanitas — Still Life with Books and Manuscripts and a Skull* · Netherlands 1663 A seemingly random array of altar items has an intentional message and setup. Collier was famed for artfully rendering the vanity of human emotions and pretenses.

Stewart Farrar · The Witch's Altar of Doreen Valiente · England · 1981 Doreen Valiente was a pioneer in speaking out about the legitimacy of witchcraft from the moment it became legal to do so. She had on her altar ritual items and a Book of Shadows.

Essay by
JUDIKA ILLES

ANCESTOR WORSHIP

Homage to the Past

Ancestor worship may be Earth's oldest religion and is still widely practiced throughout the world. For children, parents, and other family, elders may be perceived as having godlike powers with control over nourishment, comfort, and safety. Ancestor worship questions why this influence must terminate after death. Ancestors are believed to be able to intervene in the lives of the living, protecting descendants. It is a symbiotic relationship. Offerings made by descendants empower ancestors, so that they are better able to provide for the living. In many places, this is conventional practice, not witchcraft. Ancestors are simply expected to perform their duties. No communication or interaction may be expected beyond that.

The magickal practice known as ancestor work relies on the etheric web to enable communication. Messages must be transmitted on both sides of the veil separating the dead from the living. Ancestor work is a modern magickal practice, whose growth coincided with advances in genetic technology, as well as the digitalization of records that encourage ancestry tracing. Ancestor work does not require worshipping ancestors or even liking them. Instead, it relies on the magickal belief that an unbreakable bond connects ancestors and their descendants.

Ancestors are widely considered to be especially responsive, as without descendants, ancestors cease to be ancestors. They are invoked for healing, improved finances, fertility, and protection. Numerous methods are used to contact ancestors, including divination, séances, memorial candles, offering tables, and altars, but invitations may also be personalized by treating them as welcome family guests. The recently dead, whose habits may be familiar, may be offered beverages and treats that they may have enjoyed while alive, while the remote dead, who may no longer be known by name, may be summoned by gifts representing a culture, if known, or by gifts that convey respect and seek to honor them.

(page 406–07) **August Malmström** · *Dancing Fairies* · Sweden · 1866 In a whimsical image, a ring of elves dance under the moonlit midnight sky of Sweden's magickal countryside.

Kunz Meyer-Waldeck · *The Witch of Endor* · Germany 1900 A darkly imagined cauldron casting summons the ghost of Samuel. The witch is filled with excitement as Saul cowers in fear in the Hebrew biblical conjuring to predict the Philistine battle.

Sir Joseph Noel Paton
*Faust in the Witch's
Kitchen* · Scotland
1848 Renowned for
his faerie paintings,
Paton captures a scene
from Faust as he
enters the witch's den.
Surrounded by potions
and magickal tools, the
witch is said to be able
to commune the dead,
grant eternal youth, and
cast potent love spells.

John Downman · *The Ghost of Clytemnestra Awakening the Furies* · Wales · 1781 Matricide provokes Clytemnestra to return from the dead and angrily summon the nine Furies. She demands violent retribution on her son, Orestes. Downman captures the ruthless rage of this ghostly vehemence from the ancient Greek legend.

Shana Rowe Jackson · *Sisters of the Night* · United States · 2012 Witches gather in a secluded grove under a dark sky, conjuring around a cauldron, as the spirit they've called on rises above the flames.

(top) Mikhail Nesterov · *The Empty Tomb* · Russia 1889 Two women visit the tomb of Jesus to pay their respects to the deceased. Instead of his body, they find an empty tomb with an angel watching over it.

SNAKES

Transformation of the Serpent

Snakes are among the creatures most associated with witchcraft and secret knowledge. The serpent in the Garden of Eden famously convinces Eve to eat the fruit of the Tree of Knowledge, while in the Epic of Gilgamesh, a serpent steals the plant of immortality. They also represent the sacred ouroboros, the symbol associated with eternity and cycles of death and rebirth. They shed their skins, a symbol of renewal and transformation. And although snakes are associated with all types of witchcraft, they are especially connected to plant magick. Since earliest times, snakes have also been linked to divination and prophecy. The Greek title of the prophetess of Delphi was Pythia, translated as "pythoness" – a reference to the winged snakes thought to protect the sanctuary. Meanwhile, ancient Egyptian belief suggests that being bitten by a snake transmits the power to prophesize.

Observed burrowing in earth, swimming in water, wrapped around trees, and gliding from tree to tree, snakes are associated with all elements and, by extension, the quintessence.

Snakes are believed to possess all botanical knowledge and have potent associations with healing and especially women's health. Yet because many snakes are venomous, they are also associated with poison and death. *Venefica*, a Latin word for a type of witch, derives from the same root as "venom." A *venefica* is a poisoner who creates magick potions and is allied to snakes. Serpentine spirits are also frequently allied to witches. Simbi, a Congolese water spirit, now venerated in Haitian vodou, is a master magician in the form of a snake. Witch goddesses Hekate and Persephone wear snakes entwined in their hair, while snakes form Medusa's hair.

Spirit snakes are among a witch's arsenal of magickal weapons. The practice of "sending out a snake" is associated with witchcraft practices of the Caucasus and Balkans. A witch of sufficient power is able to cultivate a spirit snake, an invisible, non-corporeal pet, which she can then send through the ether to fulfill her commands, typically to attack an enemy or punish someone.

Kiki Smith · *Earth* · United States · 2012 The first of three in Smith's tapestry triptych *Earth* depicts the sun and sensuality. She works in a wide range of media: printing, weaving, painting, and sculpture.

Meagan Boyd · *Fertility Spirit* · United States · 2017
Serpents symbolize the creative life force. This vibrant
snake slithers a path through spring flowers against
a black background, invoking the mysterious void
of eternity and the continual renewal of life.

(opposite) Félix Labisse · *La fille de Tirésias* · France
1973 In striking Surrealist symbolism, we behold
the cloaked seer Manto, daughter of the oracle
Tirésias of Greek myth. Tirésias had killed two
mating snakes, resulting in a curse that turned him
into a woman who gave birth to Manto.

(following, left) Darcilio Lima · *Untitled* · Brazil 1972 Deeply surreal, the dense lithograph from the visionary, shamanic artist Lima displays his grasp of mythology, astrology, and alchemy.

(following, right) Rowan E. Cassidy · *Witch* Australia · 2018 Behind the veil of darkness, a cloaked woman of magick summons a serpent from the water's edge. Into her reflection slithers the spirit accomplice in the shadowy modern work of watercolor and ink.

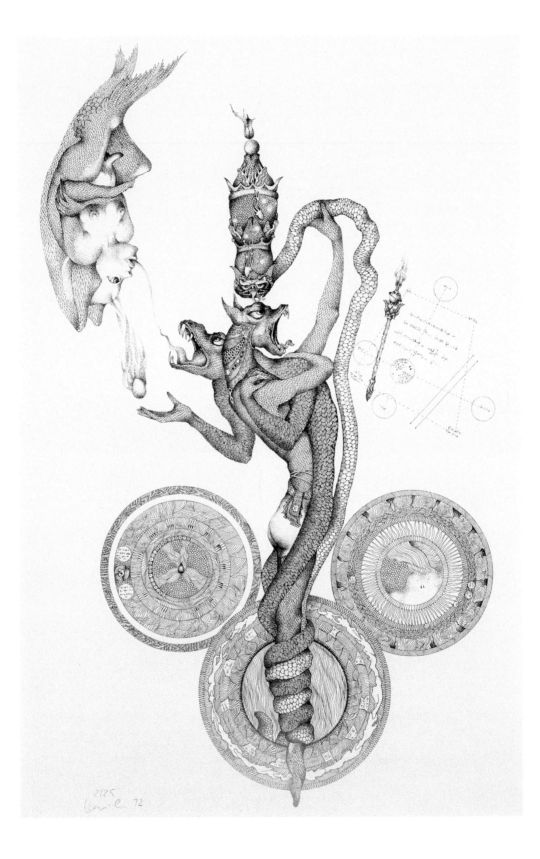

2/25
Unica 72

My maternal grandmother is of the Sinti subgroup of Roma, a diasporic ethnic group commonly known by the slur "Gypsies." She taught me card reading, palm reading, and tea leaf reading, as well as dancing, our family trades, so that I would always have work and be connected to our ancestors. Roma also have rich folk traditions centered on physical and spiritual purity that imbue everyday life, from cooking, to cleaning, to bathing, as well as herbal medicine and healing rituals. When early Roma left India around the 10th century and arrived in Europe between the 1300s and 1400s, they were met with violent oppression, from more than 500 years of enslavement, to legal hunting, to forced deportations. Due to persecution, Roma's jobs needed to fit with a nomadic lifestyle, so there were few options: craftsperson, performer, agricultural worker, horse trader, or fortune-teller. Fortune tellers and healers were labeled as witches. Mihaela Drăgan, Romani actress, playwright, filmmaker, and author of "The Roma Futurism Manifesto," explains that "witch" was a job that Romani women in particular worked for survival. She writes, ". . . since society has continued to leave us completely unarmed in the face of systemic racism, conjuring the magical and the supernatural has been our only weapon." Drăgan reclaims this role through the Cyber Witch archetype. I am part of the Roma Futurist movement too, a witch using technology for fortune telling and healing rituals, and for my art and creative writing. Roma are still disproportionately impoverished, facing hate crimes, police brutality, illegal deportations, human trafficking, apartheid, as well as health care, employment, housing, and education discrimination. Our practices and fashions are often appropriated, which negatively impacts our fight for human rights. Instead of appropriating "Gypsy" culture, it's essential for non-Romani witches to uplift Roma voices.

— JEZMINA VON THIELE,
Author, Artist, Scholar, & Witch of Mixed and Romani Heritage, 2020

Luca Ledda · *Witchcraft* · Italy · 2021 Based on a 1900s print of witchcraft and magick, the contemporary witch is in complete connection with nature and the elements.

NECROMANCY

Speaking with the Dead

Perhaps the most misunderstood form of divination, necromancy requires no visits to cemeteries or contact with skeletons. Instead, it relies on an etheric network to transmit requests and messages between the realms of the living and the dead. Just as cartomancy uses cards for divination, and pyromancy uses fire, necromancy means divination using the dead. Typically, though not exclusively, this indicates obtaining information from the spirits of the dead. Anyone who has ever played with a Ouija board or wished for a dream of a dead relative has engaged in necromancy. Ether forms a web connecting the dead and the living.

The dead are perceived as a reliable source of information, as they are believed to be privy to information that may be unavailable to the living. As they were once living people, it is widely thought that their ability to communicate with the living and to comprehend our needs and desires may be greater than that of

spiritual entities who have never experienced a human incarnation. Necromancy cautions against summoning the dead randomly, as harmful ghosts may respond. Instead, one must initiate contact carefully, taking protective measures and summoning by name. Ideal contacts are souls of loved ones who feel tenderly toward you. They may be requested to obtain information and transmit it to you through a dream or waking vision.

Crystal balls and mirrors serve as portals to the afterlife as surely as witch boards, such as Ouija boards, do. The dead may also be contacted via divination of all kinds, including pendulums or Tarot cards. Traditional rituals to contact the dead include séances and dumb suppers. A folk-magick spell recommends circling around a cemetery three times. Reputedly the dead will become visible to you, and you will be able to request information from them. Speak politely and wear an amulet.

**Frans Francken the Younger · *The Witches' Sabbath*
Flanders · 1606** Chaos ensues in Francken's depiction of the mythical sabbath, a scene of necromantic sorcery, where witches commune with the dead.

Andrea Locatelli
Magic Scene · Italy
1741 To call upon
the spirits of the dead
through incantation, a
man draws magickal
symbols in the dirt
while surrounded by
skulls, flying demon
goats, and cadavers.
Painting in the style of
Salvator Rosa, Locatelli
embraced the gruesome
in his portrayal of an
invocation of death
magick.

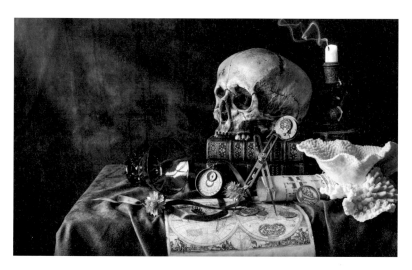

(top) Kevin Best · *Global Warming Vanitas* · Australia 2009 Presentation of our most foreboding mortal fear today: climate crisis. Every detail of every object in Best's still life is highly intentional in both arrangement and interaction, manifesting as a composition with striking symbolic efficacy.

Nikiforovich Dmitry Martynov · *The Shade of Samuel Invoked by Saul* · Russia · 1857 The Witch of Endor was summoned by King Saul to contact deceased prophet Samuel. All were startled as the specter declared the downfall of Saul's army.

Henry Gaze · *The Spell*
New Zealand · 1930s
The artist attempted to
escape the tensions of
life during the Depres-
sion by interpreting
his dreams in pictures.
Gaze fused the haunt-
ing and mysterious
with the romantic and
decorative, as in the
depiction of an act of
sorcery on a subject.

(opposite, top) Unknown · *Faust Standing in a Magic Circle Giving Instruction on Devilry* · England · 1620
The frontispiece to *The Tragical History of the Life and Death of Dr. Faustus* by Christopher Marlowe depicts Faust amid a magick circle conversing with the Devil.

John Hamilton Mortimer · *Sextus Pompeius Consulting Erichtho before the Battle of Pharsalia* · England · 1776
In the cave of the witch Erichtho, Pompeius seeks her prophecy of a coming civil war.

DIVINATION

Seeing Within

Divination refers to magickal methods of obtaining information that may otherwise be unavailable, especially through conventional sources. It offers the ability to predict the future, as well as understand the present and the past. Hidden secrets may be revealed. Better choices may be made, as divination offers access to information that may influence decisions and plans for the future.

As its name suggests, divination taps into the divine. Information ultimately derives from sacred sources, while the quintessence offers the diviner access to all spiritual realms. Divination may be a practical art or an elevated one, ranging from fortune-telling to prophecy. Virtually anything can be transformed into a divination tool, but specialized equipment includes crystal balls, Tarot cards, pendulums, runes, tea leaves, and coffee grounds. Special knowledge may be required to divine with these tools — a Tarot card is just a picture, until one knows how to read it, for instance.

The Greek word *mantis* literally means prophet or diviner. Its derivative, the suffix *-mancy*, refers to divination. Pyromancy involves gazing into fire, whether a candle flame or a burning hearth, for example, while oomancy involves obtaining oracles from eggs. An oracle associated with Mercury, the Roman deity, requires no tools at all. Instead, a small offering is made to the deity and a question formulated. The querent then covers their ears, so no sound is heard. Some sort of signal is determined in advance, so that the querent knows when to uncover their ears — a visual sign, perhaps, or counting to 10. The very first words heard after uncovering the ears provide the answer to the query, whether these words are spoken by a person or heard on the radio or television.

Siri Kaur · *Camille* · United States · 2019 From Kaur's "She Tells All" photography series documenting modern witches, Camille, an initiate of Lucumí, a variation of Santeria, poses with her ritual Tarot cards and selenite crystal tools.

Since I was a child, I've experienced intense bouts of sleep paralysis and insomnia. I'd wake up in the morning and the figures from my dreams would still be in the room with me. In that dream state I learned to visualize. I started writing poems and songs. I learned to distill all the overwhelming energies I was perceiving but didn't quite understand into music. For me, that was magick. My approach to writing songs has always been a bit ritualistic, even before I realized it. I considered some of my songs as personal chants and incantations. Over time I've more intentionally brought ritual elements into my songwriting, artwork, and live performances, from casting charms and protections over the stage, to using ritual tools and specific set designs to keep me focused and grounded. I reconnected with my intuition through this process, and from there was naturally drawn to more and more elements of witchcraft: the moon cycles and the seasons, shadow work as self-healing, performing energetic spells, doing a lot of studying, seeking, and reading, and putting what resonated with me into practice, mindful to not appropriate from closed practices. Now, witchcraft is subtly present in all areas of my life: waking and dreaming, in my work as a musician, in my creative space, in the smallest of daily rituals. Following the path of witchcraft became very central to my own healing: still is, and shall be. There's much more work to be done — healing the self for the greater good! Connecting with the divine feminine became so supportive to accepting and finding power in the parts of myself I'd always thought of as bad, wrong, ugly (thanks to growing up in this patriarchal society). I see witchcraft as such a gift — ancient wisdom brought into modern times, a balanced path of joy and shadow, endless as the cycles of the seasons.

— CHELSEA WOLFE, Musician, Artist, & Writer, 2020

Demö · *Soul Triad* · Brazil · 2020 In his wildly unique style, Demö imbues the sorceress with the power to recreate her dead family using the magick of necromancy. Their revived souls appear before her unbelieving eyes.

(following) Leonor Fini · *Le carrefour d'Hécate* Argentina/France · 1977–78 The goddess Hecate as depicted by the legendary Surrealist Fini, one in a circle of female artists of the era integrating themes of ancient myth and occult into complex and dreamlike paintings.

PART V

—

The Offering

THE CRAFT
OF CREATION

SURREALISM'S SORCERESSES

A Creative Coven

*I often feel I am being burned at the stake just because I have always refused to give up that
wonderful strange power I have inside me that becomes manifested when I am in harmonious
communication with some other inspired being.*

— LEONORA CARRINGTON, from her Surrealist novel, *The Hearing Trumpet*, 1974

At the very core of the Surrealist literary and
art movement was a radical reevaluation of
sexuality in general and of women in particular. Often aligned with the untamed forces of
nature, women were ascribed a certain imaginative potency fueled by their liberating proximity to the irrational. Alongside this was a
poetic dedication to exploring the dream-
scapes of the unconscious, often utilizing
trance techniques taken from Spiritualist
mediums, who were mostly women.
Surrealism's founder and leader, André
Breton, praised Jules Michelet's 1862 study
of witchcraft, *La Sorcière*, and was inspired to
create the term *femme sorcière* to label certain
contemporary enchantresses associated with
his Parisian group. In Surrealist works like
the 1938 *L'appel de la nuit* (*The Call of the Night*),
the Belgian painter Paul Delvaux hints at
occult goings-on as three nude women, one
draped in white cloth and holding a lantern,
seem to perform a ceremony in a landscape

replete with a skull, dolmens, and candelabra
trees. The women are beautiful and voluptuous with cascading hair that transforms
into lush foliage, making their connection
to nature complete. As much as the men
involved with Surrealism tried to envision a
new type of woman — sexually free, spiritually
empowered, and visionary — they were inevitably hampered by old tropes of seeing and
portraying the feminine.

It was the women artists associated with the
movement, both directly and peripherally,
who were to visually capture this new ideal
of the magickal and free woman, as they
themselves sought, with great daring and
difficulties, to embody it. For some of these
feminine creators, the icon of the witch, in all
her rebellious and dark glamour, held a particular fascination. In a spirit of gleeful and
wicked revision, many aspects of the witch
in art history and in the popular imagination

(previous) Leonora Carrington · *Ladies Run, There Is
a Man in the Rose Garden* · England/Mexico · 1948
The necessary task of feminizing Surrealism was
boldly carried out by Carrington, who refused to be
defined by male presumptions and brilliantly shone
as a sublime sorceress above them all.

Dorothea Tanning · *Birthday* · United States · 1942
The self-portrait of the Surrealist has her bare-
chested in a green tendril frock, accompanied by
a fantastical familiar. The painting was named by
the artist's future husband, Surrealist Max Ernst.

were revisited and reimagined with surprising twists. Gone were broomstick-riding hags and youthful seductresses, and in their place were more nuanced renditions that suggested complex relationships between nature, gender, and spiritual authority. No longer passive receptacles of outside forces, the sorceresses they portrayed were active agents channeling psychic energies and bending them to their will. Portals were opened that enabled certain mythic entities to reenter the artistic sphere – sphinxes, ghosts, faeries, demons, goddesses, and other deliciously unidentifiable creatures abound. These works portray women and worlds that cannot be controlled and so, until rather recently, were assiduously ignored and marginalized within the history of art.

A key strategy employed by women Surrealists to destabilize the male notion of the female muse as central to male inspiration was their use of abjection. Hairy,

smelly, bestial, and even monstrous figures were conjured up in literature and painting in contradistinction to the fey beauty of the Surrealist *femme enfant* (girl child) paradigm. One only has to think of the short story "The Debutante" by Leonora Carrington, where a young woman trades places with her hyena friend to attend her debutante ball, the scheme ultimately foiled by the animal's pungent odor. This story is accompanied by the mesmerizing 1939 *Self-Portrait* by Carrington, showing her in intimate communion with a lactating hyena, uproariously placed within the stultifying confines of her fancy upper-class boudoir. By the time the Swiss artist Meret Oppenheim completed the 1943 drawing *Unicorn Witch*, she found that she had "aged out" of the inner circle of desirable muses within the Parisian Surrealist coterie. With her pendulous breasts and rotund form, this cyclops witch reclines in voluptuous ease with spread legs. As if she could not render

Remedios Varo · *La llamada (The Call)* · Spain/ Mexico · 1961 Emanating forth through halls of oppressed and confined humanity, Varo's female phantom heeds a summoning into the beyond. With an alchemical retort, chemist's mortar, and flowing locks, she connects with the cosmos.

Leonora Carrington · *Grandmother Moorhead's Aromatic Kitchen* · England/Mexico · 1974 In her stunning, Surrealistic style, Carrington depicts mysterious women preparing a magickal meal over a Mexican comal, translating kitchen domesticity into a witch's wonderland.

often submerged in corpse-filled swamps or are placed in environments of decay and dissolution, as in 1949's *World's End* or 1948's *Petit Sphinx Ermite*. In *The Ideal Life*, from 1948, a wild young woman in ragged finery and feathers in her hair is surrounded by cats and debris, a modern personification of the witch and her familiars. More overt references to witches are found in *The Miracle that Sweeps (The Witch)* from 1935, where a seminude, rather masculine young woman grasps a broom, while in *The Witches*, produced in 1959, a coven of menacing older witches on brooms congregate in midair. Another series from the 1950s depicts bald androgynous women solemnly posed in ceremonial robes and holding mysterious egg forms, hinting not so subtly at both alchemy and the magick of women's bodies, as in *Guardian of the Phoenixes* from 1954. During her lifetime, Fini delighted in her own image and posed in extravagant costumes with her many cats and lovers in movie-like settings for photographs. One particularly witchy series shows her flying through the air or presiding Circe-like by the sea at the ruined Franciscan monastery near Nonza in Corsica, where she spent her summers. Surrounded by the power of the sea and in full ownership of her multivalent sexuality, Fini was a living exemplar of the Surrealist *femme sorcière*.

her monstrous enough, Oppenheim also gave her a unicorn horn, perhaps an ironic commentary on her own transition from youthful *femme enfant* to mythical beast.

Artist Leonor Fini was always fiercely independent and maintained her distance from Breton and the Surrealists, as she was not a joiner by nature. Her self-confident painted beauties lounge feline-like with mysterious and intimidating expressions, among ruins and palaces alike. Once again, abjection plays a part in their subversive message, as they are

The British-born Leonora Carrington spent the majority of her life in Mexico after emigrating there during World War II. The Spanish-born Remedios Varo had arrived in Mexico a bit earlier, also in flight from war, and the historic meeting of these two visionary artists would result in some of the most

Remedios Varo · *Witch Going to the Sabbath* · Spain/ Mexico · 1957 Invoking the occult was a given for Varo. Painting at the height of symbolic erudition, she created works that continue to stun both mystics and intellectuals.

captivating and pioneering feminist interpretations of female spirituality. Until Varo's untimely death in 1963, the two women explored numerous magickal traditions together with wide-ranging interests, from Mexican witchcraft to Gardnerian Wicca. Far from Europe and canonical Surrealism, they were free to create their own unique pictorial world, placing women at the center of the Mysteries, returning them to their rightful place after their displacement at the hands of patriarchy and the holocaust of Christianity. Known for her detailed and meticulous technique, Varo painted slender androgynous women engaged in mysterious practices and embarked upon journeys of esoteric discovery. Her 1957 *Creation of the Birds* has a hybrid owl/woman creating paint

from stardust distilled through an alchemical alembic, while in *Harmony*, made in 1956, a woman in a lab coat contacts her own materializing muse to form the musical vibrations of the universe. Carrington also equated art production with actual magick, and one of the reasons she used tempera paint was because she associated eggs with alchemy. An ardent feminist, Carrington sought to equate feminine domestic space with sacred space, dissolving the nursery, kitchen, and garden into liminal realms teeming with human/animal hybrids, among other things. In early works such as 1945's *The House Opposite*, three cloaked witches stir a bubbling cauldron while other woman/animal hybrids cavort through dreamlike chambers. Thirty years later, the numinous power of invocation is present in

Dorothea Tanning · *The Witch* · United States · 1950
Painted as a set design for John Cranko's ballet *The Witch*, Tanning's interpretation is pure spiritual Surrealism. With faces and bodies morphing into organic metal forms, the colors and darkness invoke a mysterious mayhem.

Grandmother Moorhead's Aromatic Kitchen, where embedded within a fiery red atmosphere, serious magick is afoot. Hooded figures prepare food on a Mexican griddle within a magick circle lined with Celtic incantations. The summoned white goose, representative of the great goddess (not to mention her disguise as Mother Goose), enters through an open door accompanied by a rather devilish horned character. This homage to Carrington's Irish ancestral roots gleefully mixes the seriousness of ritual magick with the savage rebelliousness of humor. No wonder Breton included Carrington in his 1940 collection, *Anthologie de l'humour noir* (*Anthology of Black Humor*).

During the 1940s, many European Surrealists were exiled in New York City, exerting a

significant influence on the art scene. Responding to the irrational horrors of fascism, Surrealism increasingly focused on the importance of myth and magick to bring about political and social change in a world lost in materialism. One particularly significant individual was the Swiss artist Kurt Seligmann, who settled permanently in the United States in 1939. Engrossed in the study of magick and witchcraft, he assembled a library of rare books on the topic that served as an important resource, and participated in discussions at that time with Roberto Matta, Carrington, Breton, Max Ernst, and others in New York. In 1948, Seligmann published his monumental *The Mirror of Magic*, an encyclopedic study of esotericism — including chapters on witchcraft, astrology, Tarot, and other such

Louis Joyeux · **Portrait of Leonor Fini** · France
1967 A portrait of artist and creative force Leonor
Fini, captured in a seductive, spellbinding pose.

topics – which would remain a great influence on artists for decades to come. Although after the war Surrealism would be supplanted in importance by Abstract Expressionism, interest in the occult would continue in America in other ways, for example, in the growing popularity of New Age thought and other alternative spiritual practices.

The American filmmaker Maya Deren experimented with Surrealist techniques, and her 1943 *Meshes of the Afternoon* gained great notoriety for its dreamlike narrative. *Ritual in Transfigured Time*, from 1946, was another experimental film whose disjointed narrative and use of freeze-framing and slow motion lent it a ritualistic solemnity. But it is Deren's unfinished 1943 film *The Witch's Cradle*, starring Marcel Duchamp and Pajorita Matta and filmed in Peggy Guggenheim's Art of This Century gallery, that more explicitly invokes the occult. A woman with a pentagram painted on her forehead moves through a spider's web in shadowy darkness. Filmed at odd angles and laced with occult symbols, it is a disturbing immersion into an indecipherable dream realm. In some respects it foreshadows Kenneth Anger's 1969 *Invocation of My Demon Brother*, especially in its use of repetition as an invocation device. Deren would soon leave for Haiti on a Guggenheim Fellowship, where she began many years of documenting the rituals of Haitian Vodou, which would result in 1953's *Divine Horsemen: The Living Gods of Haiti*.

The Chicago-based painter Gertrude Abercrombie was part of that city's bohemian jazz scene, and her free-spirited nature drew great inspiration from dreams and fantasy.

Her often small and meticulously painted canvases sport an array of specifically witchy props — owls, black cats, crescent moons, crystal balls, broomsticks, and even witches' pointy hats. What gives these works their anxious edge, in addition to the aforementioned props, is their uncanny atmosphere. Single female figures wander through desolate landscapes by moonlight, as their paths take them by lone towers, dead trees, odd clouds, and other frightful terrains associated with the witch. Titles like *Beckoning*, *Flight from Fright*, *Girl Searching*, *Reverie*, and *Owl on the Moon* reverberate with a spookiness bordering on campy humor. Her female protagonists are up to no good in interiors as well — levitating over sofas, doing magick tricks on tabletops, and even dividing as if sawed apart as on a circus stage. Here again, the titles tease: *The Magician*, *Fortune Teller*, *Floating Lady*. In 1952's *Witches' Switches*, hunks of hair — blond, gray, black, red — float in the air in an uncanny and disconcerting manner that reeks of curses, talismans, and spells. Unlike Carrington and Varo, Abercrombie was not involved with any esoteric movements; instead her work comes from an intuitive mind that channeled feminine isolation, melancholy, and resistance into images meant to confuse, unsettle, and fascinate.

Hailing from the Midwest, the painter Sylvia Fein became involved with a Surrealist group that included Abercrombie while attending the University of Wisconsin in the early 1940s. Later in the decade, Fein would show alongside such Surrealists as Ernst and Matta at the Whitney Museum of American Art's annual exhibition in New York. Like Fini and Carrington, she portrayed herself in her

Leonor Fini · *The Guardian of the Black Egg*
Argentina/France · 1955 On an arid landscape
under a fiery sky, Fini's subject sits in stillness as
a black egg gestates on her lap. She seems to
contemplate the manifestation, which symbolizes
an inner evil, or something sinister.

Kurt Seligmann · *Balancement* · Switzerland/
United States · 1931 A connoisseur of the occult,
Seligmann conveyed his exquisite understanding
of mystical truths in a Surrealistic style. A somewhat
obscure figure in the scene, he was an invaluable
influence on the world of magick.

work as wild, dressed in animal skins and set among macabre and occult signifiers such as skulls, tree stumps, cats, crows, and the like. In 1954's *The Lady Magician*, Fein portrays herself as the Magician card of the Major Arcana of the Tarot. The work is delightfully spirited, displaying a lithe Fein with her vibrant red hair in front of a table strewn with magickal paraphernalia – crystal vials, gemstones, herbs, and paintbrushes. Like the other artists discussed, she aligns magick with art making. There is a pentagram tattooed between her violet eyes while a crescent moon and stars are visible on her left shoulder. The traditionally male Magician card has been transformed to female, but with a light touch. The luminous orbs that float around her head contain birds that then fall to the ground, and the viewer is thus reminded that the feminine magician does not master or dominate nature, but rather plays alongside it.

In a more melancholy vein, the California painter Gerrie von Pribosic Gutmann worked with darker powers, such as the pain of loss, depression, and even insanity. In her haunting painting from 1952, *The Theft*, a nightmarish vision unfolds of demonic conjuring reminiscent of Hieronymus Bosch. What ungodly forces are at work here, one does not know, but the antlered feminine creature clutching a tiny child's coffin in her skeletal fingers is cinematic in its graphic horror, another abject evocation of the feminine uncanny and unsavory.

Although not strictly a Surrealist, Marjorie Cameron, a central figure in the magickal community of Los Angeles, produced

remarkable work. She can be compared to the British Surrealist Ithell Colquhoun in that their visual production was intimately tied to their magickal practices. Artist, poet, actress, and occultist Cameron embodied the counterculture of the mid-20th century. Widow of the rocket engineer and occultist Jack Parsons, she was deeply engaged with Thelemic philosophical ideals. Fully embracing all forms of liberation as part of a magickal practice that rejected patriarchal notions of sexuality, Cameron was profoundly experimental in her life, magickal practices, and art making.

Like some of the aforementioned Surrealist women, Cameron adopted a theatrical persona as witch and seer, using drugs like peyote to amplify her visionary states. In the 1955 transgressive and erotic *Peyote Vision*, she draws upon Aleister Crowley's sex-magick ideas, but makes a woman's sexual pleasure the central ritual act. Cameron's undated *Crucified Woman* embodies another reversal where the figure's pose is more about summoning and sorcery than Christian suffering. Another undated drawing in blue pencil depicts a fearsome triple-headed goddess covered in bulbous feathers that are reminiscent of the many-breasted Diana of Ephesus. The supernatural entity squats, legs spread open, while wings begin to sprout and flutter from her shoulders. Drawn on a modest sketchbook page, torn out and yellowing, this fragile sheet has the psychic potency of a bomb – that is the power of the artist, the witch, the visionary woman.

Gertrude Abercrombie · *Self-Portrait* · United States 1942 The avant-garde artist often depicted herself in surreal scenes with suggestions of sorcery. In real life she wore a pointed velvet hat to resemble a witch, and thought herself to be ugly.

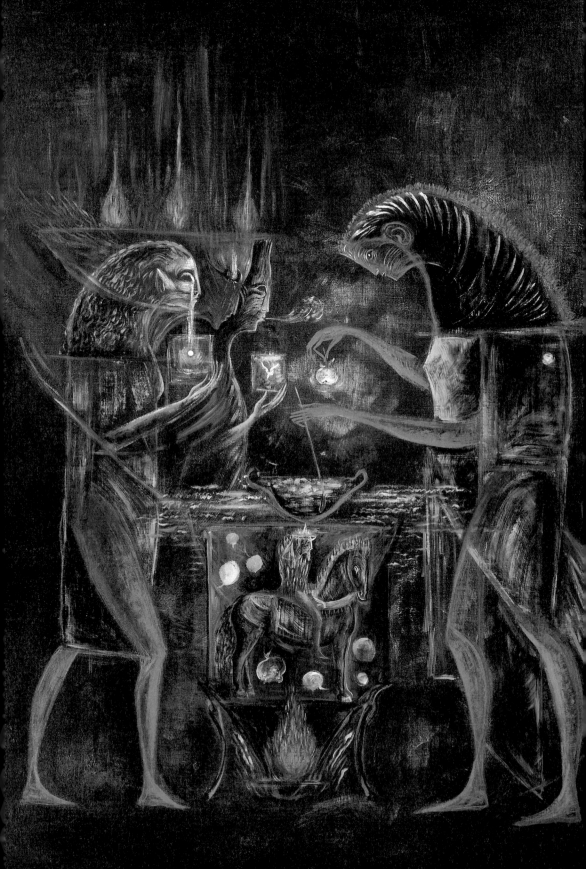

For me, being a bruja is about honoring my New Mexican mestizaje heritage as a woman of Indigenous and European, and possible Latinx, ancestry. It's about healing generational and ancestral trauma and recognizing that we carry the DNA of both the colonizers and the colonized in our blood. We reclaim natural-healing folk practices like curanderisma — once vilified as "witchcraft" by Spanish colonizers and the Catholic Church — and also recognize that we can't reclaim everything. With our histories of cultural assimilation, much of our ancestry has been lost, fractured, or otherwise tainted. So we take the medicine we can, heal what we can, and then change the narrative moving forward. Although I draw on various parts of my mixed heritage to guide my practice, some things are lost to me because of colonization and enforced cultural assimilation. My practice is a reflection of my mixed cultural identity. Being a bruja for me is about celebrating my interconnectedness with the earth and the spirit realm. It's about developing narratives beyond systemic oppression. And it's about recognizing that I have the power — the magick — to shape my own story. My advice to those interested in practicing witchcraft, and this goes without saying, is to avoid cultural appropriation. Real witches are all about social justice, not exploitation! To my mind, witchcraft is the antidote to the stressors of the modern world. Mainstream culture divorces us from our natural instincts and desires. Busy is the toxic norm. Witchcraft is the medicine that heals us from those poisons. It gets us to question unhealthy and unsustainable ways of being and return to a more natural flow of life. For me, being a bruja is about acknowledging that I am an empowered and powerful mestiza. Witches are transgressive. They push back against toxic social norms. They get us to question our own complicity in these norms and reject soulless ways of being in the world. The witch reminds us of our power and the innate magic that we are all born with, but have to relearn as we unlearn systemic and internalized oppression.

— DR. MARIA DEBLASSIE, Author, Scholar, & Bruja, 2020

Leonora Carrington · *The Ordeal of Owain*
England/Mexico · 1959 In the painter's take on
a famous Welsh folktale about the prince Owain,
a priestess and acolytes perform various Druidic
rites in a sacred grove.

ART IS A SPELL

Visual Magick & Its Makers

*Let it all be animal, my life and death, hard and clean like that, anything but human … a lot
I care, me with my red heart in the dark earth and my tattooed feet following the animal ways.*

— VALI MYERS, Artist & Witch, 1968

Like a witch, the artist conjures, shapes reality, manifests. The practice of magick is sometimes referred to as "the arte magickal" or "the dark arts." One *makes* magick. One engages in "the craft." That there is a kinship between those who craft magick and those who conjure art is undeniable. And sometimes they may be one and the same, and the Venn diagram of artist and witch collapses and melts into its own magick circle.

At its root, magick-making is a creative act. Though there are countless books of spells and how-to manuals on witchcraft, there is simply not one crisply codified body of knowledge or universally agreed-upon set of techniques. Witchcraft is rather an amalgamation of imagination, intention, and intuition – and working with whatever one has at hand. Certainly, there are rituals and invocations that have been passed down from practitioner

to practitioner, whether via grimoires or good old-fashioned word of mouth. But magick is fluid, and many who are learned in its ways tend to make room for interpretation and adaptation.

"Today we usually have to improvise as best we can," writes Gardnerian high priestess Doreen Valiente in 1978's *Witchcraft for Tomorrow*, in which she explains how to cast a magick circle: "Some people get a roll of plain carpet, on which they paint their circle….Others mark out a circle on their carpet with tape or twine. Others cut one out of felt and lay it on the floor…Use your own ingenuity; but whatever you do remember that you must consecrate and visualize the magic circle afresh each time you work. It is your effort and visualization that make a magic circle, not material things like twine or carpet."

Francesca Woodman · *Untitled* · United States 1975–76 Young and wide-open-minded, Woodman created self-portrait scenes that revealed the mysterious psyche and confounded the viewer by teetering the line between the known and unknown.

Klee

1921/52. Hexen scene

Valiente knew the value of one's individual artistic expression in witchcraft, as she was responsible for writing or adapting many of the rites and chants of Wicca that are now considered canonical, including the beloved and much-quoted invocation "The Charge of the Goddess." Her artistry and her magick were intertwined, each enhancing the other, and she encouraged her adepts to embrace this inventive attitude themselves.

Paul Klee · *Hexen-Scene* · Germany · 1921 Both distorted and mirthful, the Expressionist work of witchcraft in action incites great wonder. We see a witch in reversal under a crescent moon, as another witch and creature engage in acts of magick.

Joan Miró · *Disque* · Spain · 1956 From the artist's ceramic period with Josep Llorens Artigas, who built his kilns. These later works commonly depicted women, birds, and the moon in the automatism technique – unconscious painting to reflect the archetypal imagery of the artist's psyche.

While Valiente may have been writing her magick words in the second half of the 20th century, she and her witchy cohort can be considered the spiritual offspring of generations of artistic magick practitioners including those who made up the 19th-century bohemian occult society the Hermetic Order of the Golden Dawn. Its members were a coterie of actors, authors, and artists, including poet and playwright W. B. Yeats and legendary Tarot illustrator Pamela Colman Smith. Their rituals and ceremonial accoutrements were crafted with deep attention to color, symbol, and form. The art that was generated by members of the Order — whether used for their initiates or presented for public consumption — is notable for its lurid hues and psychedelic imagery. Though the Order drew from Freemasonry and Rosicrucianism, it also syncretized elements

Marjorie Cameron · *The Black Egg* · United States Date Unknown The artist holds a black egg – often a symbol of the devil. In her self-portrait she wears a ceremonial robe and her blacked-out eyes signify her knowledge of witchcraft.

Kurt Seligmann · *Witches* · Switzerland/United States · 1950 In his dreamlike paintings and his writings on magick and art, Seligmann manifests his knowledge of magick, philosophy, and alchemy.

FOR SHE HAS POWERS

of Egyptian mythology, astrology, and the Hermetic Qabalah, combining them all to create an altogether new path to enlightenment. For them, creativity and thaumaturgy were two sides of the same coin.

Witches and magick makers have long been embellishing their practices with a personal, imaginative touch, just as artists have been infusing their creative output with esoteric material. The early-20th-century Englishman

Austin Osman Spare injected his exceptional draftsmanship skills with occult energy, thereby developing a system of sigils – or magickally charged symbols – and incorporating them into his drawings. Spare's pictures of dark squiggles and twisting glyphs resemble a page from an ancient codex. Today, artists such as Elijah Burgher and Barry William Hale utilize sigils in their geometric pieces both in homage to Spare and to cast

their own visual spells. The marks they make are part of a living system of divine exchange. There is transference of secret knowledge, the closing of a circuit between artist, viewer, and the divine.

Likewise, entire art movements including Symbolism, Abstraction, and Surrealism were each born from women and men who sought to render the invisible visible. 19th-century

Helen Adam · *For She Has Powers* · Scotland/ United States · 1950s–1964 A Beat Generation artist, Tarot reader, and presumed witch, Adam created a run of collages showing cutouts of society women juxtaposed with supernatural or grotesque elements.

Carolee Schneemann · *Eye Body #24* · United States 1963 "Eye Body" is a series of 36 photos of the artist in which she presented her raw sensuality surrounded by objects and materials.

artists Georgiana Houghton and Hilma af Klint were Spiritualists who allowed their hands to be guided by entities from the other side. Their prismatic, nonfigurative images are now considered some of the earliest examples of Abstract art, but they each considered their work to be specimens of aesthetically enhanced otherworldly communication. Later Abstractionists such as Piet Mondrian and Wassily Kandinsky were influenced by Theosophy, and their paintings attempted to pull back the veil of the material world and visualize the spiritual structures that dwell beneath. Surrealists including Kurt Seligmann, Victor Brauner, Leonora Carrington, and Remedios Varo each had a deep interest in witchcraft, and their artwork reflects this, whether through overtly witchy subject matter or a ritualized creative process used in the making of their pictures (or, in the case of Carrington and Varo, some combination thereof). As Seligmann writes in his 1948 book, *The Mirror of Magic*, "In every man there is a child that yearns to play, and the most attractive game is occultation, mystery." This attraction to the unknown is shared among many artists, as is a desire to use their god(s)-given gifts to alchemize this mystery into matter and beauty that one can see, touch, and be touched by.

It may seem that in recent years, more artists than ever have been interested in exploring the occult, but it may be just that there is a wider embrace of it by the institutions that previously found this subject matter uninteresting, unserious, or just plain embarrassing. Exhibitions such as *The Spiritual in Abstract Art:*

1890–1985 at the Los Angeles County Art Museum, in 1985, and *Traces du Sacré* at the Centre Pompidou, in 2008, helped diminish a bit of the stigma associated with metaphysical content and paved the way for a spate of magick-themed art shows in the 2010s and onward throughout the world. There are now many living artists who openly traffic in occult tropes and bend the boundary line between craftsmanship and witchcraft, presumably because there is a more welcoming audience for it.

Some of them consider *all* art to be magick. As the artist Jesse Bransford has written, "I think magic and art are essentially the same thing. The two activities lead to a place of immanence or transcendence that point and direct all human endeavors." If a spell is intended to shift consciousness and cause action at a distance, it can be argued that any creative work falls under this rubric. Still, it must be said that there is artwork like Bransford's that is explicit about its magickal intentions. His installations and drawings consist of intricate magick circles, grimoire-inspired grids, and painted petitions to ancient deities and planetary forces. The viewer is not to passively regard a work such as Bransford's 2016 floor piece, *Circle to the Four Corners (Kali, Hecate, Ishtar, Lilith)*, but rather to interact with it as a devotional device. Its concentric rings contain various names of the goddess coupled with symbols of the four elements and other consecrated glyphs. A lit candle and flower offering signal that this is an active site of magick-making, maintained by its artist and reinforced by its visitors, who add their energy in turn.

(previous) Betye Saar *Window of Ancient Sirens* United States · 1979 Fantastical features abound in an awesome assemblage by Saar, whose mystical messages appear in her celestial and ancestral designs. Feathers and found objects create the supernatural scene.

Lezley Saar · *Reuel* · United States · 2019 Saar's show *A Conjuring of Conjurors* explored non-Western folk healers, shamans, and spiritual leaders. Saar shared about one of the figures in the show, "Reuel is a shaman and spiritual healer...a living personification of the head-on collision of Catholic and African religions." Her characters are named, embodying the true spirit of the being, as opposed to being titled and impersonal, with each identity representing a complex blend of cultures.

A magick circle is a container for spellcraft, and there is some artwork that extends this idea to a larger scale, constructing sacred spaces for the viewer to step inside. Though Judy Chicago's iconic installation *The Dinner Party* (1974–79) is most often name-checked as a trailblazing example of feminist art, it can also be as a shrine to the divine feminine. The piece consists of a hushed, triangular room with black reflective walls that evoke both a pyramid and magician John Dee's obsidian scrying mirror (or "shew stone") at once. A giant, three-sided banquet table at its center alludes to the occult symbol of the chalice, a vulva, and the triple goddess. There are 39 place settings crafted from iridescent porcelain and embroidered fabric, each stylized uniquely to honor a significant feminine deity or pioneering woman throughout history, including Ishtar, Sojourner Truth, and Emily Dickinson. Each side of the table has 13 of these settings, suggesting the number of witches said to make up a coven. The floor is adorned with 999 more names of female icons emblazoned in gold, some of whom were accused as witches. *The Dinner Party* is a memorial, but it is also an ancestor altar, allowing visitors to honor feminist phantoms of the past — and perhaps commune with these spirits here in the present.

Edgar Fabián Frías identifies as a "nonbinary, queer, indigenous (Wixárika), and Brown multidisciplinary artist" whose work explores notations of mutation, altered states, and sacred space. Their installations are neon-hued portals meant to be sanctuaries for inner reflection and spiritual respite. With 2020's *Nierika: Santuario Somático*, Frías uses video, printed textiles, and a central altar to explore the notion of integration, whether of the spiritual with the material, the ecological with the celestial, or the individual with the communal. Drawing on their own "indigenous, queer, pagan, witchy, mutagenic, and chimerica" facets, Frías takes the occult principle of "balancing the opposites" a step further, by hybridizing them into new, healing forms. By entering a space where all of Frías's identities are reconciled and remade, the viewer is invited to confront the tension between their own selves, and ultimately find peace and protection.

There are some artists who examine the body itself as a charged space, whether sacred or profane. Juliana Huxtable has referred to herself as a "cyborg, cunt, priestess, witch, Nuwaubian princess," and her self-portraits interrogate and celebrate her own transgender form. In her 2013 photograph *Nuwaubian Princess*, she is nude and doubled in a desert landscape with a glowing cosmic orb floating above her heads. It's a piece about transcending binaries, and its mystical signifiers imply that to do so is holy work. Kiki Smith has also embodied the witch throughout her oeuvre, including via her photo series *Sleeping Witch*, in 2000, followed two years later by *Out of the Woods*. An early, untitled installation of hers from 1986 is a display of glass bottles each etched with the name of a different bodily fluid, such as blood, saliva, urine, and milk. They bring to mind potions or witch bottles, and gesture toward the idea that corporeal excretions have long been considered magickal substances, since they come out of the body's most liminal zones.

(previous) **Bjarne Riesto · Louise Bourgeois's Installation at the Steilneset Memorial · Norway 2011** The late artist Bourgeois created the sculptural installation to memorialize the Norwegian witch burnings of 1621, during which 91 people were accused of witchcraft and killed. Created in collaboration with the architect Peter Zumthor, the piece was one of Bourgeois's last major artworks and is entitled *The Damned, The Possessed and The Beloved*.

(opposite, top) Edgar Fabián Frías · *Etheric Bodies* United States · 2020 In his multimedia exhibition called *Nierika: Santuario Somático*, Frías's image serves as an invocation of the sacred ancestors and an honoring of the land.

(opposite, bottom) Jesse Bransford · *Hecterion* United States · 2009 Bransford's work is a visual confluence of esoteric images and celestial iconography. This piece explores the relevance of lunar themes as they correspond with the mythological goddess Hekate.

A witch must gather the proper ingredients for her spell. She may consider the divine timing of its casting, choosing to wait until a specific moon phase or auspicious astrological moment. Some occult-oriented artists are similarly intentional about their creative processes. Betye Saar's talismanic assemblages incorporate found objects, metaphysical symbols such as zodiac imagery and Tarot cards, and culturally loaded Black American iconography such as Aunt Jemima. She shared in a 2012 interview with the Getty Museum that, for her, the sourcing and combining of her materials is as much a part of the magick as the final result: "I think of my work as being a ritual, and the first part of the ritual is the hunt: finding all the ingredients.... The second part is transformation: recycling, combining materials together, altering sometimes. Creating something out of what I found. The third part would be release: putting it out for exhibition or maybe even a sale. You just put it out there and people like it or they don't. If it doesn't feel completed, sometimes it just stays in my studio until I find the right combination."

This ritualized way of working is reliant on instinct and a sensitivity to influences beyond the realm of simple rationality. It's a feeling way of working, not just a thinking one.

Sometimes working with supernatural material can prove to be a bit *too* effective for its maker's liking. Poet and collagist Helen Adam featured harpies, witches, and demonesses (what she called her "lethal women"), and she recounted this story when discussing working on some of her dark collages: "I had been making a black magic series…[of] black magic scrapbooks, full of devils and witches, and every picture I could find related to that….And then one sunny day I was just walking along on Fifth Avenue not thinking of anything at all supernatural and suddenly I was overwhelmed by the most extraordinary feeling of evil – absolutely like a black pall coming down on me. And I remember one particular picture in one scrapbook that I'd found in one of the old bookshops, a strange print of a witch pointing at a great bed or something and a black demon coming through the window, and I don't know if it was that particular picture or the whole thing but I was so frightened I switched to angels and [threw] those scrapbooks away."

It's debatable just how "real" the magick of witchcraft imagery actually is. Do we simply respond to it psychologically, through the power of suggestion? Or does it tap into some subtle energies, manipulating them and thus affecting us? It's up to both the maker and the viewer to decide. But the fact remains that these are questions that artists continue to ask – and ask of us – by imbuing their work with magickal emblems and experiences.

Some artists have been a bit more forthright on the matter, however, not only by drawing a clear parallel between their artwork and their occult workings, but also by embodying the archetype of the witch in their everyday lives. 20th-century artists Rosaleen Norton (aka "the witch of Kings Cross"), Marjorie Cameron, and Vali Myers are but a few of those for whom the roles of creator and witch feel obviously interchangeable. They

Juliana Huxtable · *Untitled in the Rage (Nibiru Cataclysm)* · United States · 2015 Creating portrayals of sexuality beyond gender conformity and identity, Huxtable explores a rare celestial encounter between the speculative planet Nibiru and Earth.

not only populated their imaginal worlds with sorcery – and sexuality – of all stripes, but also fashioned themselves as art witches through their public personae and their own eldritch and enchanting self-portraiture.

The fine-art world's fascination with witchcraft is showing no sign of stopping any time soon. The witch remains a go-to figure for those who want to delve into the murky sea

of identity, for the witch is an ideal avatar for anyone who has felt othered or marginalized. Witch pictures allow us to interface with mystery, transgression, and transformation. By conjuring witches on walls, sigils on screens, and altars in galleries, the artist becomes an agent of enchantment herself – and allows us to fall under a spell as well.

Steven Arnold · *Gestation / Birthing in Madripore* United States · 1985 A phenomenal tableau vivant shows the visionary genius of Arnold, whose art reflected his dream states and sense of wonder and curiosity about dimensional reality.

Ed van der Elsken · *Vali Myers* · Netherlands · 1978 Muse of photographer Elsken, Australian visionary artist Myers smolders in her maniacal makeup and tattooed face. Her life, art, and performance were in themselves magickal acts.

I am a hybridized witch or brujx. I am Wixárika and have a deep connection to the sacred practices and traditions of my people, in spite of them being kept from me for most of my life. In a similar way that colonization and racism kept me from communing with the ancestral practices of my Indigenous communities, heterosexism and transphobia kept me from being able to fully commune with my queer ancestors and transcestors and our rich and vast lineages. We are collectively casting out years of oppression and bringing back the sacred intelligence of all life on Earth. First and foremost, witchcraft centers relationships and honors the inherent wisdom that we each contain. Witchraft is a space of communion, with the earth, the moon, the sun, the birds, the flowers, the bees, the faeries, our beloved ancestors, queer ancestors and transcestors, spirit guides, land spirits, and parts of ourselves we often did not know we had. We are not isolated. When we enter into ceremonial states, we are accessing the ancient memory of our ancestors and of countless witches who have cast their own circles and honored the directions and elements before us and after us. These practices dissolve the illusional boundaries of time and space. You cannot continue to reap from the destruction of the Earth if you see her as alive, and if you feel your ancient connection to her being. In your body. If you feel her cycles moving through you. If you see the resplendent magick of her forests, rivers, and deserts. That's why we need witchcraft today more than ever. A witch self-ordains. A witch inhabits paradox with ease. A witch collapses timelines. A witch expands possibilities and weaves webs within the interstices. Witches thrive within the void and understand the sacred relationship between life and death. Witches banish borders and binaries and allow for prismatic visions to take root.

— EDGAR FABIÁN FRÍAS, Founder of Our Sacred Web,
Artist, Healer, & Indigenous Brujx, 2020

(following) Judy Chicago · *The Dinner Party*
United States · 1979 The artist's installation of
an equilateral, triangle-shaped banquet table as
altar symbolizes equality. Each place setting honors
a woman of mythological or real-life significance,
cast together as powerful forces of femininity.

Elijah Burgher · *Hex Centrifuge* · United States
2015 Burgher channels mystical energies, and
infuses his artwork with them. The observer is influenced – taken out of the logical mind to experience
the esoteric imparted meaning. Art becomes ritual
in this spellbinding piece.

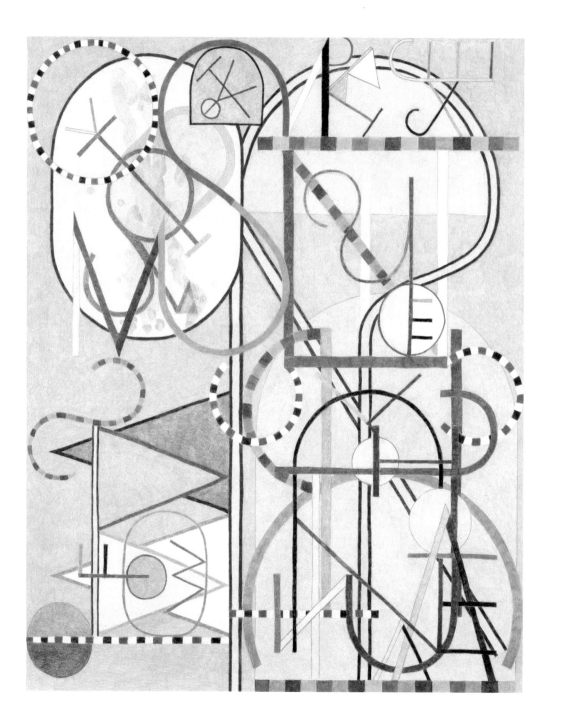

HAUTE MACABRE, HAUTE COUTURE

Witchcraft in Fashion

I was thinking about witches. Witches in the original sense of the word, in the sense of a woman having power. These are strong women that are often misunderstood by the world.

— REI KAWAKUBO, Designer of Comme des Garçons,
excerpt from interview discussing 2014 and 2016 collections

The witch has always woven an enchanting glamour, subverting the gaze of society with her cloak of magick. She wields the whip of her aesthetic with precision and clarity, both threatening and enticing in her strangeness. Perhaps one of the witch's most iconic qualities is her ability to shape-shift, to bend the energy of the universe around her to contort to her will. This is seen in the way the witch has been portrayed through history in all her dualities: as a hag in a pointed hat with a crooked nose; as a maiden seductress draped in layers of black tulle, lace, or velvet; as the rebel in an all-black ensemble protesting for the rights of the marginalized. The witch's glamour reveals society's fears and paranoias, all wrapped up in a pretty bow.

To deconstruct the garments of the witch, and the way fashion and the avant-garde have played a part in the witch's expression and revival, we need to start with how she veils herself. The word *glamour* means both "the

quality of fascinating, alluring, and attracting" as well as "magic or enchantment, spell, witchery." It's a variant of the Middle English *gramarye*, meaning "enchantment and spell." The witch is intimately familiar with this, for it's a glamour that conceals, that veils what lies beneath. When witches apply red lipstick or black eyeliner, or when they cast a spell of self-love, they are casting a glamour.

Some of the oldest witches were intimately aware of the power of fashion, of beauty, of transformation. While the ancient Egyptians used kohl on their eyes to protect them from the sun and infections, they were still working with glamour as a means of transformation.

The witch in her ephemeral power cannot be contained to one medium, so of course she has made herself known on runways around the world. One particular instance of the witch in vogue is when the famed designer Alexander McQueen honored his own lineage

Bertrand Guay · **Comme des Garçons Spring/ Summer 2015** · **France** · **2014** A witchy creation for Comme des Garçons, as modeled in the Spring/Summer 2015 ready-to-wear collection fashion show.

during his Fall 2007 ready-to-wear collection. The icon's bloodline leads back to Elizabeth Howe, a witch who was persecuted and hanged during the 1692 Salem witch trials. The collection was staged with models walking along the lines of a giant red pentagram, with heavy blue eye shadow and cat-eye liner. Some of the most striking looks in this show are literally reflective of the liminal space in which the witch exists. A sequined gold catsuit with a matching breastplate speaks of the alchemical, solar qualities of the witch, while a gauzy, sheer black dress with a high neck, puff sleeves, and a flowing train is paired with a pearl-encrusted crescent-moon headdress, singing of the lunar-ruled High Priestess in the Tarot.

But it wasn't only macabre maven McQueen who was influenced by the elusive power of the witch. Rei Kawakubo, the fashion legend behind avant-garde staple Comme des Garçons, was inspired by what she called "Blue Witches" for her Spring 2016 ready-to-wear show. Kawakubo's husband, Adrian Joffe, explained this as "powerful women who are misunderstood, but do good in the world," which is a potent piece of the archetype of the witch. In classic Comme des Garçons fashion, the show included exaggerated sculptural silhouettes – this time infused with black, royal blue, and navy velvet, plenty of ruching, and feather accents —which could very well be inspired by the ancient connection between shamanism, the goddess, and birds who can traverse the heavens and earth. The connection with witchcraft may not be so overt in this collection, but the power of witches to hold

the gaze of those who are both frightened and inspired by them still rings true.

For Hedi Slimane's first show for Saint Laurent, Spring 2013 ready-to-wear, the designer merged witch glamour with Parisian simplicity, a rock and roll-meets-Stevie Nicks sensibility, and sharp tailoring. The classic witch hat was reimagined with a wide brim, and the cloak was reimagined as a sheer mesh moment complete with a pussy bow and as a thick wool number with gold lining. Slimane's debut for the brand was one of his most iconic, and he showed that the witch can and will live on, past anyone else's outdated notion of what they may or may not look like.

Ardern Holt · *The Witch* · **England** · **1887** Featured in the book *Fancy Dresses Described*, an incredibly popular Victorian guide to party-going costumes, the witch wears a red satin skirt adorned with reptiles and rodents.

Léon Sault · *Witch or Sorceress* · **France** · **1860** Sault was known for designing dresses based on cosmic concepts and mythology. He created the illustration for Charles Frederick Worth, dressmaker extraordinaire in 19th-century Paris.

While some fashion houses are inspired by the darkness of the witch, and her ability to move through the shadows, some, like Preen by Thornton Bregazzi, are inspired by the witch's dualities and connection to the natural realm. In the brand's Spring 2017 ready-to-wear show, the inspiration came from the Isle of Man—and the wise women and healers who live there—astrology, and hippies. The resulting collection was 1970s meets 21st-century party girl. Pentagrams were a central motif of the show, pinned on shirts and jackets, worn as a sheer black fabric sewn into an abdomen-showing two-piece set, and adorned with flowers as the focal point of a white button-down shirtdress with layered puffy sleeves. Neons, metallics, and pastels were strewn throughout this collection, as were ruffles, ruching, and sheer pieces, which points to something those of us who practice witchcraft already know—magick is supposed to be fun.

Designer Rick Owens, too, seems to find inspiration in the unknown, though he may not necessarily call it witchcraft. His use of draping, all black, and overt gothic tendencies align him with both the darkness and the outsiders, which the witch knows well. Owens's wife and creative partner, Michèle Lamy, whom he calls "a magical fairy witch," exemplifies this, alongside the power of glamour. Every morning, Lamy dips her fingers in henna and draws a line of it down her forehead. Her teeth are coated in gold, and she is almost always seen wearing thick gold bangles, with her fingers covered in rings of precious metals and stones. The dedication to a signature look is one form of magick that intensifies the more you do it.

The witch hasn't just popped up on the runway out of nowhere in the last 20 years, however. Before she was a force to be reckoned with on the runways of the 21st century, she was being summoned by the likes of couturier Elsa Schiaparelli. Schiaparelli was a Surrealist-inspired fashion designer whose influence was prominent between the two World Wars. In 1938, the designer released her "Pagan" collection, merging the mystical and the material to create something extraordinary through the means of couture. The collection featured a golden choker adorned with velvet indigo bows from which gold pine cones dangled from matching chains—the pine cone being a

Unknown · *Fashion Witch* · Unknown · 1955
The 1950s were a high time for witchy fashion flair. Dressing up in tall pointy hats became glamorous and fun. From the ye-olde immoral portrayal, to modern, flirty, and amusing, the sorceress style has transcended the bounds of oppression and fear.

Robert Coburn · *Happy Halloween* · United States 1945 Columbia Pictures actor Dusty Anderson is dressed as a sexy sorceress. Her feather-duster broom gives a subtle nod to the times.

symbol of knowledge, protection, fire, and the third eye, since the pineal gland is shaped like it. Schiaparelli also included a straw hat adorned with brightly colored insects in colors like metallic green and fuchsia, and an elegant evening coat strewn with pink rosettes on the shoulders and collar, and, on the bodice, the profiles of two lipstick-clad women close together, the outline of their faces revealing a golden-edged chalice. In one collaboration with the Surrealist artist Salvador Dalí, the duo created the "skeleton dress," a fitted long-sleeved black dress that featured tailoring and raised piping that mimicked the skeleton itself, once again bringing the darkness of the witch and her awareness of the circle of life and death to the forefront.

In the 1980s, Vivienne Westwood, the acclaimed and iconic British designer credited for bringing the punk look to the runways, was also inspired by the witch, for her Autumn/Winter 1983/1984 ready-to-wear collection, aptly called "Witches." The styling was inspired by hip hop and featured three-tongued white trainers, sharp tailoring done in Westwood's graphic prints, and Chico Marx hats. But it's Westwood's series of collections titled "Britain Must Go Pagan" that show the influence of nature, magick, and romanticism in her work and, in her words, act as a call for Britain to return to the aesthetic of the pre-Christian period. Of course the collection is done up in bright colors, striking silhouettes, and in-your-face motifs, including tights stitched with a fig leaf over the crotch, an ode to sexuality, from which the witch can draw her power.

More recently, the couturier Julien Fournié made a bold statement for his Fall/Winter 2019/2020 ready-to-wear collection, called "First Spell." "I have always found witches more stimulating than repulsive," said Fournié, "Women called by that name do cultivate independence, possess a sense of adventure and stimulate the imagination, opening up to a magical world." He went on to state that witches were protofeminists who knew how to control their destiny, and shared a collection inspired by this power. Full-length velvet gowns in azure with embellished busts found their way next to an all-black ensemble with a tea-length skirt paired with a sharp-shouldered snakeskin jacket, a mandarin collar, and a single indigo feather worn as a headpiece. Cues from the natural world complement the witch's ability to merge with nature and work with elemental power, thus creating a destiny all her own.

The witch sculpts her reality with an ode to beauty, to creation, to the power that comes from perception. In this way, the witch is intimately tied to glamour, to fashion and renewal through self-expression, painting new modalities of existing through the way she dresses and drapes herself. Whether the witch is inspiring the costume design for a new film or a runway collection, her mystery and appeal will be forever present. She will continue to weave her web, and as others take the time to gaze at her mystery, she will forever be an ode to the power of the outsider.

Patti Pogodzinski · *YSL Witch* · United States · 2019
Pogodzinski has illustrated designs for many industry fashion leaders. This depiction of an Yves Saint-Laurent design seems to tap into the power and magick of the mystical feminine.

Jacques Habbah · Saint Laurent Autumn/Winter 2013 Collection · France · 2013 Imagined by the designer Hedi Slimane, this collection broke down gender barriers. This allowed a look at fashion choices of the alternative mind, beyond the mainstream limitations of expression.

Yannis Vlamos · Preen by Thornton Bregazzi Ready-to-Wear Spring/Summer 2017 Collection France · 2016 Having grown up around witchcraft on the Isle of Man, Bregazzi has a natural affinity for the witch in nature and culture, considering them relevant to fashion.

My interest in witchcraft as a practice happened very organically due to my proximity to Salem, Massachusetts, growing up. When I eventually discovered witchcraft, I learned that it was very different from the way that magick is displayed in movies and folklore. The spiritual connection with nature was something that resonated with me deeply. A lot of my creative work touches on varying aspects connecting to the practice. For example, my illustration work often depicts specific festivals or different phases of the moon, and my sculpture work can reference the witch's familiar with anthropomorphic mask making. Additionally, the jewelry company that I own with my best friend involves us gathering twigs in sacred outdoor spaces to sculpt and create organic talismans. For so many, the term witch *has been reclaimed from being something to be feared, to something that people have taken to a place of empowerment — the "outsider" being able to have their voice heard. A witch to me is a person who owns their power. They're creative, outspoken, empathetic, and connected to the earth. I do identify as one. I feel like that identity has been instilled in me from the minute my fascination with witches began. So many of us have been drawn to these individuals from movies and stories because they are often misunderstood or outcasts in their respective worlds. I inherently resonate with that being a queer person, never quite fitting a certain mold growing up. To me, the witch is an icon for anyone who feels marginalized.*

— **BILL CRISAFI,** Artist, Designer, & Witch, 2020

Elsa Schiaparelli · Necklace from the Fall
1938 Pagan Collection · Italy/France · 1938
Schiaparelli's Surrealist leanings inspired the
colorful insect necklace. As an avant-garde invoker,
fantasy and magick infuse all of her art.

SPELLBINDING

The Witch in Pop Culture

You always had the power, my dear, you just had to learn it for yourself.

— GLINDA THE GOOD WITCH, from *The Wizard of Oz*, 1939

Over the last two centuries, the witch has cast her spell over modern culture, the archetype interwoven into the conventions of popular art across most, if not all, mediums. She is *Oz*'s "Wicked Witch," shape-shifting from the printed page to the silver screen to the small screen, and finally into a colorful stack of screen prints on the floor of Warhol's Factory. She is the (not so) ordinary suburban housewife Samantha, causing mischief in *Bewitched*; she is Sabrina, the teenage spellcaster. She is a rock star, hip-hop queen, post-wave New Age chanteuse floating across the misty moors to howl at the full blood moon.

Her incarnations are as countless as her moods — seductive, beguiling, innocent, enrapturing, and wretchedly, mercilessly

evil. She is innately feminine energy but moves beyond gender into countless forms that disregard all norms and conventions. The archetype of the witch is wildly metamorphic, each reinvention shaped by and reflective of the zeitgeist of each cultural era.

Early cinema is rife with witches as narrative subject and star. Their first appearance on celluloid can be traced as far back as 1906's *The Witch*, a magickal hand-tinted experiment by the pioneering filmmaker Georges Méliès. In 1922, the truly disturbing *Häxan: Witchcraft Through the Ages* was released. The silent film, part documentary reenactment and all horror, was written and directed by the Danish filmmaker Benjamin Christensen and contains scenes that remain unsettling even to a cynical modern eye.

Virgil Apger · The Wicked Witch of the West United States · 1938 Children received their education on the evil witch/good witch dichotomy in L. Frank Baum's dark and whimsical tales. In the film adaptation of his *Wonderful Wizard of Oz*, Margaret Hamilton starred as the nasty, green-faced villain.

While *Häxan* explored the violent legacy of the witch's long persecution, back in Hollywood, the silent-era film witches were predominantly pale-skinned and kohl-rimmed, evoking a mix of camp coquettishness and flapper feminism. The archetype was portrayed by a host of legendary screen queens including greats like Clara Bow and Theda Bara. Both actresses pushed at the boundaries of the expected and at times unapologetically transgressed them – often resulting in bold femininity of their own making. Also sex symbols, they were defiantly themselves.

The most resonant and enduring portrayal of the witch on screen came a few years later, with the monumental event that was the 1939 release of *The Wizard of Oz*. Adapted from L. Frank Baum's hugely popular book series, the movie shook the foundations of filmmaking and blasted the medium into its next phase – black and white into color, sound and music combined to produce cinema as sheer spectacle. The introduction of a Technicolor Oz, the fantastical musical and dance sequences, an Oscar-winning performance from young Judy Garland as Dorothy – all pale in comparison to the portrayal of the Wicked Witch of the West by former school marm–turned–character actress Margaret Hamilton. According to the Smithsonian, *The Wizard of Oz* may be the most-seen movie of all time, making Hamilton's character perhaps the most famous of pop-culture crones, forever cackling

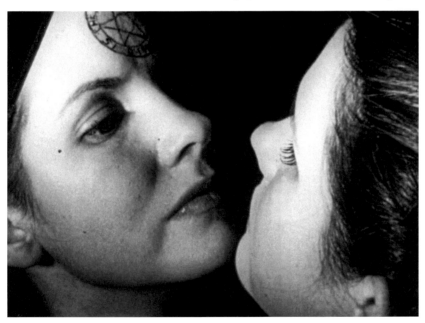

Gil Elvgren · *Riding High* · United States · 1958
Pinup artist Elvgren paints a sexy witch with a broom nestled quite erotically between her fishnet-stockinged thighs. The work is an example of the often-depicted 1950s witch as young, attractive, and seductive.

Maya Deren · *The Witch's Cradle* · United States 1944 In a still from the experimental short film by Deren, Pajorita Matta appears with Marcel Duchamp. The silent, Surrealistic witchcraft work was filmed in Peggy Guggenheim's art gallery.

gleefully over her flying-monkey minions, green-skinned, talon-nailed, and terrifying.

A few years later, the limpid-eyed Veronica Lake, gazing from behind her curtain of platinum locks, would show off her formidable comic skills as Jennifer in the title role of 1942's *I Married a Witch*. Her performance foreshadowed the screen witch to come – the independent woman, making her way in a man's world, looking for love but finding her own way to it. This approach to the modern witch plays out in the book, stage, and various film versions of *Bell, Book and Candle*. In the 1958 movie take, Kim Novak creates a slyly hip beatnik witch casting spoken-word love spells from her Greenwich Village antique

shop/bachelorette pad. She was followed by an audience-obsessed run of witches in film, the cool vamps and feral creatures of countless cult films of the era, from the B-horror classics of Roger Corman's New World Pictures to the shadowy sex nymphs of England's prolific Hammer Films. There were also the 1950s and 1960s television witches of various types – the aforementioned bewitching Samantha Stephens and *The Addams Family*'s smooth-as-silk Morticia, who evolved from Charles Addams's hugely popular illustration series featuring a macabre family of monsters.

In the music world, witchcraft would supply inspiration as well, from the slow-ride riffs

Benjamin Christensen · Film Still from *Häxan* Denmark · 1922 Ghostly witches fly in the silent movie about the misconceptions and abhorrent persecution surrounding witchcraft. The film was banned in America for its nudity, sexuality, and violence.

Angus McBean · *Macbeth Encounters the Witches* Wales · 1952 A film still taken of John Gielgud's adaptation of *Macbeth* shows the three prophet-giving witches in Shakespeare's play exploring the darker side of power.

of Black Sabbath to the broom-ride rock of
Coven. Fronted by the sultry Jinx Dawson,
Coven embraced the witch theme with unbridled theatrics, performing their songs to
ritualized stage shows replete with altars and
pentagrams, smoke and fire. Themes of witchcraft would continue to underscore musical
experiments across genres into the 2000s.

Throughout the late 1960s and into the
1970s, witches reflected the ethos of the
era, as the archetype began to transcend the
limitations of cliché. Often the characterizations sought to translate the burgeoning
women's rights movement, with the witch
represented as the empowered feminine. In
George Romero's still highly underrated

1972 release, *Season of the Witch*, an embattled
housewife stifled by the norms of conser-
vative suburbia finds a kind of redemption,
both psychically and sexually, through her
introduction and immersion into the craft.
The animated cult film *Belladonna of Sadness*,
released in Japan a year later, is a wildly
imaginative, explicit, and violent retelling of
the infamous witchcraft text *La Sorcière*, written by Jules Michelet in 1862. *The Wicker Man*,
also released in 1973, took inspiration from
the supposed ancient Celtic rite of burning
a wooden effigy, all while tapping into the
Neopaganism movement that was happening
concurrently in modern Britain and beyond.
A few years later, in Dario Argento's lushly
cinematic *Suspiria*, the witch is artist and

Unknown · Promotional photo for *Bell, Book and
Candle* · United States · 1958 The fantasy comedy
stars Kim Novak as a witch who magickally com-
pels a man to fall in love with her. Following disas-
trous hijinks, she vows to renounce witchcraft in
order to be with him permanently.

Unknown · Veronica Lake in *I Married a Witch*
United States · 1942 In the Hollywood film, Lake
plays the witch Jennifer, who was burned in the
Salem trials. She returns centuries later to avenge
the descendants of a man who condemned her
and her father.

Unknown · Barbara Steele as Princess Asa Vajda in *Black Sunday* Italy · 1960 A film still captures the vampire witch who returns from the grave to avenge her death. Having been accused by her brother of sorcery, and then killed, she seeks to curse and torment his descendants.

(opposite, top) Robin Hardy · *The Wicker Man* England · 1973 A coven of witches circle within standing stones in the popular film depicting a community of remote islanders who practice Celtic paganism.

(opposite, bottom) Akira Kurosawa · Film Still from *Throne of Blood* · Japan · 1957 In Kurosawa's cinematic translation of Shakespeare's *Macbeth*, the play's setting is transposed to feudal Japan.

artist is witch – the film a vividly feverish portrayal of female creative power made vehemently manifest. In 1974, *The Wizard of Oz* would be reimagined and updated as *The Wiz*. Featuring an all-Black cast, the modernized musical would hit the Broadway stage and later, in 1978, be released as a Hollywood film starring Diana Ross and Michael Jackson. *The Wiz* reimagined and updated the witch archetypes of *Oz*, with the Wicked Witch transformed into the bawdy sorceress Evillene.

Meanwhile, in her musical experimentations, a young Yoko Ono would respond to public criticism of her relationship with John Lennon with her seminal 1974 track, "Yes, I'm a Witch." She would also produce a

series of art pieces that lamented the horrific legacy of the Salem trials while exploring the power of the magickal feminine. A circle of musicians and artists later joined her in finding their own unique inspiration within the broader context of witchcraft, both aesthetically and creatively. Fleetwood Mac's Stevie Nicks enchanted legions of fans, inducting a global coven of young witches into a magickal circle of leather and lace stage sorcery. In England during the late 1970s and early 1980s, Kate Bush cast a spell of theatrical romance, Siouxsie Sioux pioneered a distinctively witchy cross-pollination of goth and punk music, and disco queen Grace Jones prowled the night-club dance floors with her own spectacularly unique and empowered presence. In the

Dario Argento · Film Still from *Suspiria* · Italy · 1977 Dario Argento's horror film about a coven of witches running a German dance academy revolves around ballet student Suzy Bannion, played by Jessica Harper. The film was scored by the band Goblin.

Eiichi Yamamoto · *Belladonna of Sadness* Movie Poster · Japan · 1973 The graphic and psychedelic Japanese film is about a girl who uses black magick to exact revenge upon the townsmen who tormented and terrified her.

Belladonna of Sadness

Producer: Tadayoshi Watanabe/Director: Eiichi Yamamoto/Key Animator: Gisaburo Sugii/Script: Yoshiyuki Fukuda and Eiichi Yamamoto/Art Director and Water
Color Paintings: Kuni Fukai/Music: Mitauhiko Sato/Cinematographer: Shigeru Yamazaki/Original Book: Satanism and Witchcraft written by Jules Michele/Voice
Cast: Jeanne; Aiko Nagayama/Jean; Takeo Ito/Satan: Tatsuya Nakadai/Main Theme Song: Composer: Asei Kobayashi/Lyrics: Yu Aku/Singer: Mayumi Tachibana
© Mushi Production /Color/Stereo/89min/DV/Standard/Animation

1990s, Courtney Love reclaimed witchcraft for a new generation of "Riotgrrrls." These artists were working in vastly varied genres, but they all embraced the unconventionally, unapologetically, completely defiant feminine. Today, many female performers such as Erykah Badu, Bat for Lashes, Beyoncé, Princess Nokia, Brooklynn, and Chelsea Wolfe explore their own unique expressions and connections to the spirit – witchcraft now transformed into a means of artistic catharsis, rather than a fixed identity.

Throughout the 1980s and 1990s, the screen witch would continue to take on a multitude of forms – from high-fantasy sorceresses to bawdy comic queens. There were the outcast teenagers tapping into their nascent powers in 1996's *The Craft*, the Cher/Susan Sarandon/Michelle Pfeiffer triple goddess of 1987's *The Witches of Eastwick* (based on the John Updike novel of the same name), and the mischievous matrons of 1993's *Hocus Pocus*. Anjelica Huston puts on a deliciously evil performance, prowling the screen, in the 1990s adaptation of *The Witches* by children's-book writer Roald Dahl. Later, Anne Hathaway would bring her own glamorous take to the role in the 2020 remake. The 1999 film *The Blair Witch Project* would terrify a generation with its faux-documentary take on witch cinema.

Unknown · Promotional photo of Oenothea in *Satyricon* · Italy · 1969 Donyale Luna plays the sorceress Oenothea in the Federico Fellini film of mythical Roman tales.

Curtis Harrington · *The Wormwood Star* · United States · 1955 Occult icon Marjorie Cameron starred in the short film by Harrington exploring witchcraft and occult.

Sidney Lumet · Mabel King as Evillene in *The Wiz*
United States · 1978 In this cinematic transformation of the classic L. Frank Baum narrative, Mabel
King plays a modernized version of the Wicked Witch
of the West.

Fin Costello · Stevie Nicks · United States · 1975
Known for her witchy style, Stevie Nicks has influenced many generations of witchcraft enthusiasts
with her unabashed expressions of her dark, mystical, and spiritual nature.

Neilson Barnard · Grace Jones in Concert · United
States · 2012 As a chic, gold-masked goddess,
Jones hypnotizes audiences with arcane awe. One of
the most captivating and bewitching performers, she
was styled by the equally enchanting Eiko Ishioka,
known for her costumes based on Greek mythology.

Unknown · Kate Bush performing "Wuthering
Heights" · England · 1978 The captivating Kate
Bush places a spell on her listeners in this elating
moment from a 1978 live concert.

And in the harrowing 2018 version of *Suspiria*, Argento's classic received a sleek and stylish update from contemporary Italian director Luca Guadagnino. Meanwhile, on Broadway, Gregory Maguire's 1995 best-selling book, *Wicked: The Life and Times of the Wicked Witch of the West*, would come to life as a musical in 2003 and continue on to a successful, award-winning run on the world stage.

In the 21st century, the archetype of the witch has become entirely fluid, adapted in a myriad of imaginative ways, translated by creatives of all kinds. J. K. Rowling's depictions of an enchanted wizarding world, in both her best-selling *Harry Potter* book series and their subsequent blockbuster film adaptations, are perhaps among the most influential cultural phenomena of the late

20th and early 21st centuries. Rowling's young witch Hermione is brainy and bold and knows her way around a wand. In the 2005 film version of *The Lion, the Witch and the Wardrobe*, Tilda Swinton offers viewers an icy revamp of Queen Jadis, taking C. S. Lewis's beloved *Chronicles of Narnia* book series and giving it a fantastical, theatrical spin. That same year Nora Ephron would revive the classic *Bewitched* brand, this time with Nicole Kidman in the leading role, playing opposite a befuddled Will Ferrell.

In 2015, production designer Robert Eggers would make his directorial debut with the spare, beautifully spooky costume horror *The Witch*. Shot in black and white and set in New England in the 1630s, the film follows the slow and spiraling downfall of a Puritan

Simon Fowler · Siouxsie Sioux · England · 1980
Goth goddess Siouxsie emerged as an artist of intense influence. With her band, Siouxsie and the Banshees, she subverted the role of women in music through haunting hypno-performance.

**George Miller · Scene from *The Witches of Eastwick*
United States · 1987** Cher, Michelle Pfeiffer, and Susan Sarandon star as witches who unexpectedly find themselves in the company of a stranger in town. Each is cursed to fall for him, temporarily, until they recognize him as the Devil.

In my work as a drag entertainer, the makeup process is sacred. Playing my characters comes easier to me when I have put intent and effort into the transformation. I truly believe that we can imbue magick into many aspects of our work and life when we put effort and intention into the daily rituals we must perform. I identify as a witch because I think that title exemplifies my worldview and the way in which I conduct myself in the world. Witchcraft teaches us to be mindful of our surroundings; it teaches us to listen to nature and consider the impact we have on the natural world, as well as its impact on us. Witchcraft has taught me to have greater respect and understanding for my environment, my fellow humans, and living creatures, and has consistently intersected with my worldview and belief in science — not replaced them. Ultimately, as long as we continue to think for ourselves, with an open mind and open heart, then witchcraft can fit into our world, as it already exists. A witch is someone who practices mindfulness in regards to the energy that they put out into the world. They consider the impact their actions will have on their environment, as well as other beings. They combine common sense with an open mind toward the unknown. They believe in the power that they possess as an individual, as well as a member of a larger community. The witch archetype has endured due to its close relation to the archetype of the feminine. There is a visceral understanding of the power of the feminine — which has led to both the suppression and the celebration of witches. I think whether you're celebrating the witch, or trying to root her out, you cannot deny her power.

— JINKX MONSOON, Witch, Artist, & Entertainer, 2020

Unknown · Melisandre from *Game of Thrones*
United States · 2016 Known as the Red Priestess,
Melisandre practices necromancy, imparts prophecy, gives birth to a shadow demon, and hails the
Lord of Light.

family banished from their community due to a religious dispute. On the small screen, a host of shows continue to celebrate tales of witchcraft and magick, from both the original and revamped *Sabrina the Teenage Witch*, to the murderous Melisandre, the powerful priestess known as "the red witch" of *Game of Thrones*. There was the impressive cast of actors (Jessica Lange, Angela Bassett) portraying various historical-fiction witches in 13 episodes of *American Horror Story: Coven*.

In comic books, graphic novels, podcasts and on social media, the world seems absolutely rife with shadows and spells, as a new generation continues to be enchanted by the witch. As modern culture evolves, creatives of all kinds pick up their wands to reinvent the archetype and reshape its definition in a way completely of their own choosing.

Today, there are no confines, no boundaries, just an infinite field consisting of dream and nightmare, vision, and revelation. Like all muses, the witch takes flight through our shared subconscious — their form a reflection and expression of each artist's inner self. Today and onward, the archetype will continue to beguile, to ignite our cultural and creative explorations. Each era initiates a new transformation, as the witch wields the wand and stirs the cauldron in which all ideas and imagination boil and brew.

Andrew Fleming · Film Still from *The Craft* **United States · 1996** Actors Rachel True, Neve Campbell, Fairuza Balk, and Robin Tunney raise their hands in invocation in a fire circle during a scene from the movie about high-school witches. The film's popularity spurred an explosion of teen witchcraft TV series, in turn empowering modern youth to explore their occult leanings.

Anna Biller · Film Still
from *The Love Witch*
United States · 2016
A film still from *The
Love Witch* features
Samantha Robinson as
a witch who seeks love
through cursed potions.
She racks up men one
by one, leaving a wake
of woeful casualties until
the object of her desire
finally appears.

(following, left) Nona Limmen · *C.W.* · Netherlands · 2018 Created in collaboration with the
musician and artist Chelsea Wolfe, this image by
Limmen is showcased in promotions for Wolfe's
haunting album, *Birth of Violence*.

(following, right) Rachael Pony Cassells · Natasha
Khan of Bat for Lashes · United States · 2021
A creative collaboration between photographer
and director Cassells and musician Khan, this
series of artworks and videos draws influence from
concepts of elemental magick and witchcraft.

We are going through a crisis of unprecedented proportions in today's toxic system. Witchcraft can provide us with valuable guidance to help us co-create a new, more egalitarian and sustainable paradigm. The image of the witch — learned, independent, and powerful, often feared, sometimes mocked, always shrouded in mystery, and master of her identity — is a marker of the place of women in society and the issues of each era. Since the 1960s, she has been a feminist, environmentalist, and anticapitalist icon. With the Gang Of Witches, we stand at the border of the material and spiritual sphere, of the visible and the invisible, of the conscious and the unconscious, of humor and revolt, of resistance and resilience. We travel from one to the other, creating points of convergence, opening portals, questioning the workings of our patriarchal and anthropocentric societies. Our coven is in the forest; it is what keeps us connected to the living and cosmic worlds. Witchcraft is intertwined with every aspect of life, every thought and act. It is a way of approaching life with the maximum awareness and responsibility. It is an everyday quest for staying in the flow and in balance. Yoga and awareness meditation are wonderful tools to sharpen your intuition, and stay grounded in this spinning world. Singing, writing, painting, and sculpting are at the core of our magickal practices. They allow us to connect with the mysterious forces within and to the tides of the universe, to experience transcendence, spiritual elevation, and joy.

— PAOLA HIVELIN & SOPHIE ROKH,
Co-Founders of the Gang Of Witches, 2020

(following) Lauren Lancaster · W.I.T.C.H. · United States · 2017 The Women's International Terrorist Conspiracy from Hell was founded in 1968 by feminist antiwar protesters. A renewed version of the activist group emerged throughout America in 2016.

Luca Guadagnino · Film Still from *Suspiria* Remake · Italy · 2018 *Suspiria*, the 1977 film about an esteemed dance academy run by a coven of witches, was remade by Luca Guadagnino, starring Dakota Johnson and Tilda Swinton.

FOR THE SEEKERS

A Final Note on the Library of Esoterica

The Library of Esoterica explores the expansive visual history of the arcane, showcasing artwork birthed through the expressions of a wide variety of traditions and rituals. The intent of this series is to offer inclusive, introductory overviews to these ancient rituals and to explore their complex symbolism objectively, rather than dogmatically.

In doing so, the aspiration is to draw back the veil to reveal a deeper appreciation of these valuable tools of the psyche. Esoteric knowledge offers powerful methods for self-exploration and meditation. These magickal practices have developed over centuries in order to allow for a further understanding of the inner world.

The goal of this series is to present condensed summaries of these ancient systems and from there, encourage readers to further explore the rituals, ceremonies, and sacred philosophies of various global cultures. The task is to inspire readers to seek out knowledge, to study the teachings of scholars past and present, who have dedicated themselves to the development and preservation of these ancient arts.

The hope is that *The Library of Esoterica* emboldens readers to begin their own journey down into the dark halls of the arcane, to pull the dusty tomes from the shelves, to take the timeworn cards from the satchel and spread them across the silks, to look up to the sky and read meaning in the movement of the stars.

As the author, teacher, and archivist Manly P. Hall stated so eloquently in his masterwork, *The Secret Teachings of All Ages*, "To live in the world without becoming aware of the meaning of the world is like wandering about in a great library without touching the books." Later, in this indispensable and exhaustive overview of the world's esoteric teachings, Hall exclaims, "Only transcendental philosophy knows the path. Only the illumined reason can carry the understanding part of man upward to the light. Only philosophy can teach man to be born well, to live well, to die well, and in perfect measure, be born again. Into this band of the elect, those who have chosen the life of knowledge, of virtue, and of utility, the philosophers of the ages invite, YOU."

Claude Cahun and Marcel Moore · Frontispiece for *Aveux non avenus* · **France · 1930** The collage for Cahun's book on gender exploration is topped by the Rebis, a mystical symbol of male and female as a unified whole, beyond the binary.

BIBLIOGRAPHY

Aberth, Susan. *Leonora Carrington: Surrealism, Alchemy and Art*. London, England: Lund Humphries, 2010.

Adler, Margot. *Drawing down the Moon: Witches, Druids, Goddess-Worshippers, and Other Pagans in America*. Penguin Books, 2006.

Auryn, Mat. *Psychic Witch: A Metaphysical Guide to Meditation, Magick and Manifestation*. Woodbury, MN: Llewellyn Publications, 2020.

Bedell, Colin. *Queer Cosmos: The Astrology of Queer Identities & Relationships*. San Francisco, CA: Cleis Press, 2019.

Bennett, Robin Rose. *Healing Magic Green Witch Handbook*. New York, NY: Sterling, 2004.

———. *The Gift of Healing Herbs*. Berkeley, CA: North Atlantic Books, 2014.

Buckland, Raymond. *Buckland's Complete Book of Witchcraft*. Llewellyn Publications, 2010.

———. *Wicca for One: The Path of Solitary Witchcraft*. Citadel Press, 2004.

Cabot, Laurie, and Thomas Cowan. *Power of the Witch*. London, England: Arkana, 1992.

Creed, Barbara. *Monstrous-Feminine, the: Film, Feminism, Psychoanalysis*. Routledge, 2012.

Cunningham, Scott. *Cunningham's Book of Shadows: The Path of an American Traditionalist*. Woodbury, MN: Llewellyn Publications, 2009.

Curott, Phyllis. *Book of Shadows*. New York, NY: Broadway Books, 1999.

———. *Wicca Made Easy: Awaken the Divine Magic within You*. London, England: Hay House UK, 2018.

———. *Witch Crafting: A Spiritual Guide to Making Magic*. London, England: Thorsons, 2002.

Davies, Owen. *Grimoires: A History of Magic Books*. London, England: Oxford University Press, 2010.

———. *Witchcraft, Magic and Culture 1736-1951*. Manchester, England: Manchester University Press, 1999.

de Givry, Grillot. *Witchcraft, Magic and Alchemy*. Magnolia, AR: Smith (Peter), 1999.

Dell, Christopher. *The Occult, Witchcraft & Magic: An Illustrated History*. London, England: Thames & Hudson, 2016.

Denny, Frances. *Major Arcana: Portraits of Witches in America*. Kansas City, MO: Andrews McMeel Publishing, 2020.

Diaz, Juliet. *Witchery: Embrace the Witch Within*. London, England: Hay House UK, 2019.

Dorsey, Lilith. *Voodoo and Afro-Caribbean Paganism*. Citadel Press, 2005.

———. *Orishas, Goddesses, and Voodoo Queens: The Divine Feminine in the African Religious Traditions*. Red Wheel/Weiser, 2020.

DuQuette, Lon Milo. *The Magick of Aleister Crowley: A Handbook of Rituals of Thelema*. Red Wheel/Weiser, 2005.

Estes, Clarissa Pinkola. *Women Who Run with the Wolves: Contacting the Power of the Wild Woman*. London, England: Rider, 2008.

Federici, Silvia. *Caliban and the Witch: Women, the Body, and Primitive Accumulation*. New York, NY: Autonomedia, 2004.

Freeman, Mara. *Grail Alchemy: Initiation in the Celtic Mystery Tradition*. Rochester, NY: Inner Traditions Bear and Company, 2014.

Gage, Matilda Joslyn. *Woman, Church and State: A Historical Account of the Status of Woman through the Christian Ages: With Reminiscences of Matriarchate*. Franklin Classics, 2018.

Garcia, Yates Amanda. *Initiated: Memoir of a Witch*. London, England: Sphere, 2019.

Gardner, Gerald Brosseau. *The Meaning of Witchcraft*. Red Wheel/Weiser, 2004.

Goodrich, Norma Lorre. *Medieval Myths*. Hawthorn, VIC, Australia: Penguin Books, 1988.

Gottesdiener, Sarah Faith. *The Moon Book: Lunar Magic to Change Your Life*. New York, NY: St Martin's Press, 2020.

Grossman, Pam. *Waking the Witch: Reflections on Women, Magic, and Power*. New York, NY: Simon & Schuster, 2019.

Herstik, Gabriela. *Bewitching the Elements: A Guide to Empowering Yourself through Earth, Air, Fire, Water, and Spirit*. TarcherPerigee, 2020.

———. *Craft: How to Be a Modern Witch*. London, England: Ebury Press, 2018.

———. *Inner Witch: A Modern Guide to the Ancient Craft*. Tarcherperigee, 2018.

Hults, Linda C. *The Witch as Muse: Art, Gender, and Power in Early Modern Europe*. Baltimore, MD: University of Pennsylvania Press, 2005.

Hutton, Ronald. *The Witch: A History of Fear, from Ancient Times to the Present*. Blackstone Audiobooks, 2017.

Illes, Judika. *The Element Encyclopedia of 5000 Spells: The Ultimate Reference Book for the Magical Arts*. London, England: Element Books, 2004.

———. *The Element Encyclopedia of Witchcraft: The Complete A-Z for the Entire Magical World*. London, England: Harper Element, 2004.

Jong, Erica. *Witches*. London, England: HarperCollins, 1982.

Kitaiskaia, Taisia. *Literary Witches*. Seal Press, 2017.

Lightfoot, Najah. *Good Juju: Mojos, Rites, and Practices for the Magical Soul*. Woodbury, MN: Llewellyn Publications, 2019.

Miller, Madeline. *Circe*. Little Brown and Company, 2018.

Murray, Margaret Alice. *The Witch-Cult in Western Europe*. Pinnacle Press, 2017.

Radziszewski, Ylva Mara. *A Practical Guide for Witches: Spells, Rituals, and Magic for an Enchanted Life*. Rockridge Press, 2020.

Sollee, Kristen J. *Witch Hunt: A Traveler's Guide to the Power & Persecution of the Witch*. Red Wheel/Weiser, 2020.

Spalter, Mya. *Enchantments*. New York, NY: Random House, 2018.

Starhawk. *Spiral Dance: A Rebirth of the Ancient Religion of the Great Goddess*. 2nd ed. London, England: HarperSanFrancisco, 1989.

———. *The Earth Path: Grounding Your Spirit in the Rhythms of Nature*. New York, NY: HarperOne, 2006.

Teish, Luisah. *Jambalaya*. New York, NY: HarperOne, 1988.

Valiente, Doreen. *Witchcraft for Tomorrow*. London, England: Robert Hale, 2018.

Walker, Barbara G. *Women's Encyclopedia of Myths and Secrets*. London, England: Thorsons, 1995.

Young, Serinity. *Women Who Fly: Goddesses, Witches, Mystics, and Other Airborne Females*. New York, NY: Oxford University Press, 2018.

IMAGE CREDITS

Foundation: *186, 270, 337, 347(t), 450*. Catherine Zarip: *185*. Charlotte Edey: *343*. Chris Ramirez: *81*. © Christie's Images: *159(t)*. Cornell University Library, Division of Rare and Manuscript Collections: *120*. Courtesy of the Curtis Harrington Collection at the Academy Film and Flicker Alley Archive: *495*. Demontier Meireles Vasconcelos: *426*. Denis Forkas: *241*. The Doreen Valiente Foundation: *27, 268*. Edgar Fabián Frías: *460(t)*. Elijah Burgher: *467*. Emily Balivet: *167*. Esao Andrews: *171*. Fay Avnisan Nowitz: *198, 400*. Courtesy of Fiona Pardington and Starkwhite, Auckland: *224(b), 377(b)*. © Frances F. Denny, Courtesy of ClampArt, New York City: *49, 124(b)*. © Frazetta Girls All Rights Reserved: *255, 322*. Courtesy of FULGUR PRESS: *154, 229*. Gallery Oldham, 1952, Given by Marjory Lees: *59*. Courtesy of Gallery Wendi Norris, San Francisco: *280, 437*. Ger Eenens Collection, The Netherlands: *64(b)*. Getty Images/American Stock Archive: *475*; / Bertrand Guay: *471*; /Bettman: *18, 78, 258*; /Bev Grant: *9*; /Fin Costello: *497*; /George Rinhart: *73*; / Heritage Images: *406*; /Hulton Archive, Stringer: *474*; /Neilson Barnard, Stringer: *498*; /Oli Scarff, Stringer: *10*; /Sepia Times: *107, 224(t)*; /ullstein bild Dtl.: *494*; /Virgil Apger: *483*. Gilles Grimoin: *313*. Glyn Smyth: *187*. The Goddard Center: *435*. Grapefruit Moon Gallery: *346*. Gromyko Semper: *43*. Heritage Auctions, HA.com: *100(t), 132*. Ian Howard: *299*. iStock, clu: *35*. Jacques Habbah: *478*. From The Janet and Stewart Farrar Collection: *23, 257(b), 333, 401(b)*; /Photo Ian Rorke: *355(b)*. Jean-Baptiste Monge: *127*. Jesse Bransford: *138, 139, 460(b)*. Photo Jo Freeman, jofreeman.com: *55*. Jodie Muir: *191*. Jos. A. Smith: *85*. Josephine Close: *207, 354, 373*. Josh Sessoms: *355(t)*. Julia Soboleva: *141*. Courtesy of Juliana Huxtable, JTT, Reena Spaulings Fine Art, and Project Native Informant: *463*. Karen Strang: *347(b)*. Karina Kulyk: *80*. Courtesy of Katelan Foisy: *47*. Kay Turner and Rosina Lardieri: *50*. Kevin Best: *421(t)*. © Kiki Smith, Courtesy of Pace Gallery, Photo Kerry Ryan McFate: *237, 411*; © /La Monnaie de Paris, Photo Martin Argyroglo: *31*. Kremena Chipilova: *92*. Kris Waldherr: *169*. Kunsthistorisches Museum, Vienna, Österreichisches Theatermuseum, Hermann Bahr

Bequest, Vienna: *20*. Kunstsammlungen der Stadt Nürnberg: *123*. L (Jason Metcalf): *365*. Lauren Lancaster: *51, 510*. Laura Tempest Zakroff: *2*. Courtesy of Lehmann Maupin: *315*. Leo and Diane Dillon, Courtesy R. Michelson Galleries: *88*. © Estate of Leonard Baskin: *125*. © Estate of Leonor Fini: *245, 316(b), 428, 440*. Lezley Saar: *456*. Library of Congress: *97*. Luca Ledda: *417*. © Lucien Shapiro: *371*; © /Photo Shaun Roberts: *273*. Malwine Stauss: *328*. Manisha Parekh: *262(b)*. Maria Giulia Alemanno: *320*. Maria Torres Subira: *360*. Martina Hoffman: *71, 390*. Mary Evans Picture Library: *118, 128*; /© Studiocanal Films Ltd: *490(t)*. Adapted from an article originally published in Mashable magazine: *40–45*. Meagan Boyd: *143, 217, 412*. Meagan Donegan: *194, 285(t)*. The Met/The Elisha Whittelsey Collection, The Elisha Whittelsey Fund, 1957: *21, 324*; /Purchase, Joseph Pulitzer Bequest, 1962: *296*; /Gift of Felix M. Warburg and his family, 1941: *13*; / Purchased by Harry G. Sperling Fund, James A. and Maria R. Warth Gift, in memory of Anne and Peter Warth, and Bequest of Clifford A. Furst, by exchange, 1996: *181*; /Rogers Fund, 1915: *212*. Miguel Opazo: *234*. Museu Nacional de Arte Antiga, Lisbon, Photo Luísa Oliveira, Arquivo de Documentação Fotográfica – DGPC: *239*. © Museum Mayer van den Bergh, Antwerp: *102*. Museum of New Zealand, Purchased 1999 with New Zealand Lottery Grants Board funds: *422(b)*. Museum of Witchcraft and Magic: *208, 212, 216(b), 220, 321, 366, 397*. Courtesy of © Myrlande Constant and CENTRAL FINE, Miami Beach, Photo George Echevarria: *44*. Natalya Kuzmina, Kuzmina. com: *339*. National Galleries Scotland, Purchased 1979: *404*. National Gallery of Art, Rosenwald Collection: *117*. Courtesy of the National Gallery of Victoria, Melbourne, Purchased through The Art Foundation of Victoria with the assistance of Coles Myer Ltd, Governor, 1993 (AS26-1993): *41*. © National Library of Australia: *383*. Courtesy of the National Museum of Women in the Arts, Washington, D.C. Gift from Private Collection, Photo Lee Stalsworth: *434*. Nederlands Fotomuseum: *465*. Neil Daftary: *215*. Neumann Family Collection, Courtesy Kravets Wehby Gallery, New York: *144*. The New

Thank you to the artists, authors, publishers, and scholars kind enough to share their knowledge and passion with us, and the witchcraft practitioners who offered wisdom through their insightful interviews. Special appreciation goes out to the coven of talented essayists who contributed their writing to this volume: Susan Aberth, Amanda Yates Garcia, Sarah Faith Gottesdiener, Gabriela Herstik, Judika Illes, Jess Joho, Michelle Mae, Kristen J. Sollée, Mya Spalter, Morgan Sung, and Dr. Kate Tomas.

We are grateful for the generous participation of the following people and organizations: Robert Ansell, Robin Rose Bennett, Jesse Bransford, Buckland Museum of Witchcraft & Magick, the Cornell University Witchcraft Collection, Simon Costin of The Museum of Witchcraft and Magic, Phyllis Curott, Frances F. Denny, Christina Oakley Harrington,

Ronald Hutton, the Janet and Stewart Farrar Collection, Elisabeth Krohn, *Mashable* magazine, the Philosophical Research Society, The Collection of Stephen Romano, and Luisah Teish.

Thanks to all those who have offered support throughout this project, including Matt Freeman, Alex Glass, Lara Antal, Queenright Coven, and the listeners, guests, and supporters of *The Witch Wave* podcast.

And finally, this book would not exist without the talent and dedication of Nic Taylor and Lisa Doran; the expert copyediting and proofreading of Teena Apeles and Jessica Hoffmann; and the wisdom and encouragement of Nina Wiener, Kathrin Murr, Marion Boschka, Andy Disl, and Benedikt Taschen.

— JESSICA HUNDLEY & PAM GROSSMAN, 2021

For those seeking to explore the history, art, and practice of witchcraft, we encourage everyone to support all the work of the wonderful artists, essayists, and interviewees included in this volume. The following is a brief list of individuals and institutions that offer invaluable information through their print and digital media.

Individuals · Susan Aberth, Teresa Arcq, Rebecca Artemisa, Mat Auryn, Maja d'Aoust, Robin Rose Bennett, Leilani Birely, Jesse Bransford, Bill Crisafi, Phyllis Curott, Dr. Maria DeBlassie, Frances F. Denny, Juliet Diaz, Lilith Dorsey, Edgar Fabián Frías, Janet Farrar & Gavin Bone, Erica Feldmann, Liza Fenster, Amanda Yates Garcia, Sarah Faith Gottesdiener, Christina Oakley Harrington, Gabriela Herstik, Ronald Hutton, Judika Illes, Jess Joho, Marcella Kroll, Elisabeth Krohn, Najah Lightfoot, Bri Luna, Michelle Mae, Madeline Miller, Jinkx Monsoon, Sarah Potter, Ylvadroma Marzanna Radziszewski, Stephen Romano, Empress Karen Rose, Kristen J. Sollée, Mya Spalter, Starhawk, Morgan Sung, Luisah Teish, Jezmina Von Thiele, Dr. Kate Tomas, Alia Walston, Marina Warner, Casey Zabala

Websites/Podcasts/Media Between Worlds, Fulgur Press, Gang Of Witches, HausWitch, Missing Witches, Modern Witches, Modern Women, Moonbeaming, Oracle of Los Angeles, Our Sacred Web, Rise Up Good Witch, Sabat Magazine, The Hoodwitch, The Witch Wave, Witch of the Dawn, Your Magic

Institutions · Buckland Museum of Witchcraft & Magick, Cornell University Witchcraft Collection, The Golden Dome School, The School of Traditional Magic, Museum of Witchcraft and Magic

IMPRINT

Edited by Jessica Hundley, 2021

Various essays by *Witchcraft* co-editor Pam Grossman, 2021. Captions by Michelle Mae. Timeline by Jessica Hundley.

Design: Thunderwing, Los Angeles
Research & licensing: Lisa Doran, Los Angeles

ISBN 978-3-8365-8560-6
Printed in Bosnia-Herzegovina

© 2021 TASCHEN GmbH
Hohenzollernring 53, D-50672 Köln
www.taschen.com

(front cover) John William Waterhouse
Circe Invidiosa · England · 1892

(back cover) Luis Ricardo Falero · *Faust's Dream*
Spain/England · 1878